SLAVERY AND SLAVE TRADE IN NIGERIA
From Earliest Times to the Nineteenth Century

SLAVERY AND SLAVE TRADE IN NIGERIA

From Earliest Times to the Nineteenth Century

Edited by
J. F. Ade Ajayi and Okon Uya

Safari Books Ltd
Ibadan

Published by
Safari Books Ltd
Cambridge House
20 Joop Berkhout Cresent
Onireke, Ibadan
Email: safarinigeria@gmail.com

on behalf of
The Federal Ministry of Tourism, Culture and National Orientation

First published, 2010

© J. F. Ade Ajayi and Okon Uya (Editors)

All rights reserved. This book is copyright and so no part of it may be reproduced, stored in a retrieval system, or transmitted in any form or by any means, electronic, mechanical, electrostatic, magnetic tape, photocopying, recording or otherwise, without the prior written permission of the copyright owners.

ISBN: 978-978-49089-6-2

DEDICATION

To
Professor J. F. Ade Ajayi
for over five decades of inspirational leadership in African historical scholarship.

And to the sweet memory of
Ms. Ogbe Nchonwa
the erstwhile Director of Culture, during whose tenure this project was initiated.

FOREWORD

Any kind of intellectual endeavour has always held an attraction for me. So I was most gratified when I learnt that one of the flagship projects of this ministry which I have a unique privilege to head is this book that defines a tragic but unforgettable chapter in the annals of human history. I feel proud indeed that such a noble initiative was conceived and implemented by this ministry, whose statutory responsibility is the preservation, promotion and presentation of the best aspects of our cultural patrimony.

While tons of literature abound on the trans-Atlantic slave trade and to a lesser extent, the trans-Saharan slave trade and trans-Indian slave trade, not much is known, written and discussed about the indigenous slavery and slave trade. It is therefore to fill this void that this book project was embarked on. Much has been said about oral traditions, being the bedrock of Nigerian history, however, with the advent of cutting-edge technology, there is need to explore those frontiers in order to document our history for posterity.

Indeed this book is a product of extensive networking between the Federal Government of Nigeria, UNESCO, the academia and the testimonies of the Nigerian people. That is why I consider it the original and authentic Nigerian story. I hope all who encounter this story would have a better understanding of us as a people.

Senator Bello Jubrin Gada
Honourable Minister
Federal Ministry of Tourism, Culture and National Orientation
March 2010

PREFACE

It is often said that too many cooks spoil the broth. This is writ large in many cases but in this particular instance from the conception, to the administrative procedures, financial commitments, logistics and final completion of this landmark publication, the contrary is the case. So much so that we can conceive of an adage in the true African spirit that says, "many heads are better than one". Also, managing gifted intellectuals especially those with considerable reputation is supposed to be a daunting task. In this case, once again, it proves the opposite in that what one discovers are simple, humble, most co-operative, intellectually engaging and understanding personalities who are ready to help at every stage of producing this monumental publication. Even though with different temperaments, attitudes and cultural backgrounds, a common thread among all of them have been the unflinching commitment and single-minded dedication to completing this national assignment. More than anything else, the sacrifice in terms of physical exertion is equally comparable to the academic rigours that informed the production of this book.

The process of producing this book was measured, deliberate, painstaking and systematic from the conception stage, the gathering of data and its analysis, to the formation level of draft going on to the editing and the final product, the book. Even the choice of publishers was dictated by the quest for excellence and experience. It has to be said that all this process we made use of old good techniques of face to face meetings and old methods of hard copy editing to modern use of information technology by use of internet to circulate draft and proof read same as well as text messages plus telephone calls to discuss change of dates and other sundry matters.

Ordinarily, this tragic event which necessitated a constant re-visit to that human chapter which some think should be best forgotten requires this kind of introspective soul searching that would purge the guilty of their guilt and assuage the humiliation of the victims in such a way that these negative events can be channeled to communities to release their creative impulses and latent energies towards meeting our day-to-day struggle for cultural space in a rapidly globalising world.

At the end, it is our sincere hope that readers will find this book educative, easy to read and a reliable source of information that would enrich our knowledge of ourselves towards a better understanding of our past with a vision to meaningfully engage ourselves for the task of this 21st century.

Alhaji Sheidu Ozigis, OON, mni
Permanent Secretary
Federal Ministry of Tourism, Culture and National Orientation
March 2010

ACKNOWLEDGMENTS

Someone described all the directors of culture who supervised this project as a quintessential relay team, from Alhaji Bello Bala, mni, a man with the wisdom of the proportion of the famed King Solomon to Mrs Angela Uyah whose work ethics is second to none to the organisational skill and kind understanding of Ms Ogbe Nchonwa of blessed memory and my humble self who fate has bestowed upon the role of an anchor. Our sincere appreciation must go to Mr. Augustus Babajide Ajibola, the coordinator of this project and his able assistant, Mr. Emmanuel Adeniyi Odekanyin. They are all pillars of this project.

Appreciation must be exercised in the direction of the political and administrative heads of the ministry during the period when the project was conceived, especially Ambassador Frank Ogbuewu who initiated and brought to fruition the Slave Routes project and to all those who sustained the momentum. Professor Babalola Borishade, CFR, Prince Adetokunbo Kayode, SAN and Senator Bello Gada. They all deserve our appreciation for showing considerable goodwill towards the successful completion of this project.

How can we forget or would I say measure our appreciation to the accounting officers of the ministry during the process of producing this book. *Primus inter pares* amongst this permanent secretary's is Alhaji Shehu Suleiman, OON who showed a lot of interest and during whose tenure the book project commenced. No less gratitude should be extended to Alhaji Nu'uman Barau Dambatta, OON and Dr Goke Adegoroye, OON whose interest in the project never wavered or waned. Is it therefore a coincidence or divine intervention, an historian by calling was left with the task of completing this project as it can be said that the best part was saved for the last, definitely, not the least. A big thank you must therefore go to Alhaji Sheidu Ozigis, OON, mni, during whose tenure the book was completed.

Our immense gratitude and fulsome praise must go to the Chairman of the National Committee on Slave Route, Professor J.F. Ade Ajayi for his kind disposition, perseverance, fortitude and resilience in co-coordinating all aspects of this book. No less appreciation goes to the other contributors of this defining publication: Professors Adamu Mahdi; Okon Uya; Bawuro Barkindo; Sa'ad Abubakar; Abi Derefaka; Drs I.S. Jimada and Akin Alao.

Many thanks must also be extended to Mr Adebanji Benjamin Adeyanju for his untiring efforts as research assistant to Professor J.F. Ade Ajayi and Alhaji H.A. Dari Gada for the comprehensive map clearly depicting all the slave routes in Nigeria. Neither can we fail to acknowledge the immense support given to this publication by the UNESCO office in Abuja especially the director, Dr. Joseph Ngu and our indefatigable National Programmes officer, Mrs. Zainab Ali-Biu.

More than anything else, my resounding commendation finds its root in all the staff of the Federal Department of Culture who provided the raw material for the research and photographs of this book. To all of them, we must say a big thank you for a brilliant collective effort.

Nkanta George Ufot
Director of Culture
Federal Ministry of Tourism, Culture and National Orientation

CONTENTS

Dedication   *v*

Foreword   *vii*

Preface   *ix*

Acknowledgements   *xi*

Contributors   *xiv*

Chapter 1
Introduction   1

Chapter 2
Slave and Slave Trade in Sokoto and Kebbi States   6

Chapter 3
Slave Trade and Slavery in the North East Region of Nigeria   28

Chapter 4
Slavery and Relics of Slavery in Bornu and the Three Emirates   49

Chapter 5
Slavery and Slave Trade in the Middle Niger and Confluence Area   81

Chapter 6
Indigenous Slavery and Slave Trade in the Cross River Region   101

Chapter 7
Slavery and Slave Trade in Niger Delta and Its Hinterlands   133

Chapter 8
Slavery and the Trans-Atlantic Slave Trade in
Southwestern Nigeria   160

Chapter 9
Slavery, Slave Trade and the State in Pre-Colonial Nigeria   183

Bibliography   *204*

Index   *206*

CONTRIBUTORS

Emeritus Professor J. F. Ade Ajayi

Professor J. F. Ade Ajayi has been Nigeria's foremost historian for over five decades. He is an author of many outstanding publications which includes the monumental ten volume *UNESCO History Of Africa Series*. He was the Vice Chancellor of the University of Lagos from 1972 to 1978. He has remained an iconic national figure.

Professor Mahdi Adamu

Professor Mahdi Adamu has become one of the torch bearers of Nigerian History for over four decades of impeccable scholarship. He is a pioneer of trans-Saharan studies at the University of Maiduguri, Nigeria. He is also an astute administrator having served as the Vice Chancellor, Usman Dan Fodio University, Sokoto from 1982 to 1989. He remains a constant firmament in the academia as he still teaches history at the Usman Dan Fodio University, Sokoto till today.

Professor Okon E. Uya

Professor Okon Edet Uya, B. A. (Hons) Ibadan; M. A., Ph.D (Wisconsin); FNAL; FHSN and FABI, is former Tenured Professor of African and African-American History, Howard University, Washington DC, USA and Head of History, Dean of Arts and Deputy Vice Chancellor, University of Calabar, Calabar, Nigeria. He also taught at University of Wisconsin, Madison; Cornell University, Ithaca, New York; and University of Maryland, College Park, Maryland. A widely acknowledged and often quoted expert on slavery, Atlantic slave trade and African diaspora studies, he is the author of 28 books, many book chapters and articles in learned journals. Among his books are: *From Slavery to Public Service; Robert Smalls, 1839 - 1915* (Oxford University Press, 1971); *Black Brotherhood; Afro-Americans and Africa* (D. C. Heath and Company, 1971); *African Diaspora and the Black Experience in New World Slavery* (Third Press, New York, 1992) and with others, *Slavery and Slave Trade in Africa; The Akwa Ibom State Experience* (2006). Professor Uya is currently professor of history on contract, Department of History and International Studies, University of Uyo, Uyo, Akwa Ibom State, Nigeria

Professor Bawuro M. Barkindo

Bawuro M. Barkindo is currently Professor and Head of History Department, University of Abuja. He served as the pioneer Director of Research and Documentation and subsequently Permanent Secretary, Nigerian National Boundary Commission. He later served successively as Permanent Secretary at the Federal Ministries of Solid Minerals Development, Communications and Transport. Amongst his numerous publications are *Mandara Sultanate to 1902: History of the Evolution, Development and collapse of the Central Sudanese Kingdom, Stuttgart, 1989*; "The EarlyStates of the Central Sudan: Kanem, Borno and some of their neighbours to 1500AD" in J. F. Ade Ajayi and Michael Crowder (ed) *History of West Africa*, Longman, 1985, vol. 1, 3rd ed., "Royal PilgrimageTraditions of the Saifawa in Kanem and Borno" in Ajayi J. F. A. and J. D. Y. Peel (ed) *Empires in African History: Essays in memory of Michael Crowder*, Longman, 1992; "Kanem-Borno: Its Relation with the Mediterranean Sea, Baghirmi and others states in the Lake Chad Basin" in B. A. Ogoh (ed.) *UNESCO General History of Africa*, vol. v, Africa from the 16th to the 18th century; Heinman, California, 1992. Professor Barkindo is the current president of AFTRAG – Nigeria.

Professor Sa'ad Abubakar

Professor Sa'ad Abubakar has carved an enviable niche in the annals of Nigerian history scholarship. He taught his favourite subject for many years at the Ahmadu Bello University, Zaria; the University of Maiduguri. He presently teaches at the University of Abuja, Nigeria.

Dr. Akin Alao

Dr. Akin Alao is an Associate Professor of History and currently the Director of the Institute of Cultural Studies, Obafemi Awolowo University, Ile-Ife. He authored *Statemanship on the Bench: The Judicial Career of Sir Adetokunbo Ademola, 1939-1972* published by African World Press and co-authored with Professor Tunde Babawale; *Global African Spirituality, Social Capital and Self Reliance in Africa* and *Culture and Society in Nigeria* published by the Centre for Black and African Arts and Civilisations.

Professor Abi A. Derefaka

Professor Abi A. Derefaka remains the second generation of archaeologists that have carried out with utmost distinction the great tradition of Nigerian scholars in that field of study. The best graduating history student in the Class of 1974 at the University of Lagos, Professor Derefaka has continued with excellent scholarship at the University of Port Harcourt, Rivers State, Nigeria.

Dr. I. Shuaibu Jimada

Dr. I. Shuaibu Jimada is one of the new generations of Nigerian historians whose scholarly excellence is not in doubt. He had his tutelage at undergraduate level at the University of Ilorin and continued postgraduate studies at Ahmadu Bello University, Zaria where he has continued to give vent to his academic impulses. He is the author of a monumental work on *Nupe-Yoruba Relations*.

Chapter 1

INTRODUCTION

J. F. Ade Ajayi
Emeritus Professor of History, University of Ibadan, Ibadan
and
Okon Edet Uya
Professor of History, University of Uyo, Uyo

SLAVE trade and slavery have been major subjects for historical studies by scholars, especially those in the West, for over a century, and still continue "to fascinate our historical imagination"[1]. The magnitude of the human tragedy they represented as well as the continuing relevance of their aftermath in contemporary times account for this interest. For much of that period, however, attention was focused on the external slave trade, more especially the trans-Atlantic slave trade to Europe, the Americas and the Caribbean and less so on the equally important and much older trans-Saharan and trans-Indian ocean trades. One result has been that, until very recently, little attention was paid to the indigenous internal slave trade and slavery, in many ways the "launching pad" for the external trade.

A major reason for this was the profusion of documents and records on the European and American aspects of the trade and the now familiar absence of African voices in these records. However, new methods and approaches resulting from the revolution in historiography where non-written sources, especially the use of oral history and oral traditions, are increasingly enabling us to capture not only the African voices but the indigenous memories concerning the institutions. The increasing and expanding interest in African diaspora studies since the late 1970's and the intervention of the United Nations Educational Scientific and Cultural Organisation

(UNESCO) in the form of their Slave Route Project since 1993 in which Nigeria is actively participating, have given additional fillip to the attention now being paid to indigenous slave trade and slavery in Africa. These two developments have found expression in the recent study by Akosua Adoma Perbi on indigenous slavery in Ghana[2]. Indeed, our present book is essentially modelled after the Ghana book, except that while the former was a single-author effort, ours is multi-authored, which we believe has enriched our volume.

Slave Trade and Slavery in Nigeria: From Earliest Times to the 19th Century brings together contributions from various scholars with acknowledged expertise in their region of focus. An important strength of the book is that each contributor is from the area of focus and thus a speaker of one or more of the indigenous languages. The language facility enabled the contributors to collect the oral traditions and oral histories of the groups involved as well as access the memories of the people and communities given their confidence in them. This is particularly important given the reticence and reluctance of people to share memories on a subject matter which has been intimately associated with inferiority. This has brought freshness of perspective and depth to our study and thus corrected largely some of the errors and confusion surrounding the subject matter in the works of some non-indigenous scholars such as Paul Lovejoy, David Northrup, Susan Miers and Igor Kopytoff[3].

Essentially, the book is structured to address some important themes in slavery and slave trade studies in the Nigeria region as follows:

1. The ancient nature of slavery and slave trade in our area of study.
2. The origins of both institutions in the context of the socio-economic and cultural challenges the polity in question had to confront.
3. The status and roles of domestic slaves, especially slavery as a system of social subordination and control, existing alongside other such institutions as pawnship.
4. Slavery, slave trade and the establishment and consolidation of political power in the states that arose in the region.
5. Slavery and slave trade in economic diversification, especially the growth of international trade and agricultural production.

6. Slavery and the management of the bureaucracy and military affairs of centralised states.
7. The role of slave trade in shaping the relations between the coastal African middlemen trading communities and their hinterlands from where the slaves were recruited and those between them and the Europeans.
8. The organisation of the slave trade focusing mainly on methods of slave recruitment and means of transportation of slaves to their points of embarkation to the Middle East, Europe, the Americas and the Caribbean.
9. The system and currencies of exchange.
10. The impact of both slavery and slave trade in the societies involved.
11. The impact or otherwise of the British Abolition Acts of 1807 and 1833.
12. Slave trade as the major factor in the African Diaspora to Europe, the Middle East, the Americas and the Caribbean.
13. The significance of the slave trade routes for cultural tourism; and
14. The major relics of the trade in the Nigerian region.

These themes are discussed by the various contributors and properly situated in the context of the on-going debate among historians and other scholars interested in the subject. Thus, although the different chapters of the book are authored by different experts, there is a thematic unity that runs through the volume.

The book is presented in nine chapters. The first chapter is this *Introduction* authored by the doyen of African historiography and the project leader, Professor Jacob Festus Ade-Ajayi and Professor Okon Edet Uya, an acknowledged expert on slavery, slave trade and African diaspora studies. In Chapter 2, the well known historian of Hausaland, Professor Mahdi Adamu, critically examines *Slavery and Slave Trade in the North-West Zone of Nigeria* especially in the Sokoto Caliphate and Kebbi State. *Slavery and the Slave Trade in the North-Eastern Zone of the Kanem Borno Empire and the Emirates of Adamawa, Gombe and Muri,* are examined in Chapters 3 and 4. They are contributed by two well known scholars of the region, Professors Sa'ad Abubakar and Baworo Barkindo. While Abubakar presents a general picture of the significance of the institutions, Barkindo analyses their specific intricacies in Borno. Chapter 5, contributed by a young scholar, Dr. I. S. J. Jamada, examines *Slave Trade and Slavery in the North Central Zone*, comprising mainly the present states of Niger, Kwara and Kogi. This was an important region experiencing the pool of the trans-Saharan trade to the north and the trans-Atlantic slave trade to the south. These four chapters thus focus extensively on the trans-Saharan slave trade which is not always emphasised in current books on the subject.

Chapters 6, 7 and 8, examine *Slavery and Slave Trade in the Southern States of Nigeria* which were the most important, indeed major contributors to the Atlantic slave trade. Professor Okon Edet Uya analyses the *Institutions and their Significance in the Cross River region*, comprising the present states of Akwa Ibom, Cross River, parts of Abia and Ebonyi as well as the lower Benue Valley. Professor A. Derefaka, an archeologist with substantial interest in history, examines *Slavery and Slave Trade in the Niger Delta States* and their hinterlands which formed an important part of the Bight of Biafra region of European records. Dr. Akin Alao, another important emerging scholar, subjects *Slavery and Slave trade in South Western Nigeria* to critical analysis in Chapter 8. Chapter 9, which is the *epilogue* to the book, written by Professor Okon Edet Uya, pulls together the different strands from the various contributors and attempts a bold synthesis of the significance of the two institutions for the Nigerian area. By adopting this regional approach, the book brings to light the complexity of slave trade and slavery in Nigeria, indicating the similarities as well as the differences in the institutions in the vast Nigerian area.

We believe this book represents a major contribution to studies of slave trade and slavery in the Nigerian area, synthesising current knowledge and breaking new grounds on the subject. The book should serve to modify some of the many generalisations about the importance of the institutions for our area. It is also clear that slavery and slave trade were indeed very major factors in the social, political, and economic transformation of the polities in the Nigerian area in the pre-colonial period, most especially between the fifteenth and nineteenth centuries. As two scholars have concluded in a recent and most welcome general history of our subject area: by the turn of the nineteenth century, slavery and slave trade with the Europeans had become integral aspects of the economies of states and societies throughout the greater Nigerian area[4].

Though essentially embodying very high degree of scholarship and research in both archival and non-written sources, the book is presented in a simple style and thus accessible to the general reading public. We thank the Federal Ministry of Tourism, Culture and National Orientation for the opportunity and support given to enable us finally complete this important national project.

Notes and References

[1] R. M. Miller and J. D. Smith (eds), *Dictionary of Afro-American Slavery, (1988) Introduction.*

[2] Akosua Adoma Perbi, *A History of Indigenous Slavery in Ghana: From the 15th to the 19th Century.* Accra, Ghana: Sub-Saharan Publishers, 2008. See also *UNESCO, Slave Route Project Newsletter* vol. 4.

[3] Paul Lovejoy (ed), *The Ideology of Slavery in Africa.* Beverly Hills, 1981. *Transformations in Slavery,* Cambridge, 1983; and *Slavery, Commerce and Production in the Sokoto Caliphate of West Africa,* Trenton: Africa World Press, 2005; David Northrup, *Trade Without Rulers* (1978); Susan Miers and I. Kopytoff, *Slavery in Africa: Historical and Anthropological Perspectives,* Madison, Wisconsin, 1977.

[4] Toyin Falola and Mathew M. Heaton, *A History of Nigeria,* Cambridge University Press, 2008, p. 59.

Chapter 2

SLAVERY AND SLAVE TRADE IN SOKOTO AND KEBBI STATES

Mahdi Adamu
*Professor of History, Department of History,
University of Sokoto, Sokoto*

Introducing The Area of Study

THE area of the present Sokoto and Kebbi States of Nigeria, that is, the geographic area of coverage in this chapter, was made up of portions of the former Hausa Kingdoms of Kabi (Kebbi), Gobir and Zamfara. The other Hausa kingdoms, but located outside our area of study, were Katsina, Kano, Zazzau, Daura and Rano. All these kingdoms were fought and defeated by the forces of the Sokoto jihad of 1804 during the period 1804-1808.

Gobir Kingdom was established by the Hausa people in the 8th century AD[1]. At that time, the kingdom was located in Abzin in what is now northern Niger Republic. Its capital at that time was called Bagazim. In the 9th century, Maranda, a prosperous Hausa trading centre, became its new capital. Maranda was described by the Arab writer Al-Yakubi[2] as being on the trans-Saharan trade route from North Africa to the River Niger bend area. It was through Maranda town that the Hausa kingdom of Gobir had participated in the trans-Saharan trade at that early age, and it was through it that Islam had first reached the Hausa people[3]. Gold and slaves were, as shown elsewhere below, among the commodities exported from West Africa along the route.

In the 15th century, the government of Gobir shifted its location southwards and established a new headquarters at Birnin Lalle. In the 18th century, it shifted southwards again and established its last capital at Alkalawa[4]. During the wars of the Sokoto jihad, Alkalawa was captured and destroyed in 1808 by the jihad forces[5]. Gobir thereby list its active participation in the trans-Saharan trade. In 1809, Sultan Muhammad Bello established Sokoto town[6] in the present Sokoto State to serve as the capital of the newly established Islamic state which was called the Sokoto Caliphate (see below).

Zamfara Kingdom was established in the 15th century[7], and Kebbi in the 16th[8]. Zamfara had no direct participation in the trans-Saharan trade, but Kebbi, according to Murry Last[9], had. When the Hausa kingdoms were conquered by the jihad forces, an Islamic government was not up to rule the territories of the former Hausa and non-Hausa kingdoms which were conquered by the jihadists. This new Islamic state was called the Sokoto Caliphate[10]. Its capital was Sokoto town assisted by Gwandu[11], a town in the present Kebbi State. So the present Sokoto and Kebbi State were, jointly, the nerve centre of the Sokoto Caliphate in the 19th century.

At the height of its prosperity, the Sokoto Caliphate consisted of eighteen emirates and nearly thirty sub-emirates[12]. Each emirate had its distinct boundaries and was administered by an Emir who ran the day to day affairs of the territory under him. He was answerable to the Caliph (Sultan) in Sokoto (or Gwandu in Kebbi as the case may be), who controlled the foreign affairs and the territorial defense and integrity of the empire. All Emirs were appointed by the Sultan to rule for life, but could be removed from the office by the Sultan if the need to do so arose.

The Sokoto Caliphate was thus a federation. Its main objective was to promote and protect Islam and, as much as possible, to ensure that the religion was practiced properly[13]. The security of life and property, at home and on the highway, was another principal objective of the Islamic government. To ensure that the rule of law, based on the Sharia, was observed all over the caliphate, the judicial court of the Sultan in Sokoto was made the court of final appeal in the Islamic empire. All citizens of the huge empire, male and female, free people and slaves, have access to the court if they were not satisfied with the judgements passed on them in their emirates. To a great extent, the caliphate lived up to the calling.

In the early 20th century, to complete its colonisation of the Nigerian area, the British colonial government fought and defeated the forces of the Sokoto Caliphate at a battle fought outside Sokoto town in March 1903[14]. The Sultan fled the town but he was pursued and killed in a subsequent battle. The Sokoto Caliphate was thereby dissolved and its vast territory was shared by the British and the French.

The British took the southern portion, which by far was richer and more populous, and the French took the northern portion which was not well endowed and was thinly populated. The French portion is now called the Niger Republic. The British share of the caliphate, together with Borno, became the Northern Region of Nigeria, of which Sokoto Province was a part. It was Sokoto Province which later became Sokoto State in 1976. The present Kebbi and Zamfara States were curved out of it in 1991 and 1996 respectively.

The brief discussions above show that Sokoto and Kebbi States had a long history of political relationships, apart from their being inhabited by people of same ethnic groups, that is, the Hausa and the Fulani. In addition, Islam was, and still is, the dominant religion in the two areas.

Slavery and Slave Trade in Sokoto and Kebbi

To the best of our knowledge, no scholar has yet re-constructed how and when slavery had started in the Sokoto and Kebbi areas, or in any part of Nigeria for that matter. Scholars merely took the institution as given. For the time being, that is our position here too.

A slave is a person, male or female, who performs services to another person without payment and without choice of what to do, where to do it, how to do it, or when. The Hausa word for a slave is *bawa* if male or *bauya* if female. The types of services which were rendered by slaves in the Hausa society are discussed further below. In our area of study, as indeed all over the defunct Sokoto Caliphate, free people became slaves through one of the following ways:

Capture in Wars and Raids

In Hausaland, as was also the case all over West Africa, people captured in wars and raids were regarded as slaves straight away. This point was made by all the oral informants in the field. It was only very few of the captives mostly Islamic scholars and high ranking government officials of the opposing parties, who were kept as prisoners in house arrest in the capitals of the captors for some time, and then released. Most of the Hausa kingdoms were established in the 15th and 16th centuries, and some before the 15th. As the political history of Hausaland has shown, force was used in their establishment in most cases. Throughout the 16th, 17th and 18th centuries, there was no time when one Hausa kingdom was not at war with another. Roland Adeleye[15] has discussed the various military engagements which had taken place between them. Mahdi Adamu[16] has enumerated some of the wars between some Hausa kingdoms and some of their neighbours. Yusuf Bala Usman has also done same for the Hausa kingdoms and Borno[17]. So before the jihad of 1804, there was no time in Hausaland when wars and raids were not providing channels for enslavement by some free people. In the 19th century, military engagements increased in frequency and intensity as a result of the battles and punitive expeditions of the jihadists.

In most cases, battles in Hausaland were fought outside the city walls, and so destruction to property was minimal, except when to destroy the town was part of the ground military plans of the invading force. This was what had happened to Yandoto which was burnt down by the Sokoto jihadists in 1807 and Alkalawa in 1808. Neither of these two urban centres has been re-occupied up till now. So in Hausaland up to the beginning of the 20th century when the British colonial forces pacified the region, the capture and the wounding of the soldiers of the opposing armies or their support persons, their weapons (including horses and camels) and their provisions (including livestock) were an important consideration in military strategies in battles and raids. People were made to become slaves in this way up to the beginning of the British colonial rule.

Islam has sanctioned the enslavement of war captives[18] under certain conditions, but people rarely followed the niceties of the law.

Since military engagements were a permanent way of settling political disputes in Hausaland in the past, wars and raids continued to become the dominant way in which thousands of free people had become slaves in the territory. Our principal oral informants during the field research, namely Justice Usman Dangwaggo Bungudu in Sokoto; Alhaji Haruna Jada Bashar, the District Head of Kalgo in Kebbi; Alhaji Muhammadu Sani Ango, the *Waziri* of Kebbi in Argungu; and Alhaji Muhammadu Haruna Rasheed, the District Head of Gwandu in Kebbi; were all emphatic on the position of government as the principal cause of the enslavement of free people following military campaigns.

In the 19th century, the government of the Sokoto Caliphate was the greatest cause of wars and raids in its vast territory and along its borders. Throughout the century it had to be organising military campaigns for the defence of the boundaries of the caliphate and also dispatch armies for territorial expansion.

Though the forces of the Sokoto jihad of 1804 had succeeded in defeating the forces of all the pre-1804 Hausa and Nupe kingdoms and converted their territories into the Sokoto Caliphate, they had not been able to liquidate the former governments completely. Some members of the ruling families of the defeated states who escaped death or capture, organised themselves into resistance armies and continuously harassed the Emirates of the Islamic empire which were established in their former kingdoms in a bid to recover their lost lands or at least some parts of them. So throughout the 19th century, the remnants of the former ruling families of Kebbi centered at Argungu, of Gobir centered at Tsibiri, of Katsina centred at Maradi and of Nupe centered at Pategi continuously engaged the forces of the Sokoto Caliphate nearest to them up to the establishment of British colonial rule. At one stage in the middle of the 19th century the war between the Caliphate and Kebbi had become so intense that the Sultan of Sokoto had to call for military assistance from Kano and Katsina. However, even with the help of these re-inforcements, the caliphate forces could not liquidate the Kebbi forces, and neither could they prevent the Kebbi armies from capturing some valuable bouties, the most painful of which were the traditional royal drums of the Sultan of Sokoto which are still being kept by the people of Kebbi in their museum in Argungu.

The rulers of Borno were also bitter with the loss of western Borno to the caliphate, that is, the territories of Misau, Hadejia Katagum, Gumel and Gombe Emirates. So in 1828, Borno mounted a major military invasion of the Sokoto Caliphate. The campaign was led by the ruler El-Kanemi himself. They successfully swept through western Borno and eventually entered Kano Emirate from the east. Knowing that the Emir of Kano was no match against El-Kanemi, the Sultan of Sokoto, Muhammad Bello ordered the Emir of Bauchi (Yakubu) to mobilise militias against the invaders. Yakubu defeated the forces of Borno so decisively that El-Kanemi went back home and had never returned to the caliphate. Western Borno continued to remain in the Sokoto Caliphate.

Internally, the caliphates had the rebellion of the Emir of Hadejia in the 1860s and a civil war in Kano in the 1880s. In the south and south-west, the caliphate forces, separately led by Nupe and Ilorin Emirates respectively ventured into the forest belt in a bid to expand the frontiers of the caliphate and of Islam. The Nupe forces successfully reached as far south as Auchi and halted. Though they later withdrew, they had succeeded in entrenching Islam in the society. The Ilorin forces went deep into the Yoruba territory before they were defeated and forced to withdraw to their emirate.

In all, these defensive and offensive military campaigns in which the forces of the Sokoto Caliphate were engaged could be translated into massive capture of prisoners of war on both sides and consequently the enslavement of thousands of free people. Many of the ones caught in the campaigns in the south and south-west were sold as slaves and eventually shipped to the Americas. So wars and raids were definitely the greatest cause of the enslavement of people in our area of study.

Kidnapping

Where and when security on highways was laxed, the kidnapping of people travelling in ones and twos, or of a few people working on distant and isolated farms, was done. The victims were mostly sold as slaves. In most cases, the kidnappers, called *yan-samame* in Hausa language, were highway robbers (*yan fashi*) or slave hunters.

Judicial Sentences

Some provisions of the law in Hausaland, both Islamic and traditional, provided for the sentencing of people through enslavement for certain offences such as breach of trust relating to state security or military intelligence. The convicts were sold off immediately, and banished from the land. Some of the slaves from Hausaland who were interviewed in America in the 19th century stated that they became slaves through judicial sentences[19].

Birth through Slave Parents

Children of slaves were regarded as slaves unless the father was the owner of the slave mother. Some beautiful female slaves were often made the concubines of their owners. A concubine was called *kwarkwara* or *sadaka* in Hausa. In Islam, and also in the Hausa customs, all the children of concubines were regarded as equal on all counts with the children of the free wives of the same husband. The equality included even succeeding to the father's throne[20]. On the death of the owner, the concubine who had some children with him could not be sold or inherited by any of the inheriters of the estates of the deceased owner. In most cases she would be encouraged to marry a free person in the deceased husband's extended family, or an outsider in the locality. However, if she (the concubine) had no children with her deceased owner, she would be regarded as part of the property of the deceased owner to be shared out to the legitimate inheriters. However, if she was an old woman and had stayed with her owner for some time, she would either be freed or be allowed to continue to live in the house as a slave who would be free to perform services at her will. The new head of the family would take care of her until she died.

Children of a male slave were regarded as slaves of the owner of their father, but could not be sold by any body. They would be integrated into the family of the slave owner for whom they were obliged to offer some services free of payment. In the Hausa society, such children, male and female, were called *cuncunawa*. They could own property and raise their own families who would have to live in or near the house of the owner of their slave father. They could, however, pay for their freedom if they had the money and the wish to do so.

How Slaves were Utilised

In the Sokoto and Kebbi areas, there were many ways in which slaves were utilised. The various ways are discussed immediately below.

As Domestic Slaves

Domestic slaves were kept in the houses of their owners to provide a variety of services, depending on the gender, age and skills of each slave. A male domestic slave could be called upon to do any menial work in the house at any time of the day or night. He had no freedom of choice. He would be fed and clothed (scantily in most cases) by the owner who also provided him with accommodation in his house. However, if the slave was a professional before his enslavement, he would be permitted to practice his occupation in his spare time. If he was trusted by his master, he and the master could enter into the *murgu*[21] arrangement whereby he would operate freely and on his own and be paying some fixed regular charges to his owner. Such payments were not regarded as deposits for his freedom. If he wanted to be free, he had to negotiate with his master the cost of the *fansa*, that is self-redemption. According to the provisions of the Islamic law and the customs and traditions of the Hausa people, the owner had to agree to grant the *fansa*, though he was at liberty to decide the price, which might be high to facilitate replacement.

If the domestic slave was a woman or a girl of marriagable age, one of the following five would happen to her:
- She could be made a concubine of her owner; we have already discussed concubinage.
- She could be given as a gift to an important government officer, to a high ranking military officer, to a friend or to an Islamic scholar of immense learning and respect.
- Be married to a male slave in the house, all her children would be the *cuncunawa* already discussed.
- Operate as an unmarried servile member of her master's family, performing all sorts of menial duties, such as general cleaning,

looking after the children, cooking, washing up, going on errands in the locality, and the like.
- A free person could request the owner to allow him to marry her under the terms to be negotiated between the prospective husband her owner.

The number of domestic slaves that a person would have, depended on his social or administrative status, or on his wealth. Many wealthy people used their domestic slaves in their commercial or industrial activities. All senior government officers in Hausaland were required to keep some domestic slaves, however few, because the custom of the land prohibited them from performing some physical work in public.

Domestic slaves and the free members of the owner's family lived in the same house, dressed in similar garments and ate from the same pot. The only difference would be with regard to quality and quantity. In Islamic worships, Muslims free man and Muslim slaves lined up in same rows to pray.

Through the liberal ways in which domestic slaves were handled, many non-Muslim slaves became converted to Islam. The non-Hausa among the male and female slaves gradually became absorbed in the Hausa culture. So the institution of domestic slavery was one of the ways in which thousands of people became Islamised and Hausanised.

Used as Public Officers

In Sokoto and Kebbi States, as was also the case all over Hausaland, slaves were used in the running of the government. There were certain duty posts which were reserved for slaves and people of slave origin. Such posts included *Shamaki, Shinfida* and *Jakada*[22].

The palace courtiers (*dogarai* and *fadawa*) were a mixture of free people and slaves. In his Ph.D (History) thesis, Adamu Fika has discussed cases of slaves in Kano Emirate who distinguished themselves as excellent soldiers and were consequently given important appointments in the government. In his book, *The Hausa Factor*, Mahdi Adamu has done same for Bauchi, Keffi, Nasarawa and Lafia Emirates[23].

Military Services

In the past, it was quite common to use slaves as soldiers and as attendants who would service the needs of the soldiers and their horses and camels. In a battle, these slaves who were good at the arms might be given some positions of command in the military campaigns. At the end of a successful campaign, they would be given portions of the booty. Such warrior slaves were often domestic slaves who had stayed with their owners long enough to distinguish themselves. Some of them might even own some slaves while they themselves were slaves before the law.

Use on Farms

Even before the jihad wars of the 19th century, farm work was one of the major duties of male slaves. During the planting season, the slaves would work daily on the farm (or farms) of their owner. Such a farm was usually large; it was called *gandu* in Hausa. In their spare time, however, they would cultivate their own farms which were usually small in sizes, and were called *gayauna*. In the 19th century, due to the constant military engagements of the Sokoto jihad, the number of slaves in the territory, particularly in the Sokoto and Kebbi areas, increased very much. In addition, thousands of slaves were sent to Sokoto and Gwandu (in Kebbi) as annual tributes (see below). Consequently, the senior government officials and some of the senior Muslim clerics came to own so many slaves that they settled most of them on their large private farms located outside the capitals. The slaves would cultivate the farms of their masters and also cultivate their own *gayauna* farms. Such farm settlements for the slaves was called *runji*. Around Sokoto town in the 19th century there were a number of *runji* settlements. One of them was called Runjin Sambo; it is now a built up suburb of Sokoto town. The *runji* system in and around Sokoto town has been adequately studied by Shehu Lawal and Ibrahim Jumare; reference could be made to their articles[24] for details.

In a *runji*, one of the resident slaves was often appointed the overseer. In the large ones, that is the ones containing many houses of slaves, the overseer often found himself discharging some administrative functions, including the settlements of disputes. The title of this type of overseer was *hakimi* (village head). The hardworking slaves, and also those of good behaviour, were allowed by the overseer to marry and raise families.

Deployment in the Economic Sector

Some rich traders and merchants used slaves to run their businesses. Some slaves were used in buying and selling and others in the industry, such as weaving, metal works and the making of leather goods. In Sokoto, the decendants of such professional slaves are still living in the town carrying on the professions, but doing so as free people[25].

From the brief account above, it could be seen that there was no aspect of human activities in Sokoto and Kebbi in which slaves were not used. In the 19th century, slaves in the Sokoto Caliphate, particularly in the metropolitan areas, were so numerous that the English traveler called Clappertan thought that in Kano in 1825 the population of slaves equaled that of free people? Lovejoy and Hogendorn felt that the proportion of slaves to free people was not far from that[26].

Despite the large number of slaves in the area, there was no slave class which had developed in Sokoto and Kebbi. The slaves were scattered over the various levels and sectors of the society as we have just seen. Probably that was why there had not been any general slave revolt in the territory.

Import and Export of Slaves

No records of import and export of slaves into and out of Hausaland were kept by the people involved in slavery and slave trade in our area of study. Consequently, writers and commentators have been addressing the issue in general terms only. This chapter is not an exception.

The vast majority of the people who found themselves as slaves in Hausaland were used in the locality; they were not exported. Before the 19th century, most of the Hausa slaves who were exported were marched across the Sahara desert to North Africa and the Middle East. From the beginning of the 19th century, however, the export of Hausa slaves to the coast in the south became significant[27] before it was abolished in the middle of the century. Lovejoy attributed the rise in the export to the increase in the supply of slaves occasioned by the military campaigns of the Sokoto Caliphate. Boahen[28] has stated that about 70% of the slaves exported from our area of study to North Africa were women (60%) and children (10%). However, according to Lovejoy, human cargo of Hausa origin which was shipped to America consisted of able-bodied men and women, mainly men. When the trans-Atlantic slave trade was abolished in the middle of the 19th century, many Hausa slaves were repatriated from America and the West Indies to West Africa. Nearly all the freed slaves settled along the coast stretching from the Senegal River basin to the Calabar area. Records of all such re-settled freed slaves were kept at their points of entry. It has been established that some of the freed slaves who settled along the coast were Hausa people from Kebbi State. The Hausa freed slaves, whose repatriation records were kept at the National Archives in Freedom, Sierra Leone, and were examined by the present author, had established thriving ferry services using a large coastal boat which they named Maiyama; and Maiyama was, and still is, an important market town in Kebbi State. Fishing, farming and ferry services were among the traditional occupations of the people of Kebbi State.

The manner in which slaves were transported from Hausaland to the Guinea Coast has already been discussed[29]. Mahdi Adamu has shown that it was the normal trade routes from the Savanna to the coast which were used for exporting slaves from the Savanna belt southwards. There were no routes set aside for importing or exporting slaves. A popular trade route which was used in the 19th century in the north-south trading relations was Katsina (or Kano)-Zaria-Nupe-Ilorin-Ijebu-Lagos (Eko).

With regard to the import of slaves, Hausaland has been importing slaves from the Benue River basin for many centuries before the Sokoto jihad of 1804. Kano, Zaria, Yandoto and Katsina were the main destinations in Hausaland. Using data in the *Kano Chronicle*[30], it would seem that imported slave labour was first used in Hausaland in the 14th century. The King of Kano called Yaji, son of Tsamiya, brought in numerous slaves from his successful military campaigns in the second half of the 14th century against the hill dwellers of the present Bauchi State, and against the Jukun. Some of the imported slaves were war captives and the others were purchased. His successor continued the campaigns up to the end of the 16th century. Tribute slaves were also said to have been sent from the Nupe rulers to the Hausa kingdom of Kebbi under Muhammadu Kanta in the 16th century. Most of the slaves who were imported into Hausaland from Nupe and the Benue basin were used in the country as domestic slaves.

In the 19th century, a big boost took place in the import of both the trade slaves and the tribute slaves into Hausaland. With the establishment of the Sokoto Caliphate, all the emirates which were created south of Hausaland sent their annual tributes to the Sultan in Sokoto. Some slaves were among the gifts sent by each Emir to the Sultan and to some of his senior government officers. For instance, the Emir of Adamawa sent 1,000 slaves annually to Sokoto as part of his tribute. The emir of the smaller emirate of Hamara sent 500 slaves every year[31]. Nupe and Ilorin Emirates sent theirs to the Emir of Gwandu in Gwandu town in the present Kebbi State.

All the tribute slaves and the trade slaves which were imported on continuing basis were in addition to the thousands of slaves which were generated in Hausaland itself. As already stated, most of the slaves generated internally and those imported were utilised in the locality. The situation was perhaps the main factor that led Lovejoy to describe the Sokoto Caliphate as one of the largest slave societies in modern history[32]. Without giving any statistics to support him, he opined that slaves in the Sokoto Caliphate numbered one-third to one-half of the population of the Islamic empire. This is an unwarranted exaggeration.

The Trans-Saharan Trade

Crossing the Sahara Desert to reach the West African countries is a very old affair. When and how it started nobody can tell, but it was stated that by 1000 BC, the Carthaginians, in the present day Tunisia, had started to do the desert crossing using chariots[33]. This development made the western routes across the desert more important than the central and the eastern routes. Non-perishable goods of low weight but high in value obviously predominated.

It was the introduction of the camels into North Africa from the Middle East in the 1st century AD[34] which revolutionised the trans-Saharan trade between North Africa and West Africa. At that time, the route from Tripoli going south-west ward to Gao and Timbuktu in the Niger-bend area was the most important. However, as the export from the Songhai Empire to North Africa increased, the route from Morocco going southwards once more took the premier position.

Up to the end of the 16th century, the western routes from Morocco to the Songhai territory were the most important trans-Saharan routes. In 1591, the Morrocan forces successfully invaded the Songhai Empire in a bid to have a direct control of the gold trade. The Morrocan conquest of the Songhai Empire destabilised the region, and the routes across the desert no longer as safe as they were before. The south-eastern routes, which went from Tripoli to Kanem-Borno, took the lead. According to Boahen, in the 19th century, it was the central route which went to Kano, with a branch to Sokoto, which became the main carrier of the trans-Saharan trade. This followed the destruction of Birni Gazargamu as a result of the military attacks by the Sokoto jihadists and the establishment of Sokoto town to serve as the headquarters of the Sokoto Caliphate. Katsina and Yandoto were also destroyed as market centres and as recipients of the trans-Saharan trade. Reference could be made to the article of Mahdi Adamu[35] to see how events connected with the Sokoto jihad of 1804 had led to the destruction of most of the 18th century trading centers in the Central Sudan and the rise of new ones in the 19th century.

Adu Boahen has studied the trans-Saharan trade in detail, and has concluded that the trade was at its peak in the period 1490-1590[36]. At that time, gold was the most important commodity. Slaves were also exported through the trans-Saharan trade routes, but they never took the lead in value because it was women and children that were preffered for use in North Africa and the Middle East. Crossing the Sahara Desert in those days took 70 to 90 days. The journey was harzadous and consequently not conducive to women and children. All slaves, male and female were made to trek cross the desert barefooted. Using data sourced in the 18th and 19th centuries, Boahen estimated the annual export of slaves of all categories from West Africa to North Africa as 10,000[37]. He has also given the list of the other goods which featured in the import and export trade across the desert. Ann Modougall has given an account of the various service people who were lubricating the trans-Saharan trade and thereby facilitating the export of slaves from our area. Reference to her article could be made for details[38].

The trans-Saharan trade, and also the salt trade from the Sahara, reached the end of their importance when rail lines were constructed by the British and the French colonial governments from the Guinea Coast going northwards. This took place in the first decade of the 20th century. By then slave trade had already been abolished all over the West Africa.

Relics and Social Scars Connected with Slavery and Slave Trade

Throughout the field research which was carried out to collect material for this chapter[39], no relics connected with slavery and slave trade were found. The absence of relics was a reflection of the nature of slavery and slave trade in our area of study. As noted elsewhere above, most of the slaves in the Sokoto caliphate, male and female, lived and worked in the homes and in the farms of their masters. They were not chained, and they moved around the locality without guards accompanying them. Even hand-cuffs and chains which could be attributed to slavery and slave trade were not found. They were not used to control slaves.

Slaves in Sokoto and Kebbi States were rarely paraded in market places for sale. Most of the sales were done when the slaves were in the houses of their owners or were being kept for sale by the market brokers (*dillalai*) who specialised in slaves. Such market brokers were called *dillalan bayi* in Hausa (slave brokers). So, no special slave markets had developed in the area.

During the field research, people were asked to talk on the social, economic or political effects of slavery or of the slave trade which could still be seen in their communities. All the oral informants replied that there were none in their respective areas[40]. Their explanations tallied with the research findings of Shehu Lawal who, in 1983, had carried out field study of the *runji* system in Sokoto town in the 19th century[41]. Ibrahim Jumare later carried out similar interviews in the same area and on the same theme, which was slavery and slave trade in and around Sokoto town in the 19th century[42]. Their findings were similar.

The point that the oral informants and the scholars have made is that the scars of slavery and slave trade are no longer visible in the society because of the manner in which slavery and slave trade were conducted in Hausaland. As is already noted, slaves were allowed to use their spare time to work on their occupations. It has also been noted that under the *murgu* and the *fansa* arrangements a slave — male or female — could acquire his/her partial or full freedom. The ability of the slave to raise his own family has also been noted above. So slaves and slave owners did not live as antagonists. Islam always intervened in favour of the slave and controlled the level to which slave owners could exploit their slaves, male and female.

In the Sokoto and Kebbi areas, as already alluded to, slaves and the free people lived together in the same houses, dressed in the same way and ate the same food. Unless one was told, one could not easily distinguish the slaves from the free people. Some slaves who were in government, or who were commercial agents of some rich people, lived more comfortably than many of the free people who were not in such privileged positions.

The relationships between slaves and their owners in Sokoto and Kebbi States were so liberal that when slavery was abolished by the British colonial rule in the 20th century, many ex-slaves and their families continued to attach themselves, socially and politically, to their former masters and their successors, but did so as free and equal partners in progress. So later in the 20th century when the ex-slaves had died out, vestige of slavery died with them. In both Sokoto and Kebbi States, there are presently many descendants of former slaves who are now holding very important public posts. Some of such people were among the informants who were interviewed at the palace of the Sultan in Sokoto in February 2008. The criterion for holding public responsibility is no longer one's social or traditional origin but one's level of education and the strengths of one's character.

The Bara System

In discussing slavery and slave trade in Sokoto and Kebbi States, care must be taken to distinguish between the slave, called *bawa* in Hausa, and the servant of no fixed remuneration, called *bara* in the Hausa language. Both *bawa* and *bara* systems had existed in the Sokoto and Kebbi areas long before the Sokoto jihad of 1804, and continued to co-exist until slavery was abolished by the British. The *bara* system is still operative all over Hausaland[43]. The *bara* is a person, male or female, who renders a variety of services to another person without fixed or immediate remuneration for the services. The master, the *maigida* or *ubangida*, would give him whatever he wanted and whenever he chose to make the donations. Whenever the *bara* had expensive engagements, such as marriages or naming ceremonies, the master was expected to make an appreciable contribution in cash or in kind. Most of the *bara* were men, but a few women, widows or wives of some poor people, specially attached themselves as *bara* to some women of influence (wealth or status of husband). A *bara* could be well off if his master was rich and was generous.

Conclusion

In conclusion, it should be stressed that slavery in Sokoto and Kebbi States differed from slavery in most places such as the Americas where slaves were used mainly as farm labourers in the plantations, or in North Africa and the Middle East where the female slaves were not given the privileged positions of being concubines but were used only as house maids to carry out all types of menial duties in the houses of their owners. The *murgu* and the *fansa* systems further distinguish slavery in Hausa land from slavery in many places. Islam has also stepped in to give the slaves some measure of protection from extreme exploitation. It is therefore not surprising that by now, when all the ex-slaves must have died, relics, no vestiges or social scars connected with slavery and slave trade can be seen in our area of study.

Notes and References

1. Illa Maikassua, "Some suggestions relating to the contributions of Gobir migrants to the transformation of the neighbouring communities" *History Research at A.B.U*, Vol. VI, 1981/82
2. Al-Yakubi, *Al-Tarikh* (1960 edition, Beirut).
3. Mahdi Adamu, "Sufism and empire building in West Africa," International seminar on Sufism and the cotemporary time in Nigeria, held at Sokoto, Nigeria, 26-28 October, 2007.
4. Illa Maikassua, *Some Suggestion*; Adeleye, R. A: "Hausaland and Borno", Chapter Four in Ade Ajayi and Michael Crowder (eds), *History of West Africa*, vol. I.
5. Murray Last, *The Sokoto Caliphat*, (London, 1967).
6. Saleh Abubakar, *Sokoto Birnin Shehu*, Ph.D, Zaria (1982).
7. Garba Nadama, *The Rise and Collapse of a Hausa State: A Social and Political History of Zamfara*, Ph. D, Zaria (1977).
8. Bello Alkali, "A Hausa Community in Crisis, Kebbi in the Nineteenth century", M. A. Zaria (1969).
9. Murray Last, *Before Kebbi; Written Evidence for a Rima Valley State at Gungu before 1500 AD*, paper presented at an international seminar held on archaeology and early history of Sokoto States, Sokoto, 1983.
10. For detailed discussion on the establishment and management of the Sokoto Caliphate, see: Murray Last, *The Sokoto Caliphate*; Hamid Bobboyi and A. M Yakubu (eds), *The Sokoto Caliphate, History and Legacies, 1804 -2004* (Kaduna, 2006); Ahmed Kani and Kabir Gandi (eds), *State and Society in the Sokoto Caliphate* (Sokoto, 1990). Also see the same sources for the cause and the conduct of the Sokoto jihad of 1804.
11. Though Birnin Kebbi was the capital of Kebbi Kingdom before the jihad conquest, Abdullahi Fodiyo, who was given charge of the western emirates of the Sokoto caliphate (Nupe and Ilorin) by his brother Shehu Usmanu Danfodiyo, chose the nearby Gwandu town as his capital. All the Emirs of Gwandu in the 19th century operated from Gwandu. It was under British colonial rule that the seat of government was transferred to Birnin Kebbi.

12. The Emirates were: Kabi (Kebbi) centred at Gwandu, Zamfara, Katsina, Kano, Daura, Bauchi, Zazzau (Zaria), Katagum, Gumel, Hadejia, Misau, Jama'are, Gombe, Adamawa (Fombina), Hamarua, Bagirmi, Nupe, and Ilorin (Yarba). There were over thirty sub-emirates who were sending their annual tributes to some senior emirs for transmission to Sokoto. Of the sub-emirates, Keffi, Nassarawa and Wase were the most important. The first two were supervised by the Emir of Zazzau, and Wase by the Emir of Bauchi. Adamawa and Nupe too had a number of sub-emirates under them. See (i) Murray Last, *The Sokoto Caliphate*, (London 1967), pp. 53-4.; Adamu, *The Hausa Factor in West African History* (Zaria, 1978), pp 91-106; Sa'ad Abubakar, *The Lamibe of Adamawa: A Political History of Adamawa, 1809-1901*(Zaria, 1979).
13. The Sokoto jihad of 1804 was executed to give the Islamic reformers of the late 18th century and the early 19th century a conducive political and administrative platform for their enforcing the reform and expansion of Islam in Hausaland in line with their reform ideologies. Shehu Usmanu Danfodiyo was the leader of the reform movement, assisted by his brother Abdullahi Fodiyo and his son Muhammad Bello. When the Sokoto Caliphate was firmly established, Muhammad Bello became the Sultan of Sokoto and Abdullahi the Emir of Gwandu. For details see the sources listed in note 10 above.
14. For details, see H. F. Backwell (ed.), *The Occupation of Hausa Land* (Lagos, 1927); Adeleye, *Power and Diplomacy in Northern Nigeria, 1804-1906* (New York, 1971).
15. Adeleye, "Hausaland and Borno, 1600-1800," In: Ade Ajayi and Micheal Crowder (eds) *History of West Africa*, Vol. 1, Chapter Four.
16. Adamu, *The Hausa Factor*, pp. 23-27.
17. Yusuf Bala Usman, "A Reconsideration of the History of Relations between Borno and Hausaland before 1804," being Chapter Nine in Usman, Y. B. and Alkali, Nura (eds), *Studies in the History of Pre-colonial Borno* (Zaria, 1983).
18. Abdullahi Fodiyo, *Tazyin al-waraqat*, Translated and edited by M. Hiskett (Ibadan 1963).

19   Paul E. Lovejoy, *Slavery, Commerce and Production in the Sokoto Caliphate of West Africa* (Africa World Press, (Trenton, 2005), p. 64.
20   Sultan Aliyu Babba and his younger brother, Sultan Aliyu Karami ,were both sons of Sultan Muhammad Bello and were both born by the same concubine of Sultan Bello. On account of this provision on equality, they each became Sultan of Sokoto in the 19th century even though sons of free wives were many in the palace in Sokoto. Field research at the Sultan's palace in Sokoto, August, 2009.
21   For some discussion on the *murgu optem*, see Adamu, *The Hausa Factor*, pages 11-12; Lovejoy, *Slavery Commerce and Production*, pages 207-222.
22   Group interview at the Sultan's palace, Sokoto on February, 2008. See appendix.
23   Adamu Mohammed Fika, *The Political and Economic Reorientation of Kano Emirate, 1882-1940*, Ph. D, (London, 1973); Mahdi Adamu, *The Hausa Factor*, Chapter IV.
24   Shehu Usman Lawal, *The Economics of Slave Use in Runjin Sambo Slave 'Plantation' of Sokoto*, a seminar paper presented at the Department of Histroy, Usman Danfodiyo, University, Sokoto (1984); Ibrahim Mohammed Jumare, *Slavery in Sokoto city 1804-1936*, M. A, Zaria, (1988). *Slavery and the Development of Ribats in the Metropolis of the Sokoto Caliphate*, DEGEL, the Journal of the Faculty of Arts and Islamic Studies, Vol. VII, (2007).
25   Group Interview at the Sultan's palace, Sokoto, February, 2008.
26   H. Clapperton, *Journal of a Second Expedition into the Interior of Africa from the Bight of Benin to Soccatoo*, to which was added the *Journal of Lander from Kano to the Sea Coast* (London, 1829); Lovejoy, *Slavery, Commerce and Development*, p.3.
27   Philip Curtain, *The Atlantic Slave Trade: A Census* (Madison, 1969).
28   Boahen, Adu, *Britain, the Sahara and the Western Sudan, 1788-1861* (Oxford, 1964), page 128.
29   Mahdi Adamu, "The Delivery of Slaves from the Central Sudan to the Bight of Benin in the Eighteenth and Nineteenth

Centuries", a chapter in H. A Gemery and J. S Hogendorn (eds), *The Uncommon Markets: Essays in the Economic History of the Atlantic Slave Trade* (New York, 1979).
30 H. R. Palmer, *The Kano Chronicle* (Lagos, 1928), p. 106.
31 Sa'ad Abubakar, "A Survey of the Economy of the Eastern Emirates of the Sokoto caliphate in the Nineteenth Century", Chapter Five in Y. B Usman (ed), *Studies in the History of the Sokoto Caliphate* (Zaria, 1979), page 124, endnote 57.
32 *Love Joy, Slavery, Commerce and Production*, p. 3.
33 Boahen Adu, *Britan, Sahara and the Western Sudan, 1788-1861* (Oxford, 1964), page 103.
34 Boahen Adu, *Britain, Sahara and the Western Sudan*, p.103.
35 Mahdi Adamu, "Destruction of Trading Centres in the Central Sudan in the 18th and 19th Centuries", Chapter Four, in Y. B Usman (ed), *Studies in the History of the Sokoto Caliphate*, (Zaria, 1979).
36 Boahen Adu, *Britain, Sahara and the Western Sudan*, p. 104.
37 Boahen Adu, *Britain, Sahara and the Western Sudan*, page 128.
38 E. Ann Mcdougall, "Camel Caravans of the Saharan Salt Trade", in Catherine Covery-vidrovitch and Paul Lovejoy (ed), *The Workers of African Trade* (Sage Publications, London, 1985)
39 The people who had carried out the field research to collect data for this chapter were: Professor Mahdi Adamu, Miss Rose Mershak, Mr. Richard Makan and Mr. Dauda Alkali. The informants are in the appendix attached herewith.
40 The records of all the interviews conducted during the research are currently being kept by the Federal Ministry of Tourism and Culture, Abuja.
41 Shehu Lawal, "The Economics of Slave Use".
42 Ibrahim Mohammed Jumare, "Slavery in Sokoto City".
43 Mahdi Adamu, *The Hausa Factor*.

Appendix

Oral underviews during the field research carried out in Sokoto and Kebbi States in February, 2008 with the following informants:
1. Alhaji Muhammad Bello, The Director, Waziri Junaidu History and Culture, Bureau, Sokoto.

2. Professor Mahdi Adamu, Department of History, Usman Danfodiyo University, Sokoto.
3. Justice Usman Dangwaggo, Bungudu (retired), Marina, Sokoto. He died some months after the interview.

Group Discussion at the Sultan's Palace, Sokoto.
The interview was arranged by the secretary of the Sultan of Sokoto. It was attended by some courters and some royal drummers, singers and trumpeters of the Sultan. Some of the people were descendants of former slaves and some descendants of free people.
1. Their leader was Garba Na-Garba, the *Dangaladiman Sarkin Dawaki* of Sokoto. He descended from free people whose ancestors were living in Alkalawa before that capital of Gobir Kingdom was captured and destroyed in 1808 by the forces of the Sokoto jihad of 1804.
2. Sidi Dan-Atto, Kofar Atiku, Sokoto. He was aged 83 years at the time he was interviewed in February, 2008 at the residence of Professor Mahdi Adamu. He was still engaged in some commercial activities in Sokoto. He descended from a Sokoto based family of traders and merchants.
3. Alhaji Haruna Jada Bashar, the District Head of Kalgo, Kebbi State.
4. Alhaji Muhammadu Sani Ango, *Wazin Argungu*, Kebbi State.
5. Alhaji Muhammamdu Haruna Rasheed, the District Head of Gwandu, Kebbi State.

The interviews were conducted by the following researchers:
1. Professor Mahdi Adamu, Department of History, University, Sokoto.
2. Miss Rose Mershek, Department of Culture, Federal Ministry of Culture and Tourism, Abuja.
3. Mr. Richard Makan, Department of Culture, Federal Ministry of Culture and Tourism, Abuja.
4. Mr. Dauda Alkali, Department of Culture and Tourism, Abuja.

Chapter 3

SLAVE TRADE AND SLAVERY IN THE NORTH EAST REGION OF NIGERIA

Sa'ad Abubakar
Professor of Nigerian History, Department of History, University of Abuja

Introduction

THE term North East geo-political zone of Nigeria applies to the six states of Adamawa, Bauchi, Borno, Gombe, Taraba and Yobe; an extensive region and heterogeneous ethnic groups with a rich and diverse history dating back into antiquity. Looking back, at its political history, the earliest polity in the region was Kanem, located to the east of Lake Chad, which was abandoned as a result of dynastic instability when the Saifawa moved into Borno on the western part of state in c.1400[1]. Mai Ali Ghaji Dunamami established a new capital at Ngazargamu, now in Yobe State, in c.1470. Therefore, our discussion of slave trade and slavery in this region must start from that time. Even before then, in 1392 for example, in a letter to the Sultan of Egypt, Mai Uthman Biri ibn Idris complained that some Judhama Arabs had been capturing,

> our free subjects - women and children and old people, and our relatives, and other Muslims...selling them to the slave dealers in Egypt and Syria and elsewhere, and some they keep for themselves[2].

The other major polity in the region at about the 14th century was the Jukun Kingdom of Kwararafa, which probably was located further away from their present base, modern Wukari. The kingdom achieved fame through extensive long distance expedition against the Hausa states to its northwest and Borno to the north. However, due to lack of authoritative sources and because we know how its successor state of Wukari organised itself, it is true that while internal slavery existed in their society, slave trade was not very widely practiced. Therefore, from the 15th to the beginning of the 19th century, the two states of Borno to the north and Kwararafa (Wukari) were the dominant polities in the region before the emergence of emirates of the Sokoto caliphate beginning from 1809, about four hundred years later. The latter include the seven emirates of Adamawa, Bauchi, Gombe, Jamaare, Katagum, Misau and Muri. Since their emergence down to the end of the first decade of British colonial rule, these emirates and Borno promoted "slave trade" in their domains until it became virtually impossible to do so in the region. The British creation of a territory known as Nigeria, their curving out of provinces, divisions and districts made it dangerous for slave trade to be openly practiced. In fact, the British one year after declaring a protectorate over Northern Nigeria in January 1900, had abolished "the legal status of slavery prohibited slave dealings and declared that all children born after the 1st of April 1901 were to be free"[3]. However, as we shall see later, it took quite some time for Britain to abolish slavery in Borno and the emirates.

The Antiquity of Slave Trade and Slavery

No one can suggest precisely the beginning of slave trade and slavery in this region. Even in Borno where a document indicates Arab enslaving its people in the 14th century, slave trade, not to talk of slavery, had been going on for over a millennium before then. On the whole therefore, slavery was an extremely common institution in the north east region, if not the entire country and the world. How then do we define *slave* and *slavery*? Ordinarily, the term slave applies to a captive, to someone who lost his freedom through warfare; who could therefore be bought and sold like any movable property and a person who had lost his rights and privileges after being moved to a different society. Slavery on the other hand refers to the act of being in captivity and serving a master without receiving legal payment or compensation for the work rendered. In Borno and later the seven emirates in the zone, slavery was greatly influenced essentially by the stipulation of their religion, which permits enslavement of non-believers as a means of converting them to the faith. In this regard, the law obliged the owner of a slave to watch over his religious well being. The situation was more or less like a trusteeship that might be exercised over a ward or a young minor as he developed. Among non-Muslims in the region *slavery* were a social rather than an economic institution, and a means of recruitment into an appropriate social group in society.

After the Saifawa moved into Borno in the 14th century, warfare for expansion became very common giving rise to acquisition of captives, some of who were sold as slaves and a number retained by the officials of government as *domestic slaves*. Therefore, warfare was the major source of slave acquisition in Borno and right to the time of British conquest in 1902, there was no time that wars and raids had stopped completely thereby providing avenues periodically for the enslavement of the large pagan population surrounding the empire, especially to the west, south and southeast. Then in the 19th century, the tempo of warfare and enslavement increased seven fold with the foundation of seven Muslim emirates that acknowledged the suzerainty of the caliph at Sokoto. As a matter of fact, the emirate governments in Adamawa, Bauchi, Gombe, Katagum, Misau, Jamaare and Muri, were the greatest initiators of wars and raids in the vast territories surrounding their domains. Similarly, each emirate was on its toes by constantly monitoring its borders and organising warfare to defend its boundary, to punish recalcitrant groups and to extend territorial control over their neighbours.

There were also internal conflicts, especially between the emirates and Borno, which the jihadists had failed to conquer and take over the task of governance in Ngazargamo in 1808, 1809 and 1811. It was this failure that compelled the jihadist to retreat westward and southwest wards where they eventually established the emirates of Hadejia, Jamaare, Katagum, Misau and Gombe. Under al-Kanemi, Borno militarily confronted the emirates and in 1826 led its forces against Kano, but was intercepted by the Emir of Bauchi, Yakubu, who defeated the invaders and forced them to retreat. Since then al-

Kanemi and Borno never again attempted to lead an expedition against the emirates of the Sokoto Caliphate. But to the southeast cross border skirmishes between officials of Borno and Adamawa emirate continued down to the advent of Rabih in the 1890s. From the forgoing therefore, and given the frequency of warfare in the region, the ground remained very fertile for major enslavement of people and the resultant slave trade and slavery in the region down to 1901 when Britain, on beginning to conquer the area, abolished them completely.

Other methods of enslaving in Borno, the emirates and non-Muslim areas in the region, although on smaller scales, included kidnapping, legal sentencing and biological reproduction while in slavery. In the 19th century, with the absence of good roads and lack of general security outside towns, organised robberies were common. It used to be unsafe for individuals to travel long distances alone or in small groups because of the possibility of being kidnapped and subsequently sold out as slaves by organised gangs of robbers. In fact, in some places they also waylaid caravans to steal and also enslave their members and sell them into slavery. Usually in these robberies there was no distinction between non-Muslim and Muslim as the robbers were merely interested in capturing who ever fell into their way for enslavement. Therefore, on most trade routes that traversed the region it was dangerous for small groups to undertake inter emirates or state travels as they risked being captured and sold into slavery. As a result, travels consisted of very large groups led by *madugai* (merchants), who knew the routes very well and were accompanied by well armed escorts for protection en-route their journeys.

Among the non-Muslims, enslavement for some came as judicial punishment for offences against society. These included murder, incessant stealing, and breach of trust, including betrayal of the community's military secrets as well as witchcraft and fornication. There was no system of sentencing people to prison; therefore, convicts of serious offences usually ended up being sold and removed out of the society by those that had bought them. This practice was more widespread amongst the large number of other communities outside Borno and the emirates, such as Margi, Higi, Gude, Pabir,

Mumuye, Chamba, Tera, Manga and many others.

With regard to biological reproduction by slaves, there is need for differentiation because not all children of slaves were regarded as slave, especially in Muslim communities. For example, where an owner took one of his slave women as a concubine, her children in Islam were free and therefore equal on all grounds to those born of his free wives. This was common in Borno and the emirates, before the British conquest. Once a concubine had children there was no way she could be sold. Even after the death of her owner, she could either be inherited along with the estate of her dead owner, or marry any member of the owner's extended family. But where the concubine had no children she still would not be sold, rather she would become part of the owner's estate for distribution to his inheritors. It would become the duty of the owner's inheritors to look after her, as a slave until death. As for male slaves, their children were still considered as slave of the family that owned their father but they could not be sold by him or anyone else. Usually, they grew up as members of the owner's family owning property and marrying wives to give birth to third generation slaves. On the other hand, if they wished, especially where they became wealthy, it became easier for some of them to buy back their freedom and live as free men in society.

Slave Capture and Exploitation in the Region

In the era of slavery and slave trade, the latter was definitely "an economic institution" that provided income, which supported the livelihood of a large number of the population in Borno, the emirates and other chiefdoms in the region. Indeed, organised states — such as Borno and the emirates — were for a long time in the forefront of slave capture and slave marketing in the northeast. The demand for slaves was certainly very gigantic. As a result, the raiding of non-Islamic groups in the hills and the wide Savannah zone was a major activity of all the Islamic states, not just in the region but throughout the Central Sudan. Usually, raids were carefully planned and then launched, sometime secretly by an overwhelming force, either at day time or at dawn. Consequently, villages were surrounded making it difficult for anyone to escape. Depending on the disposition of the raiders, the aged and infirm would not be allowed to live; they were usually slaughtered. For example, in Borno, Barth actually saw a spectacle when 170 men in their prime were abandoned and bled to death. These and similar acts by the forces of the Shehu and emirs had given rise to a serious charge against Islam, "that it has encouraged and given religious sanction to slavery"[4]. Slave markets existed in the major settlements of the zone, although today information is very scanty on their organisation and transactions. But in the absence of a common currency, the price of a slave varied from one area to the next depending on proximity to the source of the slaves. In Yola of Adamawa Emirate, for example, the price of a slave in mid-19th century was 2,000 *chede daneje* (cowry shells) or four *turkudi*, even though *leppi*, (stencilled locally woven cloth) which was the preferred currency of exchange and was more acceptable than the cowries.

Generally, European records portrayed slavery and the slave trade in nineteenth century Adamawa as the worst of their kind in the Sokoto Caliphate. In fact, the region "was looked upon by the Hausa states and particularly by Sokoto as the Eldorado of the slave trade"[5]. There was certainly slave trading on a large scale in the nineteenth century. This was perhaps because the emirates emerged in a wholly non-Muslim region through religious wars aimed at establishing Islamic polities. In a jihad, Islam sanctions the fighting of anyone who refuses to accept Islam or to live in peace with Muslims. Thus, the by-product of this fighting was prisoners of war — jihad captives — and Islamic law permits their enslavement[6].

In Hausa land, the jihadists took over established Hausa states with highly developed economic systems of traders and merchants, and a monetary system. The situation was different in the emirates established in the north east zone. After the emirates and sub-emirate governments emerged, they had very limited sources of income to support them. Similarly, a majority of the jihadists were not farmers and could not farm in conquered territories without changing their ways of life. Thirdly, the jihad conflicts had created hostility between them and their previous suppliers of agricultural goods. This then necessitated the founding of slave settlements to produce agricultural produce for them. In short, the prevalence of slavery in Adamawa and the other emirates arose from economic necessity.

In the early years, the jihadists put captives into economic and military uses, and they played important roles in the economic, political, and military life of the emirates. The ruling classes acquired slaves in two ways: either by their conquests of non-Islamic communities and rebellious *amana'en* (trustees), or as tribute and gifts (*shahu*) from the rulers of sub-emirates. In Yola, the bulk of this tribute came from the large and powerful sub-emirates of Rai-Buba, Bibemi, Ngaundere, Tibati and Banyo-Koncha[7]. The sub-emirates in north Adamawa, especially Maru'a and Madagali, also sent some few slaves. According to Dr. Barth, the tribute coming into Yola from the sub-emirates in mid-19th century amounted to about five thousand slaves annually[8]. The Yola ruling class as well as those of other emirates also acquired slaves through their local expeditions commanded by senior officials, including brothers of the heads of government.

It was customary for the emirs to send a tribute to the caliph. In Adamawa, the ruler used to despatch one thousand slaves annually. After any successful expedition, a large number of slaves were retained for the palace, the females as either concubines or domestic servants, and the males as personal servants, courtiers, and soldiers. Some slaves were also reserved for the leading officials either as rewards for services or as gifts designed to obligate them to the emirs. Ownership of slaves was not limited to the emirs and the sub-emirs; their officials and warriors too acquired slaves during raids and expeditions in which they had taken part. In some emirates even common citizens owned slaves, and some rich men owned even up to a thousand slaves and more.

While slavery was prevalent in the emirates, slave trading was on a lesser scale. The reason was that the vast majority of people retained slaves for other needs instead of selling them. This was because it was in the owner's interest to keep them in permanent deployment in the slave farmsteads (*dumde*) or train them in other vocations. Usually, only stubborn and uncouth slaves were sold at the slave markets of the emirates or if there was a compelling need for money and materials. Slaves were also sold by the ruling classes in all emirates by the emirs, sub-emirs, and their officials — in order to obtain luxury items brought into the emirates by traders from distant places[9].

In all the emirates and sub-emirates, the ruling classes used slaves in different tasks. In the households of officials, the female slaves (*horbe*) performed domestic jobs such as grinding corn to make flour, and the preparation of daily meals, thereby lightening the burden of the legally married women (*reube tëabe*) who were superior to the concubines (*sulãbe*). Each *debbo teado* had a number of *horbe* who did other jobs, such as sweeping, spinning cotton, and plaiting hair, on her behalf. The male slaves (*maccube*) performed heavier household jobs, such as fetching water and firewood, but their real importance lay in the military and economic fields. As earlier discussed, each member of the ruling class had farmsteads (*dumde*) in which slaves lived to farm for their masters. In the environs of Yola settlements such as Chomoyel Abba, Doulabi, Golomba, Langui, Wuro dole, Kirngabu, Konkol, Pette, and Yolel started as *dumde*,[10] as did nearly most of the villages in Namtari, Girei and Gurin districts[11]. Some of the slaves who lived for a long time in the *dumde* worked at crafts; some wove cloth - the narrow loom — some were brokers in the market and some sold salt, kola nuts, sugar cane, sweet potato, etc. However, newly acquired slaves only lived and farmed at the farmsteads.

The *dumde* produced most of the food consumed by the families of the ruling group. This was in addition to the foodstuff brought in from the villages of the free non-Fulbe peoples either as tribute or *jizya*. The agrarian slave settlers lived under a sort of contract with their masters. The latter owned the land and in this capacity, they received part of the produce of the *dumde*. However, where a master was responsible for the upkeep of the slaves, he received all the produce of the farms. Alternatively, the slaves lived as tenants and they laboured in return for their occupancy, or gave part of the farm produce to the landowner. An alternative contractual relation was for the slaves to maintain two farms, one belonging to their owner, which they cultivated in the mornings and evenings, and the other, which was their own, they cultivated in their spare time[12].

In the military field, slaves formed the basis of the power of the ruling class - the emirs, sub-emir and their officials. Even though a slave officer class such as had existed in Borno did not emerge in the emirates, there were many notable warriors of slave origin. The number of slaves at his disposal determined the power of each official. Therefore, the *dumde* served as military garrisons of the leading officials in the emirates. The emirs relied upon their officials to raise the necessary personnel for expeditions whenever required. At such times, each official engaged in war had to lead his slaves from the farmsteads into the field as soldiers. According to Dr. Barth who visited Yola in 1851, many private individuals possessed more than one thousand slaves kept in the *dumde* and their homes. When occasion arose, the *dumde* slave owners deployed them into the battlefield as soldiers. Therefore, the slaves in *dumde* served dual functions: they were farmers in the wet season, and soldiers in the dry. They also indirectly maintained their powerful masters in office, for the more slaves an official had the greater was his influence and power. Thus, the emirs and the sub-emirs in the sub-emirates owned more slaves, which was not only for their security but also for the enforcement of their orders.

The Europeans described slavery in the emirates of the Sokoto Caliphate as evil because their understanding of it was associated with the American one, which was an advanced and refined type of human exploitation unparalleled in history. However, in all the emirates and Borno, the case had never been "once a slave always a slave". Long before the British conquered the region, it was possible for slaves to acquire freedom, wealth, prestige, and power. For example, persons of slave descent held important emirate titles, such as, *Ajia, Baraya, Majidadi, Dan Rimi* and *Shamaki*. While in Borno some members of the state council —the *kokenawa* — the *kachalla*, were of slave origin. Indeed, there was slave labour within the emirate system, but the forms of economic exploitation of the time were limited to jobs which freeborn also performed such as farming, domestic jobs and participation in campaigns. The exploitation was not of the plantation type geared towards profit making on a large scale. In both Borno and the emirates, majority of non-Muslims were not enslaved arbitrarily, but either because they had rejected Islam or refused to submit to Muslim rule. Moreover, after enslavement, the conditions and status of slaves gradually changed whenever they embraced Islam. On the whole, being slave was not like belonging to a caste system, rather, he occupied the lowest status in the social hierarchy of the nineteenth century but emergence from that status had always been possible.

Slave Routes in the Region

It is generally agreed that one of the important results of the emergence of the Sokoto Caliphate was in opening a vast land of diverse people to trade and communication. Before 1804, apart from Borno, the gigantic northeast region remained virtually little known because access into it was difficult, if not impossible. By 1809, the situation changed following the establishment of the new emirates and as the century advanced more parts of the region were better known as links with the outside world became well established. Trade routes linked the emirates one to another and also with Sokoto, the seat of the caliph, as well as with Borno in the Chad Basin. But chronologically Borno, being in existence going back to a millennium, deserves premier consideration before looking at the emirates, which came into being only in the 19th century.

By 1808, when the Fulata attacked and sacked Ngazargamo, Borno, as earlier discussed, had had well established relations and commercial contacts with Egypt and other North African countries across the Sahara Desert. There were also good commercial relations westward with Kano and the other Hausa states; so too was there trade with the people of the south Chad basin extending possibly down to the Benue River. All the various regions were traversed by trade routes, through which slaves were exported from Borno. However, the most important slave trade route from Borno across the desert was the Ngazargamo to Kawar to Fezzan to Tripoli, which according to Arab geographers was in use by the 9th century[13]. According to Bovill, this route was essentially a slave trade route and as Boahen indicated, "from about the beginning of the 17th century until the 1820s, the Fezzan Borno route was the most active of all the Saharan routes"[14]. Indeed, as European travellers suggested, thousands of human skeletons were strewn at the major stops from Borno to Tripoli. These included skeletons of young women and girls, which were numerous around the water points, having died of exhaustion and thirst as a result of tracking on foot from the point of their purchase in Borno. Generally, slaves from Borno and Hausa land were very popular and demands for them were very high in North Africa essentially for local use and also for further export to Egypt and Turkey in the east. Indeed, the preference for slaves from these regions was because of the skill and intelligence of the men and "women for their good looks, cheerfulness and neatness"[15]. This then explains why slaves from Hausa land and Borno used to attract better prices. It also explains the volume of slave export as the number of skeletons en-route North Africa suggests.

However, as from the third decade of the 19th century, the importance of the Borno to Kawar to Fezzan and Tripoli route declined. This was due to the fall of the Karamanti dynasty in Tripoli, which had maintained strict control over Fezzan and developed amicable relations with Borno. Their successors, the Turkish Governors appointed by the Porte found it not too easy to make their power felt in the desert region. As a result of this, an Arab group, the Awlad Sulaiman moved just to the north of Lake Chad where they raided and plundered at will thereby disturbing the peace and security of the region. Similarly, wars and conflict between Wadai and Borno became more frequent and devastating. Certainly, these led to some decline in the export of slaves along this route to North Africa. By that time, Kukawa — Borno's new capital founded by al-Kanemi — became one of the three entrepots of the trans-Saharan trade. The slave dealers ensured that their slaves were in good condition before setting out to cross the desert. The male slaves, most of them young men, were coupled with leg-irons and chained by the neck, while the girls and young women walked without the chains or leg-irons. It was difficult to march across the desert; as a result by the time of their reaching Fezzan most of them became living skeletons. Then, the slaves were allowed to rest and underwent a fattening process before they were sent to the markets at Tripoli and Benghazi to be sold at very high profit.

Traffic in eunuchs, although on a small scale, had big local and foreign demand as "guardians of the *harem*". In most states —Borno inclusive — robust and healthy boys were usually captured and held to foster trade in eunuchs, and some were as punishment castrated and kept as palace slaves. The process, which was brutal, was performed in the crudest possible manner. Borno enjoyed reputation in this trade where Turkey, Egypt and the Barbary states were the major buyers, paying as much as 250 to 300 dollars per person. At the beginning of the 19th century, according to Denham, the Shehu in Borno had 200 eunuchs in his *harem*[16]. The total number of slaves annually exported across the Sahara Desert was about 10,000 and by 1860, the number for Tripoli was 5,000; Morocco, 2,500; and the rest were smuggled into Tunis and Algeria. Then, about half of those exported to Tripoli were re-exported to Turkey[17].

There were also east-west slave trade routes leading from Borno into the Hausa states going back to centuries. The major route passed from Ngazargamo to Nguru and through Hadeji'a into Kano, which was an important slave market. Because of Kano's commercial dominance, traders moved out into various regions bringing back slaves, which were sold to trans-Saharan traders. Similarly, slaves from other parts of Borno found their way into Kano and then finally exported. Some of the slaves were moved across the desert to North Africa and some southwards to the coast for shipment to America.

The major trans-Saharan trade route, through which slaves were exported, was from Kano to Iferuan, Ghat and Ghadames. Then, from there the route either went to Tunis in the north or Tripoli in the north east. Traders bringing slaves from Borno to Kano did so because of the variety of products in the latter to exchange for their slaves and because of the fame of the traders that plied the trans-Saharan route from there.

The emirates to the west and south of Borno — Misau, Katagum, Jamaare, Bauchi and Gombe — were closer to Hausa land and had more or less better contacts and more established trade routes. Gombe, for example, had its route through Darazo, Gwaram, and Birnin Kudu before entering Kano city. It was an import-export road for the emirate, including conveyance of slaves to the famous slave market at Kano. The emirate of Bauchi also had trade routes linking it to Kano and Zaria through which slaves were transported to their markets. The major route ran through Ningi before joining the route from the other emirates in the region. The other emirates of Misau, Katagum and Jamaare to the northwest of Bauchi have been very near Kano and the trade routes were shorter, which meant constant commercial relations with the Hausa states, particularly Kano.

When the emirates sprang up in the 19th century, slave trade expanded. Before then, the external trade of the region was on a very limited scale, but the conquest of the area by the jihadists and the subsequent establishment of emirates some with dependent sub-emirates changed the situation. A vast and extensive region became an integral part of the Sokoto Caliphate, which, consequently accelerated trade and intercourse with distant neighbours. As Dr Barth rightly pointed, the jihadist had "succeeded in giving to distant regions a certain bond of unity...making the land more accessible to trade"[18]. Certainly, the establishment of a single authority over the heterogeneous Adamawa peoples facilitated regular entry of outsiders. The Kanuri from the north and the Hausa from the northwest and Kakanda from the south west began to enter the emirate in large numbers in the nineteenth century and eventually dominated its trade. Thus, by mid-19th century an enterprising Hausa community of traders — including slaves — had fully developed in Yola.

Trade routes linked the emirate to Borno and the other western emirates of the Sokoto Caliphate, just as they linked the various sub-emirates together. The route to Borno, which Barth followed to Yola, was from Kukawa, through the Margi country to Sorau and Benue Valley. It was Adamawa's highway to the north through which slaves and other products were transported. The route was well protected during the early years of the jihad. There were *ribats* along the route, especially in the northern Benue plains, to protect caravans, although the original motive was to protect Yola. There had always been a general fear of a possible attack from Borno, especially during the conflict between the Fulata and the Kanuri following the former's rebellion against the Mais. Therefore in most of the *ribats*, trusted slaves were encamped as a fighting force against possible attacks from Borno. It was also a dangerous road, which used to witness high way robberies and indiscriminate killings. In 1854 for example,

Sherif Ahmed el-Baghdadi, an Arab traveller, was slain and killed on the route from Yola to Kukawa[19].

By mid-nineteenth century, the importance of the route was purely for commercial reason, as trades with Borno become fully established. The valued products that came from Borno consisted of potash for watering cattle, salt for human consumption and luxury goods, such as European and North African textile materials. In return, Adamawa exported slaves, cattle, and ivory northwards to Borno. Trade in slaves was next in importance to ivory. Adamawa in the nineteenth century was the leading exporter of slaves in the Sokoto Caliphate, with majority of the slaves being exported from the sub-emirates in the south. In fact, a large number of slaves from those sub-emirates were exported westwards along River Taraba and across the Benue to Kano. The importance of Adamawa in slave trade was that even as late as 1894, Monteil in Sokoto received a bill for 72 slaves drawn on Yola for merchandise he sold to Caliph Abdurrahman. The bill was negotiated and paid for at Kano by a man who accompanied him from Sokoto[20].

Trade route linked Southern Adamawa to the middle Benue valley in the west, which went along the River Taraba valley through Gashaka, Bali, and Bakundi down to the Benue River. There were also trade routes that linked Yola, the capital of Adamawa, to the neighbouring emirates of Muri, Gombe and Bauchi. The route to Bauchi for example, went through the Bata country, then along the valley of the Gongola to Gombe[21]. From there, the route went via Gwaram to Kano. There were two routes to the emirate of Muri. These were the Mumuye and the Bachama axis. The former went via Mayo Ine, Chukkol into Mumuye land to the river port of Lau on the Benue River. The Bachama route on the other hand, was from Yola through Ngurore, to Numan, but it was unpopular because of the hostility of the Bata and the Bachama of the western Mayo Ine plains. The most important trade commodity was salt; especially the brown salt of Bomanda, which Muri exported, while slaves formed an important segment of export.

The routes linking the northern and the southern parts of Adamawa converged at Yola. The main link between the capital and the southern sub-emirates of Banyo, Tibati and Ngaundere, was the Daka route. The Funange route linked Yola with the sub-emirates of Guider, Binder, Kalfu and Maru'a. From Maru'a, other routes led to Borno and Mandara in the west and Bagarmi in the east linking the emirate to the Sudan. The other most important route was the river Benue, the natural highway that linked the emirate to the River Niger. Before the nineteenth century, the river was not popular as a means of transport, but after the establishment of emirate administration, it became a major highway for the Nupe who engaged in the slave trade, and the Kakanda who were anglers and traders in fish. The rulers of the emirates were particularly concerned with trade between their domains and other parts of the Sokoto Caliphate, as well as with Borno. The trade routes were vital not only for trade but as a means of contact and communication within the emirates and with their neighbours. In all emirates, there were local officials responsible for commercial activities, including slave trade.

Slavery and Colonial Rule

The contact between the northeast region and Britain goes back to the 1820s following the visit of Denham to Borno but it was not until 1901 that they started to subjugate some parts of the zone when Yola fell and in 1902, Borno followed suit. Indeed, right from 1807, Britain had abolished slave trade and throughout the nineteenth century their travellers to the region rarely engaged in it. Many had received gifts of some slaves from traditional rulers only for them to set them free and then travel with just a few as free companions. In Yola, for example, Dr. Barth refused a gift of two slaves from Emir Lawal, but he eventually returned to Britain with two young Margi youths he obtained in Borno. But after they had some training in Britain, they returned and settled at the British Consulate at Lokoja. There is therefore no record of British travellers within the region engaging in slave trade and this continued even after they had conquered and brought it under colonial rule. As already indicated, the British first act in the newly declared protectorate was to declare the abolishing of slave trade and slavery and that all children born as from 1st April 1901, shall be free. Since that date both slavery and trade in slaves were driven underground, as the slave markets folded up but people knew how to get slaves from the underground before it finally disappeared altogether. In 1903, officials of slave descent in Muri emirate had nothing to pay for merchandise brought by merchants from Kano so they raided and captured slaves from an aman community without the consent of the emir[22]. Consequently, when the British resolved to come and enquire, the emirs lost his life mysteriously thereby closing the matter indefinitely.

With regard to ending slavery, this affected essentially the ruling classes and wealthy individuals, the owners of farmsteads where the slaves usually resided and served their owners. Majority of such slaves, even after becoming legally free, did not welcome it because it meant vacating their habitat and scouting for a new means of livelihood for the future, which was quite difficult. Thus, in most emirates, the change meant little to them as majority of the slaves continued to live in the farmstead as before and went on giving part of their produce to their former owners as *payment* for the land they used. Certainly, this indicates that they enjoyed living under powerful and influential masters. For domestic slaves in the homes of leading officials, their freedom was also meaningless as they lived in comfort, and they had power and prestige, which they had to lose once they vacated the personal homes of their previous owners. In reality, what had happened in Borno and the emirates was a stop in the use of the term slave to describe all those that were domestically deployed, which then allowed most of them to live and practice their vocation as before. In an emirate outside this region, a powerful slave group opposed their emancipation because it meant "loss of their privileges and influence"[23]. However, the recruitment of new slaves for the farmsteads had ended since the British put a stop to it in 1901. Moreover, the fact that British officials resided in the Provincial and Divisional headquarters largely accounted for the gradual decline of the *dumde* type of slavery.

Relics and Monuments of Slavery and Slave Trade

It is not impossible for relics and monuments of slave trade and slavery to still exist in some parts of the northeast region. Borno is a very good example, given the long history of slavery in that ancient empire. Unfortunately, the present capital of Maiduguri was founded after the British conquest in 1902. Before then, Kukawa, which was also established in 1814, as the capital of Borno by al-Kanemi, was abandoned after the invasion by Rabih from the Sudan in the 1890s. Similarly, Ngazargamo, the capital established by the Mais early in the fifteen century ceased being one after the Fulata invasions, the last of which was in 1811. Thus, at present there are no relics or monuments as such in Maiduguri and in the case of Ngazargamo and Kukawa, it is possible for an archaeological excavation at a future date to come up with things that may be relevant to slavery and slave trade of the past. In the emirates there are a number of farmsteads that still exist where slaves were kept for farming and other activities. These therefore are contemporary monuments of the slavery and slave trade era that ended over one hundred years ago.

Community relations at the end of slave trade did not change immediately because majorly the slave raiders belonged to the ruling class and because they were still in power under colonial rule they saw themselves as an upper class in society looking down on all others. In Jalingo, for example, the Djen, Apawa, Mumuye, and a number of other smaller groups lived under aman and so even at the time of slave trade they were usually spared from being caught and enslaved. At an early age, this writer knew that annually the Apawa people used to come to Jalingo to repair the emir's palace walls, staying in the town for some months. Similarly, the Mumuye people were untouchable as the emir treated them with favour and allowed them free access into the palace for whatever they wanted to do. Indeed, apart from the episode of 1903 discussed earlier, which the emir opposed, non-Fulbe groups within the emirates, including Kona after 1892, were not to be enslaved. Instead, expeditions went further south across River Taraba into Tiv land periodically for slaving activities. Common citizens may look down on non-Muslim groups socially but, as already indicated, a caste system never emerged. Although the community to which I belong participated in slave catching, it is difficult now to articulate who the actual participants were because during wars or expeditions the people where rulers lived were conscripted to participate. The only thing that is fair is that no major family that has been in Jalingo by 1903, could claim not being involved in raids for slaves and also disposing them when the need arose. Unfortunately, there is no communal archive on slavery and slave trade in the community for further reference.

Slavery — in the sense of keeping and making others to work at farmsteads or similar activities — does not exist today anywhere in the northeast. However, during the first two decades of colonial rule, the system of conscription of labour for executing government projects — building roads, railways, office and houses, etc., — with little or no pay was indeed a form of *slavery*. Emirs generally were asked to gather the men needed for such projects. Similarly, during the First and Second World Wars, traditional authorities were involved in forcefully mobilising groups for enlistment into the colonial army to be despatched to the war front. The other type of *slavery* practiced in other parts of the country — a system of enticing young women and getting them sent abroad for prostitution by organised *pimps* here and in Europe — also does not now exist in the region.

One of the effects of slavery and slave trade on ethnic group relations in the region, especially nowadays, is the way majority of non-Fulbe perceive non-ethnic Muslims that were in power from the 19th century down to independence. Firstly, the non-Hausa Fulani people still harbour ill feelings essentially because of the way their ancestors suffered under emirate administration, because of the way they were enslaved and treated before the British ended it by their conquest. Besides, because the British arrival allowed missionaries to freely establish in the non-Muslim areas, which ultimately opened them up and now with popularly elected governments, they had opportunity to participate in governance. In some emirates, the non-Fulani saw the Hausa Fulani as "oppressors", and "exploiters" who, because of economic advantages, deliberately "refused" to spread the Islamic faith in their groups. This explains the presence of undeclared hostility and tension between non-Muslim, non-Hausa Fulani Muslims and Muslims in various locations in the region. This was all the more so because, until fairly recently, the latter had the advantage of higher social standing and better economic control throughout the zone. Majority of businesses and contracts from governments were monopolised by the same Hausa Fulani elements. Thus, for the non-Hausa Fulani peoples in the zone, these disadvantages came about because of their disadvantaged pre-colonial disposition.

Conclusion

In conclusion, slavery and slave trade had been on going in the northeast region for over a millennium before the 19th century. Because of the prominence given to the trans-Atlantic slave trade, and slavery acquired a very bad name and many scholars, particularly Africans, call it the most inhuman action of man against man ever witnessed in history. However, a deeper examination of that trade, especially in this region, would reveal the following. In the first place, there was virtually no Europeans' hand in the slave trade in northeast Nigeria right from its beginning up to the time when Britain ended it at the beginning of the 20th century. In fact, the contact of the region with Europeans started only in the third decade of the 19th century when Clapperton, Denham and Oudney visited Borno in the 1820s. Therefore, the major traders in slaves were Arab from North and Northeast Africa. It is true that in the 19th century, many slaves from the region were exported by African traders to the Atlantic coast, from where the Europeans purchased and exported them across the sea to the New World. But this was against the tide of British opposition that had in 1807 abolished slave trade for its citizen and had even started to interfere with slave shipment across the Atlantic. Thus, whatever blame one may make against the slave trade and slavery in the northeast zone should therefore be shared by the indigenous peoples and the Arabs.

Human society, rather than being static, has always been dynamic. Our contemporary society is therefore the most civilised, the most enlightened and technologically advanced ever. This was achieved through evolution over time. Five hundred years ago, the situation was different and the society less advanced, which explains the dependence of Europeans on slave trade and slavery as they struggled to expand their plantations in the New World. As a matter of fact, the abolishing of slave trade, first by Britain and later by other European countries, was not necessarily out of humane consideration; it was not because they wanted to end the suffering of the black races, but essentially because the industrial revolution brought about the need to source for new raw materials rather than human cargoes. Some of the new source and materials — palm oil, ivory and cotton — existed in Africa. Therefore, it is possible to argue that even if European nations did not abolish slave trade and slavery, a time would have come at a future date when the trans-Atlantic slave activities would have collapsed through human evolution.

Notes and References

1. H. R. Palmer, *History of the First Twelve years of the Reign of Mai Idris Alooma of Bornu*, p.2.
2. Thomas Hodgkin, *Nigerian Perspectives* (London, 1960).
3. Sa'ad Abubakar, "The Northern Provinces Under Colonial Rule: 1900-1959" in O. Ikime, *Groundwork of Nigerian History* (Ibadan, 1980), p.454.
4. F. D. Lugard, *The Dual Mandate in British Tropical Africa* (London, 1923), p. 465.
5. Passarge, *The German Expedition to Adamawa*, Geographical Journal, vol. 5 (January 1894).
6. F. H. El-Masri, (trans/ed) *Bayan Wujub al-hijra* [Uthman ibn Fudi] (Khartoum 1977), pp.141-6.
7. Henry Barth, *Travels and Discoveries in North and Central Africa*, vol ii.
8. *Ibid.*
9. Passarge, *op. cit.* p.52.
10. Abubaka, *Lamibe Fombina*, p. 201ff.
11. Namtari D.N.B., *Local Authority*, Yola.
12. W. O. Rosedale, P. *History of Balala*, NAK, Acc. 77 p.8
13. Bovill, E. W. *The Golden Trade of the Moors* (London, 1968) p. 245.
14. A. A. Boahen, *Britain, the Sahara and the Western Sudan* (1964), p.128
15. Bovill, *op. cit.*
16. Denham, D., Clapperton H. and Oudney, *Narrative of Travels and Discoveries in Northern and Central Africa in the Years 1822, 1823 and 1824.* (London, 1826).

17 Boahen, *op. cit.*, p. 128.
18 Barth, *op. cit.*, p. 510.
19 Henry Barth, *op. cit*, vol. ii, p. 284.
20 P. L. Monteil, *De Saint-Louis a Tripoli par le Lac Tchad* (Paris, 1895), p. 248-55.
21 H. B. Ryan, *Report on Yola Province*, 1911. NAK, J.2.
22 Waziri Saadu Abubakar, Jalingo, October 2009.
23 That was the batakulki in Katsina at the time of Emir Abubakar. See Y. B. Usman, *The transformation of Katsina* (Zaria).

Chapter 4

SLAVERY AND RELICS OF SLAVERY IN BORNU AND THE THREE EMIRATES

Bawuro M. Barkindo
*Professor of History, Department of History,
University of Abuja, Abuja*

Introduction

SLAVERY has become an emotive term since it has been criminalised by the European powers in the 19th century. All branches of scholarship seem to have a conception of what the term means and how it could get manifested. By extension we now have all sorts of misdirected practices that are termed "modern day slavery" which is not the aim of this article to delve into. My aim here is to briefly look at slavery in the pre-colonial period in our area of concern and then see if there are still relics or vestiges of it with us today. Slavery here means all facets of the term: slave-raid, slave-trade and domestic slavery. We agree with the general definition that says slavery is the condition whereby one human being is in total control of another and can dispose of him or her in any way the owner wants just like owning a horse or a donkey. There were several ways of obtaining a slave in the period under discussion, the most important of which were through slave raid, gift, purchase, kidnapping or inheritance. Others included pawning and personal placement in order to escape punishment or utter deprivation.

Slavery was a phenomenon of social stratification in a settled community. The first manifestation of slavery came when deviants like witches, adulterers and others "rejected" by the gods were rid off to cleanse the society. This may be the case of the pre-Islamic Kanem whose king was said to have been in the habit of enslaving his people without recourse to war. At first, those rejected may have been killed, mutilated or banned. Eventually, as may have happened in our case, a more agreeable way presented itself. Some foreign elements offered not only to off-load the rejects and take them permanently away but also compensate the ruler for doing so. Not only that but the articles of payment, especially the foreign garments, helped to enhance the position of the ruler in the eyes of his people. Certainly, that must have contributed to the brisk commerce between North Africa and Kanem through Fezzan during this early period as we shall examine further below. The adding of camels and horses to the imports of the Kanem ruler which later arose, was not only the result of socio-political development, a means of bringing more people into the expanding state but also of enslaving all those who either refused to be included, were rebellious or considered enemies to the state. In whichever case, slaves were captured, but rather than all of them being sold as before, some were kept to help in the development of the social stratification. The adoption of Islam, the religion of the foreign traders, most of who were also proselytizers, in the 11th century AD, helped in accelerating socio-political and cultural developments. Expeditions were jihads against non-Muslims or *razzias* against enemies of state. In whichever case slaves were caught, the increasing economic development of the state meant a steady rise of the nobility with competing personal economic and political tastes with the ruler. This was the time when the rulers started to involve their trusted slaves not only in the army but also administration as a counter to the challenge of nobility. On the other hand, the involvement of the slaves in the affairs of state enhanced their positions so much so that most would come to prefer remaining slaves than to lose their socio-economic status by regaining their freedom.

The above, which has world wide application, seems to be the model that appears in Kanem and carried into Borno by the Saifawa and applicable in all the cases examined in this study (Barkindo 1985, 225-250). Captured slaves in excess of the domestic needs of the ruler and the nobility by the time when social stratification developed fully, were sold off to buy luxury goods. Second and subsequent generations of slaves — unless those considered unfit or in time of dire need — would not be sold in the market although they could be given as gifts.

The North-eastern region of Nigeria is not only extensive but also one of the most heterogeneous in the country. The previous chapter has treated the region holistically. This chapter will limit itself to metropolitan Borno and three of the four south-eastern Emirates of Sokoto, namely Adamawa, Muri and Gombe. Metropolitan Borno is now located in the Emirates of Borno and Dikwa in Borno State as well as the emirate of Gazargamu now in Yobe State. The three emirates to be dealt with are now found in Adamawa, Taraba and Gombe States respectively.

All the four were Muslim states and thus their systems of obtaining and utilisation of slaves were largely similar. In addition, they were all actively engaged in serious conflicts with their largely non-Muslim neighbors up to the colonial period. Thus, the question of slavery, slave captives, slave trade and domestic slavery, continued to dominate the history of this area for a long period. Part of the explanation is that, for Borno, the government of the Saifawa-longest surviving ruling dynasty in the Western Sudan- had collapsed in the mid-19th century due to political and ecological factors. The kanemi successors of the Saifawa were not able to fully consolidate their powers before colonialism. Similarly the emirates of the Sokoto Caliphate under discussion, were struggling to establish centralised polities in areas where none existed. To make it more difficult was the fact that the emerging emirates were based on a new religion, Islam. This meant not only an effort to build mega political systems where none existed but ones based on a new religion as well. This was unlike the Hausa states which were largely Islamic with only backsliding rulers. Once those rulers were supplanted by the jihadists, the ferocity of the conflicts subsided. In short, in our area of study, conflicts and the capture of slaves continued in most of the area until the inception of the colonial period.

Slavery in Kanem and Borno

Slavery under the Saifawa in Kanem and Borno

Kanem was one of the most ancient states in Africa south of the Sahara. It came together in the ninth century AD through the fusion of nomadic and sedentary populations whose early rulers were recognised as sacred. The people, we are told, stood so much in awe of ruler that he was said to have enslaved whoever he wanted amongst them without recourse to war (al-Yakubi and al-Muhannabi, 1981 pp22,71), a phenomenon so widely spread in Africa that does not need to detain us here. We are, however, not informed of what the ruler wanted to do with those he allegedly enslaved but piecing the internal and external sources together the answer became clear. We are told that by the ninth and tenth century AD, there was a regular trade of major significance along the route from the Mediterranean littoral to the Lake Chad via Fezzan (*ibid*:al-Yakubi). By the tenth century AD, we are told that although the majority of the people of Kanem were still clad in skins, the attire of their ruler had undergone a tremendous change. He was dressed in trousers of wool over which he wrapped himself in excellent garments of wool, silk and brocade. Further, he was also said to have owned horses and camels (*ibid*:al-Muhannabi). In fact by then al-Yakubi reported a brisk commerce between Zawila and Kanem through Kawar which was in the hands of Ibadi Muslims (*ibid*:al-Yakubi).

To pay for the exotic items, the rulers exported slaves to be used as domestic slaves and soldiery of the Muslim rulers in North Africa. In the Diwan or chronicle of Mais of Kanem and Borno, Mai Arki (1023-67) was said to have owned numerous slaves of which he settled 300 each at Dirki, Kawar and Fezzan (Diwan in Lange, 1977: 65)

In the following centuries there followed rapid urbanisation and culturisation that saw the adoption of Islam by the Saifawa ruler Mai Hume (1075-86). Hume's successors from their capital at Njimi (now in Chad Republic) were able to build an extensive government on Islamic principles. He was advised by a council of twelve, some of who were sons of slaves. The rulers continued and even further strengthened relations with the Muslim rulers of North Africa and

Egypt through royal pilgrimages to Mecca and Medina, diplomatic correspondences and commerce (Barkindo, 1992:1-20).

To pay for the exotic items, Kanem rulers continued to export slaves most of who were increasingly captured in the south, i.e. Borno. In fact much of the trade was dominated by the Mais as in the pre-Islamic period, only it was expanded to include other demands by the Mai and his chosen nobility. Kanem export also included special slaves such as beautiful girls and eunuchs for harems of the North African rulers.

Developments in the Kanem period of the Saifawa set the model for slavery in our area of study: raids into non-Muslim areas by the Islamic state in which slaves were amongst the *ganima* or booty. The slaves were utilised in the political, military and social developments of the state and the excess exported to acquire exotic items for the use of the ruler and the nobility.

Economic, political and other factors led to the loss of effective control of Kanem in the 14th century. Mai Idris b.Ibrahim (c.1342-66) on the advice of the Ulama abandoned Kanem and together with his family and partisans shifted the gravity of the state westwards to Kaga in what is now modern Borno where they had already been preceded by their followers and leading title holders. Borno was more endowed then Kanem which was largely desert and semi-desert. In the succeeding five centuries, the Saifawa were able to build a strong regional economy and a more centralised state that was able to dominate not only most states around the Lake Chad but nearly all of Hausa land as well.

Certainly, the many conquests of the Kanuri against many groups in their efforts to build the state or mellow down rebellious groups brought in many more captives than in the Kanem period although some were also received as tributes. A large number were, however, utilised for the political and economic needs of the state and for export. Most of the male and female slave titles including the titular royal concubines in the Kanuri Empire of Kanem and Borno seem to have emerged during this classical period. To be sure, exporting slaves across the Sahara in exchange for exotic needs of the Mai and his close associates, continued. Birni Gazargamu grew to be one of the major entrepots of the trans-Saharan trade where a large community of foreign merchants lived near the palace in a special quarter called Wasiliram handling commodities that included slaves. They also dealt in other luxury goods such as ivory, ostrich feathers, leather and gold dust (Lavers, 1980:205-6).

Slavery under the Kanemis and Rabih in Borno

From beginning of the mid-eighteenth century, Borno started to be faced by numerous problems: aggressions from outside forces, revolts of subordinate states and recurrent famines. There were steady immigrations of the tubu and Shuwa Arab nomads into the metropolitan province to escape the attacks by neighboring aggressive states. These developments forced the Fulbe (Fulani) to migrate into western Hausa states and into the areas to the south with disastrous consequences to Borno; for these formed the active vanguards of the jihad of Shehu Usman dan Fodio when it broke out in the beginning of the 19th century.

In spite of all the above, perhaps the over one thousand year Saifawa dynasty might have contained the situation; but the jihad of Shehu Usman was to give the *coup de grace* as it were. The jihad of Shehu contributed to the loss of the western parts of the empire and the supplanting of the Saifawa dynasty by Sheikh Muhammad al Amin el-Kanemi (a widely traveled Muslim scholar who at that time was settling at Ngala-now in Borno State) who thereafter established the dynasty of the Kanemis or Shehus. The latter, from 1846 when they formally took over power, were in turn faced with a number of problems which were not over up to the arrival of first Rabih b Fadal Allah closely followed by the European imperialists which added to the chaos in Borno.

We are lucky for the many narrations of a number of European travelers who visited Borno during its turbulent history in the nineteenth century although we have to be cautious of some of their reports. All of them were sent to see the nature of slave trade, among other things and explore how these could be replaced by the "legitimate trade". They tended in many instances to exaggerate their descriptions.

For example, Heinrich Barth had noted that, Mohammed el-Bashir b. Ahmed Tirab, the *Wazir* of Borno during his visit had, before he was put to death in 1853, had between 300 to 400 slaves and left 73 surviving sons not to talk of daughters (Barth 1965, ii, 42). In 1866, Gerhard Rolfs had estimated that Sheikh Umar el-Kanemi's personal slaves to around 4,000 (Fisher, H. J. 1991:124). However, in those days it would be difficult for the European travelers to differentiate between the royal functionaries, retainers and personal slaves of the ruler. In fact, Nachtigal had to admit that some of the numerous slaves that he found at the Borno court during his visit were actually government functionaries.

Secondly, some of the raids which many of the travelers actually accompanied were aimed at achieving more complicated designs than merely catching slaves. One of this was the Borno-Mandara joint attack against the Fulbe of Diamare in northern Adamawa in 1823 which the Arab escorts of the English traveler Major Denham were lured to join out of greed of catching slaves; and which Major Denham accompanied and nearly lost his life (Barkindo 1989:205-9).

Despite the above, however, this was one of the most turbulent period in Borno history. There were many raids against rebellious non-Muslim communities, who most often retaliated with equal disastrous consequences such as those of the Buduma mentioned further below, through which a number of slaves were acquired. And, with the increasing demands of the nobility for luxury items from the North Africans who in turn wanted principally only slaves, there appear to have been very brisk slave trade business in this period.

As we have noted, however, many a times, the Muslim were the losers especially against the dreaded Buduma "pirates" who inhabited the islands in the Lake Chad. They were said to have had the habit of suddenly busting out of the reeds and abducting a lonely man or woman and carrying them into their islands. In some villages near the lake, the marauding behavior of the Budduma took on the form of war on the Muslims. At the end of 1870, Nachtigal claimed to have recorded a Budduma raid on a substantial Shuwa Arab village near the lake where they massacred all the male population and carried away all the women and children, which was estimated over 100 into slavery (Fisher, 1991:204).

One interesting manner in obtaining slaves, which we already mentioned, was through gifts. Nachtigal himself admitted that he was offered many slaves by the rulers. Those include two boys from sheikh Umar of Borno, and two women from the ruler of Bagirmi, a former dependency of Borno during the Saifawa period now in the Republic of Chad (*ibid*:127) The two Bagirmi gifts included a wife of the king (probably a concubine) who- had been surprised in an indiscretion-and a recently captured girl of 16 years (*ibid*:128).

Organisation of Trade in Slaves in Borno in the 19th Century

In the early years of el-Kanemi rulers, they actively encouraged trade as a cardinal policy of state. Although the early el-Kanemis were a scholastic family, some of them were involved in active trading; and their transformation to political power seems to have rekindled their interest in foreign trade (Mo Kyari, 2005:112-5). Yakubu Mukhtar had demonstrated that the el-Kanemi court was some times directly involved in foreign trade ventures well into the colonial period (Mukhtar, 1998:5-10). An individual named Haj Muhammad al-Sudani was reputed to be a companion trader to el-Kanemi before he became the ruler. He continued to be in charge of el-Kanemi's trading interest in Fezzan and North Africa even after el-Kanemi became the ruler of Borno. After al-Sudani was finally appointed to the council of state (Majlis) by el-Kanemi, this function was assigned to Sidi Bukar (Moh. Kyari, 2006: 114). In fact the Kanemis not only continued but further consolidated the diplomatic and commercial relations between Borno and North Africa.

Although Barth in early 1850s claimed that there was no standardised medium of exchange in Borno, Nachtigal by the time of his visit found that the el-kanemis had succeeded in having a standard of exchange. The currencies were cotton strips (*gabaga*), cowry shells and Maria Theresa Dollar. The latter, by the 1890s, was a little above two shillings and one and half pence (*ibid*:118). Prizes are discussed further below.

A titled slave Zanna Arjunoma, catered for the interests of the North African traders (*Wasiliram*) who were still treated as state guests, was retained by the el-Kanemis. Under Shehu Umar (1837-81) and Shehu Hashimi (1884-93), the post was given largely to North

Africans who introduced the *wasilwa* and represented their interests at the court, mediated between them and the ruler and generally catered for their interests. The external commerce between Borno and North Africa was funded by the Jews in North Africa located in Tripoli (*ibid*).

Slaves continued to be the major article of export to North Africa. There were, of course, other items such as ivory, ostrich feathers, wax, etc. In exchange, the North Africans brought cloth, and clothing, burnouses, kaftans, shawls, fez caps, rugs and carpets, scents, sandalwood, etc. Looking at all these, Kyari Mohammed rightly noted:

> The Borno ruling class had developed a taste for luxury goods which only the North Africa traders could supply while the North Africans demand for slaves was insatiable...Thus the demand for slaves was externally stimulated leading to frequent raids to meet the demand. Even when trade in other items like ivory and ostrich feathers were affected by change in taste, declining demand and other market conditions in North Africa and Europe, the demand in slaves trade was not seriously affected (*ibid*).

Al-kanemi told Major Denham in early 1820s that the Arabs who came to Borno would have nothing else but slaves. Denham stated that Yusuf Karamanli of Tripoli, since the ascension of al-Kanemis to power, obtained slaves almost exclusively from Borno and that:

> The number of *kafilas* between that country and Fezzan had, within the last five years, greatly exceeded any former period; and in equal proportion did the respectability of those traders who now accompany them exceed that of merchants previously in the habit of passing through Borno (*ibid*).

In May 1851, Barth described a caravan leaving Kukawa to Fezzan for onwards journey to Tripoli, North Africa. With the caravan went Haj Hasan, a member of the Kanemi family:

> This was the largest slave caravans which departed during my stay in Bornu; for, if I am not mistaken, there were seven hundred and fifty slaves in the possession of the merchants who went with it. Slaves are as yet the principal export from Borno, and will be so till the slave-trade on the north coast is abolished (Barth, 1965, ii: 34-5).

Decline in Borno-North African Trade in Slaves

In the 1880s, Kyari Mohammed pointed out, North African demand for slaves decreased considerably partly due to the European intervention and suppression of the trade (Mohammed Kyari, 2006:120-1) An attempt to adjust to concentrate more on the "legitimate" trade in say ivory and ostrich feathers was frustrated by the economic depression in Europe. Another course of the decline was the down turn of the internal economy of Borno itself due political and economic causes. Already, by the 1870s, the North African traders were finding it difficult to collect their debts from the nobility.

The result was what appears to have been a glut of slaves in Borno resulting to the ownership of very numerous slaves by the nobility. Humphrey Fisher, citing Nachtigal who was in Borno in the 1870s, noted that:

> The rulers certainly owned slaves on a large scale. When Lamino, perhaps the most powerful man in the Borno apart from the head of state, Sheikh Umar, died, in February 1871, his estate was said to have included several thousand slaves. Nachtigal described the dwellings of the great men, with outer courtyard, accommodating male slaves, inner courtyard accommodating female slaves. The slaves served their wealthy masters as soldiers and attendants for horses, as builders and cooks, as weavers, as spinners and as tailors, and as fan-wavers, parasol bearers, even as zoo keepers, slave women surrounded their overweight masters massaging his legs...(Fisher,1991:124-5).

However, we have to note the fact that many of the "slaves" may have been servants or clients. Despite that, it seemed there were so many slaves during this period of Borno history that even commoners were able to own few slaves to work for them. Some of the male slaves drove domestic animals to pasture and cut fodder for them and the female slaves helped the mistress of the house in her domestic chores (*ibid*:124). Although Barth did not report of seeing any slave for sale in the market of Kukawa, when Nachtigal visited the market some two decades later, he saw slaves for sale in big rows, some chained and others not. For prices, Nachtigal gave the following: old man 5 dollars, 40-100 for concubine and 50-80 dollars for a boy eunuch. For comparison, he showed that with 5 dollars one could buy a good donkey, a good cow, a very poor horse or a modest Tobe (*ibid*:126).

When Heinrich Barth and Mr. Overweg brought the horrors of slave trade to Al-Bashir, the Vizier, he readily agreed, but only from environmental and economic point of view. On his way on pilgrimage, he told them, he lost forty of his slaves due to extreme cold and swore that he would never take slaves for sale if he were to travel again (Barth, ii, 44). He could not reason that at the end of their destination, the exported slaves could have received a different treatment as their domesticated counterparts from equally Muslim countries. He agreed to an establishment of a direct trade with the English in order to reduce the reliance on the North Africans. His main suspicion was that it would open the floodgate to un-Islamic goods especially spirituous liquors and Bibles (*ibid*).

Before the Shehus could solve the problems and bring law and orderly government, another, even more sinister one had arrived in the area. This was the arrival of the adventurer Rabih b. Fadl Allah who invaded Borno in 1893, captured Kukawa the capital, killed the reining Shehu and took over reigns of the government (Moh Kyari, 2006a). From that time to 1901, when he was killed by the French, Rabih attempted to establish his own government in Borno.

Rabih needed enormous resources to execute his battles in expanding and consolidating his hold on the country, and for establishing the machinery of government. But his initial invasion dealt a fatal blow to slave trade with North Africa bringing it almost to a halt. During the invasion and immediately after, about fifty North African traders — almost a half — were said to have lost their lives. Some lost their lives during the attack while those who survived had their properties confiscated and were tortured. Even those who fled were brought back to face similar treatment. The total loss of the North African traders was estimated 40,000 to 60,000 British pounds (Mohammed Kyari:1992:294-5). In 1895, an attempt by Rabih to revive the trade with North Africa came to naught since it was the very year that the Jews of Tripoli, the main financiers of the Borno-Tripoli-trade, decided to withdraw from it due to their enormous losses and the dangers involved(*ibid*). Rabih's rule ended the centuries old Borno North Africa trade in which the export of slaves from Borno was the main article of trade. By the time when Rabih was killed by the French in 1901, his rival European imperial powers were already there to practicalise their colonisation of the area.

Many aspects of slavery in Borno were adopted or at least influenced those in the Hausa states and most others in the Lake Chad Basin including the three emirates which adopted directly or through the Hausa states.

Slavery in the South-Eastern Emirates of Sokoto Caliphate

We have already pointed out the major difference between Kanem and Borno and the emirates. The Fulbe (Fulani) who declared the jihad in the south of Borno were a tiny minority who launched attacks against the predominant non-Muslim populations. In addition, the jihadids in the south east were attempting to found new polities based on Islam where none existed. We should, however, point out that our effort here is to outline only what happened at the metropolitan province of each of the emirates with the understanding that similar developments were taking place in the sub-emirates or districts. This was more in Adamawa where over forty sub-emirates developed with some of them like Tibati, Koncha, Ngaundere, and Banyo becoming richer and more powerful than the central emirate government at Yola itself.

Isa Alkali Abba analysed the 14 questions in the Masail Muhimma or what came to known as the "Manifesto of the Jihad" (Abba, 1985:90-91). Let us look at those aspects which are relevant to this work; (i) the basis of religion is Islam (iv) those who support the pagans should be regarded as pagans (vii) the jihad on the pagans is obligatory (ix) Muslims should help each other to repel the aggression of the enemy (x) the enslavement of the Fulani is unlawful because the majority are Muslim.

The above gave the Fulbe scholars, each of who had received a flag from the Shehu, reasons to mobilise Muslims in his area to launch the jihad. The first stage of the jihads in all the three emirates was similar in the sense that the Fulbe were struggling to establish bases of fledgling states from where future conquests could be conducted with the aim of building large-scale polities. Thus, it was after the emergence of the states that we can talk of the organisation of slavery. Certainly, slaves were captured during the initial conflicts but it was in the succeeding reigns that the organisation of slavery as an institution was said to have emerged.

Sources of Slaves

There were several sources of acquiring slaves. The first of course was through the jihad against non-Muslims or those who rebelled against the state. It was not only the rulers who carried out these attacks but also subordinates and warriors. Adamawa emirate, for example, had over 40 sub-emirates each involved in the jihad where large number of captives were realised. The emir of Adamawa is said to have realised about 5,000 slaves annually from raids, gifts from subordinates and warriors, tributes and of course purchase. Apart from organised raids, warriors also undertook raids against non-Muslim areas who had no *amana* (peaceful co-existence) with the state and proceeds of which were shared with the rulers.

The Role of Slaves in the Administration of the Emirates

It was in the reign of the Muhammadu Kwairanga (1844-1882), the 3rd Emir in Gombe, Muhammadu Nya (1874-96) the 7th ruler in Muri and Lawal (1848-72), the second Lamido in Adamawa that slaves started to be employed in government administration. The first titles in all the three emirates were those of *Ajia*, (the treasurer in all the emirates) *Shamaki*, *Baraya* and *Turaki*, Majidadi. These slave titles and subsequent ones, whose functions slightly varied from one emirate to the other, had one thing in common: they were all given to very trusted slaves of the emir. In addition, their creation, or substituting the free borne occupant with that of a slave was also similar.

Lamido Lawal's earliest slave appointment was *Ajia*, the treasurer, whose appointment according to Sa'ad was:

> As a result of flourishing economic activity in the emirate, it became increasingly necessary for the Limido to appoint a custodian of the wealth derived from tribute, gifts and taxes on trade. Thus, the *Ajia* was the officer in charge of the wealth of the government, and was a trusted and favorite slave of the Lamido (Sa'ad, 1977:96).

Njeuma (1978:94) even collected traditions in Yola which insisted that the *Ajia* kept written financial record. In Gombe, the first bearer of the title *Ajia* was one Kachalla Umaru, a Fulani and in-law to Buba-Yero the first emir. During Muhammadu Kwairanga's reign (1844-1882), *Ajia* title was conferred on a slave of the emir, a practice which has since remained. In fact, Gombe conquests and expansion effectively ended with the rule of Kwairanga due to several factors, one of which was the infusion of slaves not only in government (especially *Ajia* and *Turaki*) but in many cases given powers above the nobility including those of the royal house (Abba, 1985:154, 178-9). In Muri, *Baraya* administered the capital as well as being the absentee district chief of Dakka; and, together with *Ajia* and *Turaki* were members of the council of state (Hamman, 2007:103). In Yola, the *Baraya* was first appointed by Lamido Lawan. He gave the title to one of his closest and favorite slave from whom grew the function of the confidential adviser of the Lamido on personal and palace matters (Sa'ad 1977:97). *Turaki* was, in most cases, the chamberlain but because of his closeness to the emir played a leading role in the affairs of the state. According to Yola traditions (Mabudi Musa Bako) the following titles were first conferred by the following Lamidos: *Ajia*-Lamido Lawal; *Shamaki, Sarkin Zagi*-Lamido Sanda (1872-1890); *Sarkin Arewa*-Lamido Zubairu (1890-1901); *Kofa, Sarkin Rafi, Wambai*-Lamido Bobbo Ahmadu(1901-1909). Some of the surviving slave titles in the emirates are listed further below.

Some of the administrative titles also connote military functions but there were also slave military titles like *Garkuwa* (chief of shield bearers), *Sarkin Tuta* (the bearer of the jihad flag), *Sarkin Sulke* (chief of chain mill beares), *Sarkin Bindiga* (chief of the gunners), *Sarkin Libidi* and many others each of whom had his hierarchical followers.

In fact in all the emirates, a vast majority of the slaves were not sold because a large number was retained for the palace duties; as personal servants, courtiers, soldiers and to work at the *dumde*. The female slaves (*horbe*) performed domestic duties in the homes or become concubines (*chulabe*) (Sa'ad, 1977:103). Some female slaves were also sent to the *dumde* (discussed below) to help steady the populations there since any child born out of the unity between the male and female slaves was a slave of the owner. It was only the unwanted surplus or those considered unsatisfactory which were sold in exchange for luxury items brought by the Hausa and Kanuri and other traders (*ibid*).

Slaves as Tribute

We have noted that the Emir of Adamawa assembled about 5,000 slaves in a year. The powerful southern sub-emirates of Rai-Buba, Tibati, Banyo and Ngaudere alone sent an annual tribute of 1,000 slaves to the Lamido and the Caliph (Sa'ad, 1977:115). It is estimated that about 1,000 slaves were sent to Sokoto as gifts/tribute. This was not sent at the same time but taken with him whenever he visited Sokoto or when emissaries were sent or received. Muri's tribute to Sokoto was between 100 to 500 slaves (Hamman, 2007:2). In Gombe, the number varied (Isa Abba, 1985:140).

Wurno was established as *ribat* (fortified settlement) by Caliph Muhammed Bello to help in expanding the economy of the caliphate, but it also soon became a large slave settlement. According to John Phillips, the first *Wambai*, the most senior slave official in Wurno, was a man called Sahabu and that he and the people in his ward were originally slaves from Adamawa. The main duty of the *Wambai* was to travel to Adamawa to collect slaves, horses and other tribute (John E. Phillips, 2004, 113.) In Muri, the main link with the caliph was the District Head of Rabah through whom most of the tributes-cum gifts were channeled (Hamman, 2007:102).

Role of Slaves in the Economy

Dumde or Slave Settlements

All those who have seriously studied the three south-eastern emirates have concluded that their economic prosperities in the nineteenth centuries were tied, first to the *rumde* system and second, by long distance trade in which slaves formed the main articles (Njeuma, 1978:40,148; Sa'ad, 1977:100-104; Hamman, 2007:111-2). Below is a briefly outline of each.

Dumde (sig.*Rumd*) means agricultural slave settlements. On the origin of *dumde* in Adamawa, Sa'ad Abubakar stated that:

> The Fulbe were not farmers and could not farm conquered land without changing their way of life. The jihad had created hostility between them and their previous suppliers of agricultural goods so they founded slave settlements to produce for them. Thus, the prevalence of slavery in the emirate of Fombina (Adamawa) arose from economic necessity (Sa'ad 1977: 102).

The *dumde* produced most of the agricultural needs of the Fulbe ruling group, their retainers, and other functionaries of government as well as the individuals who owned them (*ibid*:141; Hamman, 2007:111). It however needed the permission of the ruler to establish a *rumde*. The inhabitants of the rumde were at the disposal of their owners not only to produce food for him but also to render any other service needed by him. The number and size of the *rumde* which a person or family has, was his index of wealth, influence and status (Njeuma, 1978:141). Those put at the rumde were the slaves who were not required for domestic or military service in case of men or conversion into concubine in case of female captives (Sa'ad, 1977:103). The *rumde* is organised like a local village, the difference being that the inhabitants were owned by an individual or a family under a trusted servant or slave. In the environs of Yola alone, according to Sa'ad Abubakar, Chomyel Abba, Doulabi, Golomba, Lagui, Wuro Dole, Kirngabu, Konkol, Pette and Yolel as well as nearly all the villages in Namtari, Girei and Gurin districts started as *dumde* (Sa'ad,1977:103).

Mahmud Hamman estimated that by the end of the 19th century there were over 40 *dumde* in the vicinity of Muri town alone where some of them had as many as 100 slaves each. The largest concentration was the area south of Muri up to the bank of the Benue. These included Kabini (*rumde* Liman), Kalaboro, Wuro Guga, Wuro Walowol, Gungiti, Belel, Wuro Tapaje, Konki, *rumde* Lamido, Wuro Ibbi, Alluga, *rumde* Feri, Ndunga, Koksel and Kokael Jabam. There were also, he added, few *dumde* to the east of Muri town at Laro, Mballuwa, Wuro Peuri, Wushadi, Wuro Ardo and Bade Koshi (Hamman, 2007:112). Thus Barth who was in Yola the capital of Adamawa on 20-24 June 1851 noted that:

> Muhammed Lawal (the 2nd ruler: 1848-72), has all his slaves settled in *rumde* or slave villages, where they cultivated grains for his use or profit (Barth,1965:ii,190).

Slave Trade

It was during the rule of Lamido Sanda (1872-1890) that long-distant trade in which slaves featured as one of the articles of export from the south-eastern emirates assumed it significance (Njeuma, 1978:141). After its foundation as the capital of Adamawa in 1841, Yola became an entrepot of short and long trade routes converging from all directions (*ibid*). However, even during the rule of Lamido Lawal, Barth mentioned the presence of trade in slaves in Adamawa noting that the most noticeable articles of export were slaves and ivory and that:

> Four good *turkedi*, bought in Kano for 1,800 or 2,000 *kurdi* (cowry shells) each, will generally purchase a slave, and a *turkudi*, will often buy an elephant's tusk of a tolerable size (Barth, 1965:191).

Sa'ad Abubakar pointed out that European goods such as *turkedi*, stripped Manchester cloth, beads and salt became more available from the latter part of Lamido Lawal's reign. Barth claimed to have been told that Koncha and Chamba outstripped Yola and its environs in long distance trade in slavery. This was because those districts' nobility obtained all their food requirements from their subjected non-muslims and so did not require tying their surplus slaves to the *dumde* (*ibid*).

The long-distance slave traders operating in the emirate of Adamawa and Muri were the Hausas coming from Hausaland in north-west and Kanuri and Arabs from Borno in the north. Njeuma noted that:

> The establishment of Fulani hegemony in southern Borno radically altered not only the political relations but also Adamawa's trading pattern and response to long distance trade including the trans-Saharan trade (Njeuma,1978:141).

Like Borno, Adamawa had a special title holder who looked after the interests of the long distance traders. The Shuwa Arabs, the Arabs from North Africa and the Middle East, those from Wadai and Baghirmi as well as all Europeans were looked after by Ardo Gamawa whom the 19th century Europeans called the most important councilor in Yola (*ibid*).

Unlike Borno, for example, a major part of the long distance trade of the emirates radiated within what is now the Nigerian area. This may be because the major traders were Hausa followed by the Kanuri. It should also be noted that the emirates being far-flung from the main terminals of the trade route had to rely on those areas and the southern outlets by the end of the 19th century for the commerce in slaves and other goods. In fact Hamman Yaji, a sub-emirate ruler of Madagali, situated at the northern tip of the Adamawa emirate actually carried on slave raiding and slave trade under the rule of the Germans, the French and the British in his twenty five year rule from 1902 until August 26, 1927, when he was deposed. He sent his captives to be sold at Kano, Maiduguri and the French Cameroon to buy more ammunition and luxury goods. Hamman Yaji himself chronicled his daily affairs up to a day before he was deposed (Vaughan and Kirk-Green, 1995).

Tangible Relics of Slavery in Borno and South-Eastern Emirates of Sokoto Caliphate

Tangible relics which today exist in the areas of North-eastern geopolitical zone include the following:

Slave Titles

In all the relevant emirates and Borno, there are many titles which are still reserved to people of slave descent. What are given below are not the exhaustive titles in each of the emirates and no attempt has been made to explain the function of all the titles. However, all of them are attached either to the person of the Shehu of Borno or the Emir concerned. There are also a few who are now salaried officials of the emirate councils. An attempt is made in a few cases to show offices which were originally borne by slaves but now being borne by free borne people and vise-versa. No attempt has been made to include titles which were either created or borrowed after 1910.

The surviving Borno slave titles which were kindly drawn for me by Dr. Kyari Mohammed speak volumes on titles which had been proudly borne for centuries by people of slave class and still remain relevant to the society. That we can speak of the same titles in the emirates may call for a rethink on the status of domestic slavery in the preceding century. Although slavery is stigmatised and even slave descendants normally frown at being referred as such, it is a fact that there are thousands who are proud to openly display themselves as such in order to preserve their slave titles, and thus position of honor and respect in the society or to qualify for succeeding into them. In fact they do not suffer any stigmatisation in the society. I have not listed titular concubinage in the emirates where, unlike Borno and Hausaland from where they adopted their statecraft and societal culture, the south-eastern emirates did not appear to have them. This means just like the legal wives the concubines are also strictly secluded from public. We know, however, that most of the rulers have concubines and there are many advantages of a descendant of a slave being made a concubine by a ruler or a nobleman. Any son borne out of that marriage is a free borne and of equal status to those of the legal wife; and, many of the former have succeeded their fathers to become emirs or other members of the nobility. In her study on the Royal Palace of Kano, Professor Ruqayyatu Ahmed Rufa'i, has shown not only the presence of concubines (*Sadaku*) in the palace but the active roles of the so many titled concubines in the day to day administration of the palace. She listed the most senior titled concubines headed by the powerful Uwar Soro who is still the first title holder in the hierarchy in the palace administration in Kano (Rufa'i, 1995:72).

Slaves Titles in Borno

There were three categories of slaves in Borno. These were the Kalia, Zusanna and Adim.
1. Kalia: Those who were captured in war or purchased in the market. These were legally chattels that could be sold or given away at the whims of the master (owner).
2. Zusanna: These were second or later generation slaves who had been born into the owner's possession. They were not legally saleable but they can be given away.
3. Adim: These were eunuchs usually employed in the female quarters of the household.

All of these categories are eligible for titles and many rose to prominent positions. The highest status to be held by a slave was to be titled at the King's court. These were the household slaves of the king including Digma, Yuroma, Mustrema, Zaifada and the slave generals or Kachellas.

The next were slaves who held titles within the noble household. These slaves usually held fort at the fiefs or provinces on behalf of their masters. Slaves appointed to these positions enjoyed a status superior to that of the village heads over whom they superintended. There were also untitled slaves who corresponded to the mounted *furma* (mounted warriors) who used to fight on horse back in the pre-colonial period. Finally there were household servants who corresponded to the peasantry.

Table 4.1: Some of the Slaves Titles in Borno

	Title	Functions	Remarks
1	Kaigama	Commander in chief of army under Saifawa	Reduced to policing duties under al-Kanemi
2	Kachella	Commander in chief of army under al-Kanemi	Very influential in the politics of 19th century
3	Digma	Took charge of the king's correspondence and catering to his guests	
4	Yuroma	Highest ranking eunuch in charge of women taken along on military expeditions	
5	Mustrema	Second in charge to Yuroma. The commander of women's section of the palace and governor of all non adult princes and princesses	Tijani calls him "the chief eunuch of the *harem*"
6	Zarma	In charge of royal stables and responsible for the king's personal security	
7	Zaifada	Royal messenger	
8	Fugoma	Used to govern the capital in the absence of the king including power of life and death.	

		He was in charge of Ngurno when Nachtigal visited Borno in 1897	
9	Mainta	Manager of the royal stores of grains	Invested with various villages from which he drew his income
10	Makinta	In charge of King's stores of wood, charcoal, dried fish, onions, tomatoes and • generally palace kitchen	Invested with various villages from which he drew his income
11	Sintelma	Supervises the butter, honey, fresh and dried meat, rice and wheat of the royal household	Invested with various villages from which he drew his income
12	Mulima	In charge of the king's horse stable	
13	Mala	The third highest ranking eunuch, custodian of royal palace itself and all goods and chattels in it	
14	Shettima	A fourth eunuch much inferior in rank to the others. Only an aide to the Yuroma	
15	Udima	Also eunuch used to receive caravans from the north and dispatched others on opposite directions on behalf of the king	

Female Slave Titles

16	Kirjiloma	First concubine of the king	
17	Surakagu	Second concubine of the king	Title out of use
18	Chindiram	Third concubine of the king	Title out of use

Source: Compiled by Dr. Kyari Mohammed based on his own studies, observation, and consulting the following sources:

Alkali, M.N. (1983), "The Political System and Administrative Structure of Borno under the Seifuwa Mais", in B. Usman and N. Alkali, eds., *Studies in the History of Pre-colonial Borno*, Zaria, 1983, pp. 101 - 126.

Brenner, L. (1973), *The Shehus of Kukawa*, Oxford.

Nachtigal, G. (1987), *Sahara and Sudan*, Vol. ii, (ed. and trans.) Allan G.B. Fisher and Humphrey J. Fisher, London, 1980.

Tijani, K. (1980), "Political and Constitutional Changes in Borno under the Shehu Muhammad al-Amin al-Kanemi: The Case of the Majlis" in B. Usman and N. Alkali, eds., *Studies in the History of Pre-colonial Borno*, Zaria, 1983, pp. 127-139.

Slaves Titles in Muri Emirate

List of titles still borne by people of slave origins:
1. Sarkin Dogari
2. Shamaki
3. Ajiya
4. Baraya
5. Majidadi
6. Barade
7. Turaki
8. Sarkin Sulke
9. Sarkin Bai
10. Garkuwa
11. Kachalla
12. Galdima
13. Sallama
14. Mabudi
15. Gado
16. Sintali
17. Kofa
18. Dan Rimi
19. Masu
20. Kuyamban

Titles formally borne by slaves but now borne by peoples of free origins:
1. Ajiya
2. Garkuwa
3. Majidadi
4. Kuyambana

Slaves Titles in Adamawa Emirate

Some of the surviving slave titles still being given to people of slave descent
1. Magaji
2. Wambai
3. Shamaki
4. Ajiya

5. Maji Dadi
6. Dan Rimi
7. Mabudi
8. Sintali
9. Sarkin Arewa
10. Sarkin Bindiga
11. Sarkin Sulke
12. Garkuwa
13. Sarkin Gini
14. Kofa
15. Sarkin Zana
16. Sarkin Tuta
17. Sarkin Dogarai
18. Salma
19. Sarkin Rafi
20. Sarkin Libidi (sudde)
21. Sarkin Zagih

The following were those responsible in organising most of the major activities in the palace such as (Hawan Daba, Sallah festivals and other relevant activities):

Garkuwa was the chief in charge in organising any festival such as Salla festivals durbars and other relevant activities. He is assisted by *Sarki Sulke* (*sulke* means chain mail) and *lamdo chudde* (chief of quilted amour). The mere appearance of the latter signals the start of the activity.

Majidadi was formally a slave title, then given to a free born before reverting back to a slave title.

Makama title formally given to people of free origin (non slaves) but now given to people of slave origins.

Slaves Titles in Gombe Emirate

Some of the titles still being borne by people of slave descent
1. Turaki
2. Shamaki
3. Makama
4. Shatima

5. Libidi
6. Dawaki
7. Barwa
8. Ajiya
9. Barde
10. Sintali
11. Durbi
12. Masu
13. Sarkin Bayi (chief of the untitled slaves of the emir)

Majidadi was a formally a title reserved to people of slave origins, but now is being given to non slaves. It is now part of the (Borori, i.e. servants) chieftaincy title.

Those with special duties among the titled slaves
1. *Turaki* - ushers people into audience hall to see the emir.
2. *Shamaki* - organises horse-riders during special occasions such as Sallah festivals.
3. *Libidi* - chief and leader of the quilted-horse riders.
4. *Sarkin Sulke* - chief of chain-mail riders

Physical Reminders of Royal Domestic Slavery

In the palaces of all the three emirates discussed, there are two gates, one called the *Kofar Fada* i.e. the main palace gate and the other *Kofar Bayi* or the slaves gate. In Adamawa, for example, *Kofar Fada* faces south and *Kofar Bayi* east of the palace. The main functions of the gates as given by Muri informants (who also supplied pictures of the two gates) is typical of all of them.

Kofar Fada
1. Main entrance to the palace.
2. Serve as official gate to the palace.
3. Serve as administration section of the palace.
4. Serve as the reception of all important guests to the palace.

Kofar Bayi
1. Used as emir's unofficial exit.

Kofar Fada

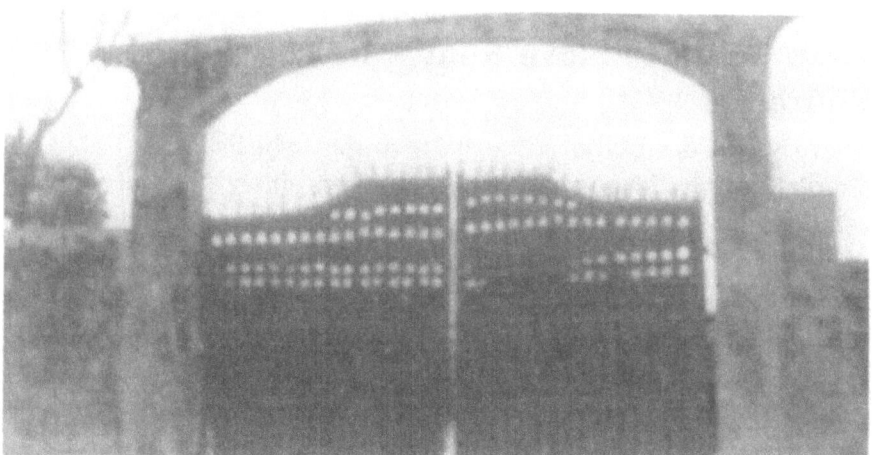

Kofar Bayi

Figure 4.1: The two gates of the Palace of Emir Muri at Jalingo, Taraba State. Kofar Fada and Kofar Bayi
Courtesy: Secretary, Muri Emirate Council, Jalingo, 17-9-09

2. Used by emir's slaves as exit point.
3. Used for durbars, horse races (*Kilisa*) and musical and other similar functions.

Slave Settlements

We have referred to the many *rumdes* or slave settlements in all the three emirates. Many of these have grown to big towns occupied now by people of many origins. Many of the slaves have been absorbed into many professions and calling. In fact, although there are many descendants of slaves, some of who want to be identified as such, as we have noted, there is no longer an exclusive slave settlement in all the four states we have examined. In Muri Emirate, however, the following settlements are still said to be largely settled by descendants of slaves most of who are now farmers and fishermen: Mayo Soi, Mayo Ranewo, Tau, Namnai, Shagarde, Kurnayi and Sibre.

Long-Distance Slave Routes In The South-Eastern Emirates

There is little doubt that some of the routes to be listed predated the jihad although a large number of them were either offshoots or were established and kept open during the jihad campaigns. The interest of the Hausa in trade from the north-west became inextricably bound up with the jihad campaigns and in order to open up new areas for trade, the Hausa traders often acted as the spies and scouts of the Fulani armies. Kanuri traders from the north-west who had some established trade with some parts of the area also began to come in large numbers. For example, after its foundation in 1841 as the capital of Adamawa, Yola became the focal point, or entrepot, for routes converging from all the cardinal points that served not only the emirate but some times also those of the neighboring emirates. There were several trade routes of considerable importance radiating from Yola. It should be pointed out, however, that although slaves were exported from Adamawa and other south-eastern emirates, it was not the only article of export. In fact, as Sa'ad Abubakar noted, Adamawa by the nineteenth century was, beside slaves, also the leading producer of ivory in the Sokoto Caliphate. Thus, slaves passed through all the routes but are only emphasized here if more than one published source and the oral data during the field work say so. The reproduction below is done largely from Njeuma (9178, pp141-3) with additional material from Sa'ad Abubakar (1977, 100-102), Abba (1985, 191) Hamman, 2007:167-9) and the field data.

The Northern Route

The northern route led from Yola through Mubi directly to Kano, or passed along either the western or eastern slopes of the Mandara mountains to Bornu, where it joined the main thoroughfare of the trans-Saharan and trans-Sudan routes to North Africa and the Middle East. This route was densely populated by both Fulani and non-Fulani settlements. It was one of the most frequented routes and Barth was led through it during his travel from Bornu to Yola. The main imports through this route were natron and salt, camphor, perfumes, paper, turkedi, beads, striped Manchester, calico, and quilted cotton, horse kits and chain mail. Horses came down through this route chiefly from Darfur and Uba following the official ban which both Borno and Mandara placed on exporting horses to Fulani regimes until 1854. The export consisted mainly of slaves, food stuffs, ivory, kolanuts, ostrich feathers, some iron and animal skins.

The Eastern Route

From Yola, the eastern route followed closely the course of the Benue to Garua, Bibemi and Rai Buba or Bindir, thereafter leaving the emirate to Logone and Baghirmi; or alternatively, it ran from Yola to Gurin, across the river Faro to Turua, Chebowa, Adumri, Rai Buba or Bindir. The Garua-Bibemi-Rai Buba route was often used by traders coming from the north who did not wish to report first at Yola, and also by those who wished to use river transport during the rainy season.

There was an alternate route through Cheboa which was preferred because it passed through many towns. The imports were generally the same as on the northern route, but a remarkable export was ironwork, arrow and spear heads, and iron bars from the Dama region-as well as honey, wild animals skins and ivory.

The Southern Route

The Southern route left Yola to Gurin, crossed the river Faro into Bundang, then following closely on the valley of the river Faro, it passed through Be and Mayo Bantaji until it finally reached the plateau regions of Ngaundere. From Ngaundere, one branch of the route went to Tibati through Tignere and either continued to the south through Yoko, or, eastwards through the Fulani settlement of Banyo, and further south, to the sultanate of Bamun. The second branch from Ngaundere went eastward through the densely populated Baya regions to the Congo. In 1891 the French explorer, Louis Mizon, passed through this route to join de Brazza in the Congo, and reported that before him, the German Flegel had used the route between Yola and Ngaundere. The main exports through this route were cattle, slaves, honey, fruits and kolanuts, and the imports consisted of European manufactures from the Atlantic Coast.

The South-Western Route

The south-western route led from Yola through Gurin to Chamba, leaving the river Faro to the east, it followed the course of the river Deo and avoided the rough precipices of the Mambila ranges until it reached Kontcha from where it descended to Banyo and then to Igboland and the coastal regions. Alternatively, from Yola it went to Wukari in Hammarua, turned sharply to the south to Takum through Munchi (Tiv) country to Gashaka on the eastern slopes of the Mamhila and then finally to Kontcha, Banyo, Igbo country and the west African coast. It was a popular route for slaves, ivory, kolanuts and beniseed, finished works of art from Bamun, sandals, mats and ropes.

The Western Route

From Yola, the western route led westward along the Benue valley through Bachama country from where it assumed a northerly direction through the emirates of Gombe and Bauchi into Hausaland proper. This route was considered more secure and shorter than the northern route into Hausaland, but its disadvantage lay in the fact that it was uninhabited for most of the way. The traffic on these routes would appear to have been considerable owing to the extensive demands for products like ivory, kolanuts, potassium, raw cotton, tobacco, ostrich feathers, nimal skins, and above all, slaves in the distant markets of Bornu, Kano and Darfur

Yola to Kano and the Benue through the Neighbouring Emirates

Yola was linked to the neighboring Gombe, Muri and Bauchi. The road to Bauchi went through the Bata country, then through the Gongola valley to Gombe. From there, the road went to Kano via Gwaram. From Yola, there were two routes that went to the emirate of Muri through Mayo Ine, Chukkol to the river port of Lau on the Benue. The other route went through Ngurore.

The Gombe to Borno and Kano Route

Gombe was linked to Borno through Nafada, Fika to Borno. However, after the growth of Darazo in the latter part of the century, Gombe Abba was affected. The main ruote was now Bauchi-Darazo-Fika-Borno or Bauchi-Darazo-Kano thus drastically cutting Gombe's trade contacts with outside world. Its main outlet was then only with Adamawa which a times passed through Muri.

There were naturally many problems associated with long distance trade in the emirates. These include porterage, ill health, discipline and insecurity — such as armed robbery on the routes. Insecurity was caused by either traders converting their role to raiding bands or by highway robbers. There were instances when robbery was even said to have been master-minded by important persons in some of the emirates. The emirs and the subordinates took strong measures to keep the routes safe.

Conclusion

The aim of this short discourse is to outline the origins and status of slavery in the pre-colonial period in Borno and the emirates and what relics of it has remained. Few extensive descriptions are given especially in the case of Borno whose history we know so much not only from internal and external sources going as far back as the first millennium AD, not to mention the reports of the numerous European travelers who visited the state in the 19th century AD. Borno is a model in all aspects of statecraft and culture including the development of slavery in government and the economy which had influenced the Hausa states and other areas of the Lake Chad Basin. The Fulbe emirates in our area of concern whose development of statecraft came only in the first half of the nineteenth century, first borrowed their ideas from Borno from where the first Jihadists migrated. Later on, they adopted most ideas and practices from Hausaland, especially Kano, where the earlier emirs always sojourned on their many trips to and from Sokoto to see the Sultan.

Slavery is an enigmatic term. No non-slave wants to be associated with slavery whatsoever. In fact even descendants of slaves try to hide that identity in public. However, to those who could aspire to slave titles or be concubines to the royalty or nobility, their slave origins are even flaunted because it brings position of honor accepted by people. We have already noted the position of the concubine to a ruler or nobility whose offspring had the chance of succession as equal as the children of the freeborn wives. Many of them still do.

Notes and References

I. A. Abba (1985). *Changing Pattern of Local Authority and the Evolution of the District Head System in Colonial Gombe Emirate, c.1804-1960*, PhD Thesis, Bayero University, Kano.

B. Barkindo, (1985). "The Early States of the Central Sudan; Kanem, Borno and some of their Neighbors to 1500 AD" in J.F. Ade Ajayi and Michael Crowder (ed.) *History of West Africa* (Longman, 1985, Vol.1, 3rd ed.).

B. M. Barkindo, (1989). *The Sultanate of Mandara to 1902, History of the Evolution, Development and Collapse of a Central Sudanese Kingdom*, Stuttgart.

B. M. Barkindo, "Royal Pilgrimage Traditions of the Saifawa in Kanem and Borno" in Ajayi J.F.A. and J.D.Y. Peel (ed.) *Empires In African History, Essays In Memory of Michael Crowder* (Longman, 1992).

H. Barth, *Travels and Discoveries in North and Central Africa*, (London, Centenary edition, vol., 1965).

H.J. Fisher, "Slavery and Seclusion in Northern Nigeria A Further Note", in *Journal of African History*, 32, (1991), pp123-135.

E.J. Phillip, "Slavery on two Ribats in Kano And Sokoto", in Paul E Lovejoy, *Slavery on the Frontiers of Islam*, (Priceton, 2004).

Hamman Mahmoud, *The Middle Benue Region and the Sokoto Jihad, 1812-1869, The Impact of the Establishment of the Emirate of Muri*, (Ahmadu Bello Press, Zaria, 2007).

Lange Dierk, *Chronoligie et Histoire d'un Royaume Africain*, (Wiesbaden, 1977).

J. Lavers, "Kanem and Borno to 1808" in Obaro Ikime (ed.) *Groundwork of Nigerian History*, (Heiniman, Ibadan, 1980), pp187-209.

Mohammed Kyari, "Trade as Diplomacy in Nineteenth Century Borno" in *Maiduguri Journal of Historical Studies*, vol.iv, Nos 1&2 (2006A) pp112-114.

Mohammed Kyari, *Borno in the Rabih Years, 1893-1901*, Borno Sahara and Sudan Series (University of Maiduguri, 2006).

Y. Mukhtar, "Continuity and Change in the Commerce of Borno: Shehu's Court in the Pre-colonial and Colonial Periods" in *Borno Museum Society* Newsletter, 36 &37 (1988) pp. 5-10.

G. Nachtigal, "Sahara and Sudan, trans." G.B. Allan and H. J. Fisher (London, 1980).

M. Z, Njeuma, *Fulani Hegemony in Yola (old Adamawa) 1809-1902*, Yaounde, Cameroun, 1978.

Rufa'I, A. Ruqayyatu, *Gidan Rumfa: The Kano Palace*, Triumph Publishing Company (Kano, 1995).

Sa'ad Abubakar (1977), *The Lamibe of Fombina: A Political History of Adamawa, 1809-1901* (Ahmadu Bello Press, 1977).

J.H. Vaughan, and Anthony H.M. Kirk-Green, (ed.), *The Diary of Hamman Yaji*, (Indiana University Press, 1995).

Al Yakubi and al-Muhannabih in Levtzion, N. and J.F.F. Hopkins (ed.), *Corpus of Early Arabic Sources for West African History*, (Cambridge, 1981).

Field Data

Muri Emirate

Group interview conducted on September 17, 2009 by Alhaji Muhammadu Sulaiman at Jalingo with officials of Muri Emirate council led by Secretary to Muri Emirate Council, Alhaj Usman Gassol. Other officials include: Alh. Jauro Aliyu Mafindi, Jauro Sanda Tafida, Bello Sarki Gado, Buba Majidadi, Abdullahi Turaki, Muhammadu Galadima, Salisu Dankom Garkuwa.

Gombe Emirate

Oral interview conducted by Faisal Waziri on September 12, 2009 at Gombe with *Turakin Gombe*, Alhaji Muhammadu Gidado, 73 years old.

Adamawa Emirate

Oral interview conducted by Faisal Waziri on September 29, 2009 at Yola with *Mabudin Adamawa*, Musa Bako, 75 years old.

Chapter 5

SLAVERY AND SLAVE TRADE IN THE MIDDLE NIGER AND CONFLUENCE AREA

I. Shaaba Jimada
Department of History, Ahmadu Bello University, Zaria

CONTRIBUTIONS on the subject of slavery and slave trade in the middle Niger and confluence area may start out from a systematic knowledge of the nature of environment and location of the area. In particular, the importance of the area to the history of slavery and of the slave trade in Nigeria is attributed to geographical realities. The area is located at the centre of modern Nigeria and was a major route and gateway between the peoples of Northern and Southern Nigeria.

The area is also located by the Niger River, a major water way that was the hub of intensive commercial and trading activity for several centuries in the Nigerian area. Indeed, the irony of the location of this area in geographical and ideological terms was that it was much open to the destructive effects of European commercial capitalism as it was to creative regional forces.

Though, certain studies exist on some aspects of slavery and slave trade in this area1, the studies are not detailed of the complex nature of slavery as it relates to the communities. It is important to note slavery was shaped by local conditions. In some instances, the studies failed to distinguish between domestic slavery and the trade slave or the trade initiated by European commercial capitalism at the instance of trans-Atlantic slave trade. Reverend Samuel Ajayi Crowther, himself an ex-slave who later became a Bishop and a participant and eye witness of the events in middle Niger and confluence area in the mid-nineteenth century, recorded explicitly condition of domestic slavery. He noted that:

> The domestic slave and master live together as a family, eats from the same bowl, dress alike and are intimate companions without distinction[2].

On the other hand, the trade slave or the human being that became the article of trade especially in the trans-Atlantic slave trade, was a chattel, without base, uprooted from his society, degraded, abused and held in bondage. And herein lies the origin of the ideology of race and racism from the seventeenth century as a basis for categories of hegemony and subordination. This chapter is a gap filling attempt to consider the nature and extent of indigenous slavery and slave trade in the middle Niger and confluence area; this strategic trade and commercial hub of Nigeria. The study examines the nature of slavery among principal groups such as the Nupe, Igala, Yoruba (Ilorin, Offa, etc.,) and the Gbagyi located in Niger, Kogi and Kwara States and their involvement in the slave trade.

Slavery and Slave Trade: A Conceptualisation

Even in contemporary times, it is often not difficult to wonder on what slavery actually entails and how it originated in the African context. Modern writers have tried to describe the concept of slavery[3], but specific data about the origin of the word slave has been lacking. One modern scholar suggests that the word originated from the English word slave from the old French word esclave which can be found in the Medieval Latin sclavus and that the term is related to the Greek Sklabos, from sklabenoi, slavs of Slavic origin. The word Sklabenoi is closely linked to the Old Russian Slovene, and the contemporary word slave is directly related to the Slavic people many of whom were sold into slavery[4].

At any rate, there are considerable uncertainties and difficulties in reaching a clear definition of the complex and varied institution of slavery. Several writers have provided some illuminating insights into the concept of slavery[5], and as such a general and broad definition can be attempted. The slave was someone who was owned by some other person, whose labour was regarded as having economic value,

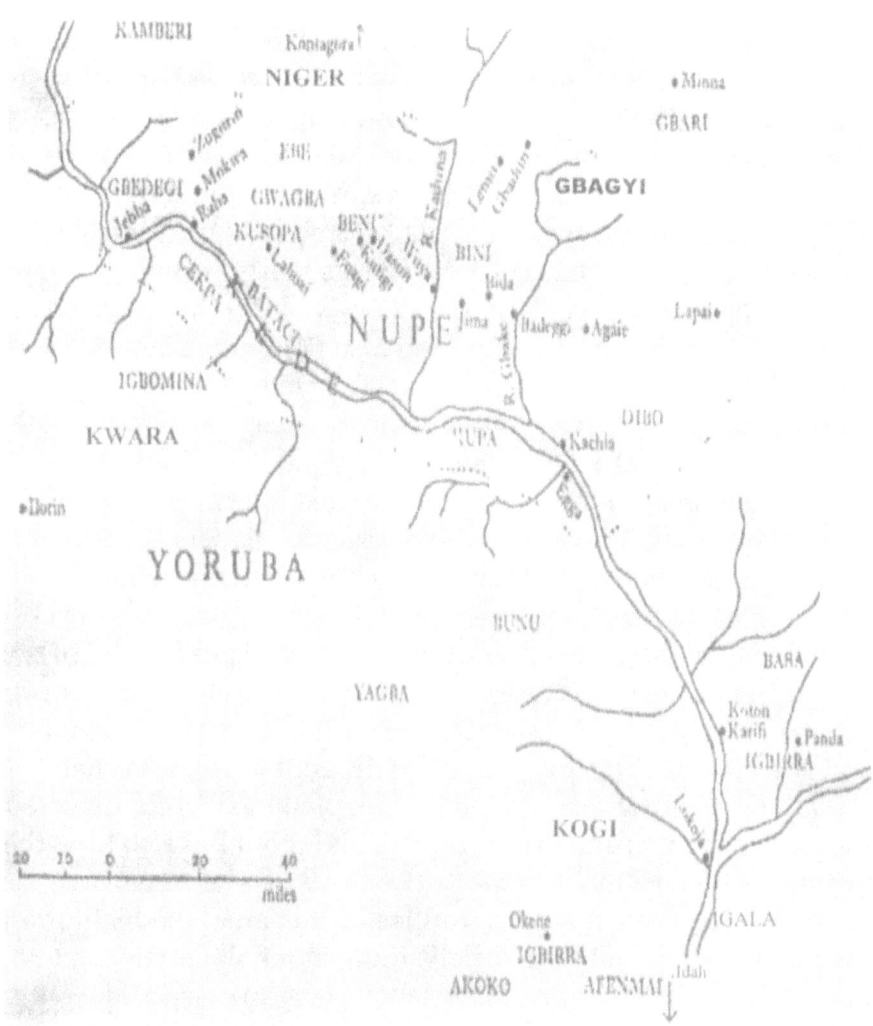

Figure 5.1: Map of the Study Area

and whose person had a commercial value[6]. This definition is clearly incomplete, as it neglects the military, political and social dimensions in considering the value of the enslaved. It is a notion that deals especially with the nature of the trans-Atlantic slave trade and not situated in the context of indigenous slavery. In the context of the region under study, the slave was of prime military value, being engaged in fighting wars on behalf of his master's state; of social value, being in charge of his master's household; or the liason officer between his master and others; and also held important political power, being often an important official of state. Among the Nupe, Yoruba, Igala and other communities in the area, the domestic slave was an important official of state[7].

The slave also did not enjoy rights of freedom; infact, the lack of freedom dominated the slave's whole existence. His person, his family, his labour, his time and his skill all belonged to his owner. Thus, slavery in the indigenous sense, was bondage; the slave was bond to his owner, the property of his owner and subject to the will of the owner. In some extreme cases, the slave was entirely dependent on his master for his daily subsistence and the fulfillment of his sexuality and powers of procreation. It was this dependence which generated a relationship of extreme servility and exploitation which divorced the slave not only from the product of his labour but also from the product of his fertility.

Nonetheless, in the communities of this area, the institution assimilated slaves into the society. Indigenous slavery was a vital part of the social structure. Slave labour was an essential factor in the productive life of a wide range of communities in the area. A general pattern comprising a number of common elements is observable concerning the nature of slavery, and an attempt will be made to expose the functioning in, and effects upon, the society and economy of the area.

As distinct from the domestic slave, the trade slave was uprooted from his society and traded as a commodity to far and often unknown lands. From about the sixteenth century, it is possible that peoples of this area were enslaved to other lands and across the Atlantic to the Americas. The trade slave was a chattel, property. The ideology of trade slavery, of which Africans were victims, was more sinister than ritualistic racial bigotry, as it was oppressive, abusive, dehumanising, and degrading of other humans; as *property value*. One might claim that the enslavers of the trans-Atlantic slave trade considered African slaves traded as commodities, as peoples without spirit, emotions, desires and rights. The chattel could have neither mind nor spirit[8].

While in these communities indigenous slavery was more like indentured servitude since slaves could buy their freedom, own properties and could achieve social promotion, trade slaving by Europeans of Africans was not only racist but was a crime of opportunity. The chattelisation of Africans in the slave trade ensured the theory and invention of race; "the white race", and the commodification of the "black" or the African. European slavers who knew that they were not black invented and created a new reality; the reality of race "the acquisition of whiteness". Thus, slavery in the context of the trans-Atlantic slave trade become a pernicious activity, a matter of greed, immorality and fundamental hypocrisy all in attempts to degrade other humans as less than human.

The most striking refutation of the conventional definition of slavery is found in the work of Asante, who sees slavery as the dissonance between personal greed and personal morality, and racism as the fundamental basis of chattel slavery. Africans became not labourers, but "slaves" and "slaves", in the mind of the capitalist-colonialist enslavers, were less, much less, than labourers. They were nothing but chattel, property value[9].

The Ideological Foundations of Indigenous Slavery

Few writers have been able to write on the communities of the Middle Niger and Confluence area without making constant reference to the stratified nature of the states, kingdoms and chiefdoms in the area. Could social stratification be the distinguishing feature in the origins of slavery and slave trade in this area? If so, what could be the theoretical explanation of the nature and extent of slavery and slave trade in the area especially from the seventeenth to the nineteenth centuries, and at the instance of European commercial capitalism?

Like most communities in the Nigerian area, three social classes were evident among the principal groups of the Nupe, Igala and Yoruba. The Gbagyi, though having considerable numbers, were stateless, many of the people being scattered in small communities in the central Nigerian area and became victims of local enslavers, due to the decentralised nature of their society.

The principal states where classes featured were broadly: Nupe, Igala and Yoruba. In these states, slaves (Nupe-*Wuzhizhi*, Igala-Adu, Yoruba-*Awoneru*); freemen (Nupe-*talakazhi*, Igala-*talaka*, Yoruba-*mekunu*) many of whom were clients (i.e. Nupe-*Barazhi*, Igala-*Ashadu*, Yoruba-Ilorin *bara*); and nobles (Nupe-*Sarakizhi* or *Agabi*, Yoruba-*Awon Oloye*, Igala-*Amajofe*) were found. Though the historical development of these classes cannot be traced with certainty, if it is accepted that the words *bara, saraki* and *talaka* are derived from Hausa, it is possible that social stratification in this area was accelerated through trade and commercial contacts with the north[10].

In the principal communities of the area, in the period before the fifteenth century and after, most slaves were employed in agriculture. Others were found in the palaces as servants and as members of the titled slave elite (slave order) in the markets, and on the roads as traders, in the police and army as armed representatives of their master's influence and in the craftsman's sheds weaving or providing the menial labour for the smiths, glass makers, wood carvers, etc.

From the evidence, it is plausible to suggest that probably before the fifteenth century, some form of indigenous slavery had taken root in the area. The acquisition of slaves was probably among the important activities of the elite which ruled these communities from early times. The *Kano Chronicle* suggests that from as early as the time of the father of Amina, Queen of Zazzau, probably in the sixteenth century, slaves were sold by the ruling elite of the states in this area in return for horses from Hausaland[11]. As trade goods, slaves were undoubtedly sent from these communities to the Atlantic littoral as well as the Northern savanna states.

There are abundant archaeological, oral and written evidences on the origins and nature of indigenous slavery in this area of Nigeria. These sources complement each other. Among many groups in the

Central Nigeria area, indigenous slavery appears to have started as the societies were transforming and there was rapid demand for cheap labour largely for agricultural and industrial purposes and the need of the states to expand territorially. Among the peoples of this region such as the Igala, Nupe and Gbagyi peoples, those who were indebted had a member of their family members sold to the creditor in order to pay off the debt. And of course, the creditor was most likely a member of the elite. The slave could of course be ransomed by his kinsmen. In other instances, slaves were acquired from criminals; those who committed crimes such as stealing, adultery, murder, insubordination to a chief or king were sold as slaves to neigbouring communities[12]. It is also possible that the unfortunate were enslaved. One modern writer notes that:

> If a man was known to be a wicked member of the Mbastav group, which had immense powers that could not be challenged, he was considered a threat to life in his lineage group and was sold into slavery through conspiracy by his kinsmen[13].

At any rate, a general picture of the nature and extent of indigenous slavery among the communities of this area is recalled by traditions. For instance, selling people that were suspected to be witches, or wizards and miscreants, was common place, to safeguard the weak and ensure the survival of the community. These were sold to distance places up North or down South to prevent their easy return home. In most of the communities in this zone, people were sold into slavery during periods of famine; in exchange for food[14]. Other likely sources of indigenous slaves in the communities included raiding and internal crises between lineages or communities where the more powerful lineage or community sold off the captured peoples of the other weaker lineage or community into slavery. Wars of expansion from about the seventeenth century were major sources of slaves in this area. In some few instances, children were sold into slavery when they were considered to be "too stubborn" and refused to take correction. Instances of extreme poverty[15], in many of the communities forced people to enslave their own. Poverty, debt and inability to pay taxes were linked, which leads to what is conventionally accepted as the dependency theory, which is structured by poverty when the weak needs the support of the powerful to survive.

Contemporary European accounts of the *modus operandi* of slave raiders in this area come from the early nineteenth century and might be regarded as the description of a process familiar for several centuries. Oldfield noted that:

> The slave raiders travel very quickly, taking the unsuspecting by surprise. They seldom fail in capturing hundreds of prisoners as well as cattle, horses etc. The slaves are disposed of to the "Arabs"; some are sold at towns on the banks of the Niger and eventually reach the seaside[16].

A prominent feature of the nature of slavery in this strategic area was the presence of several slave markets. From Bussa, to Ilorin, through Jebba, Mokwa, Rabba, Bida to Lokoja and Idah was a hub of slave markets. Baikie observed in 1862 that, there were normally 300-400 slaves in the Bida market daily; and that the number might rise to 800 as a result of successful campaigns[17]. Between 1830 to 1845, Rabba was a prominent slave market supplying slaves to Nigeria states to the north and south. Oldfield saw several slaves shackled at the market of Rabba for sale to merchants from the north and from the south.

Besides being sold in the market places, some slaves were incorporated into the domestic economies of the states. Many served in the armies, while some with specialised skills were engaged in duties such as rope making, barbing, as surgeons, or took care of horses. The Olokunesin that the Landers met in the Ilorin area in 1830 was a slave from Hausa, Nupe or Borno[18]. Many slaves of northern origin were especially sought for to tend horses, and perform the role of surgeons; duties for which local inhabitants may not have been qualified[19]. Clapperton and the Landers recorded the role of slaves in the transformation of states in this area in the early 19th century.

Probably, from as early as the sixteenth century, the populations of this general area had become heterogeneous as a result of indigenous slavery[20]. Traditions suggest the presence of slaves from various parts of the Nigerian area and beyond. It is possible that the emergence of the principal states as centralised states in this area was as a result of slavery. There are reports that slaves performed crucial roles in the king's court in Nupe, Igala and Ilorin. In Nupe as well as in Idah, the palace slave order led by the Gabi Seidi (Nupe) or Ashadu (Igala) performed important adminis-trative, political and military duties[21]. Johnson's reports on Oyo and later Ilorin showed the nature of power held by slaves in affairs of the state[22].

Before the nineteenth century, many kings in this area established slave settlements, which later came to be called *tunga* (hamlets) (i.e. Nupe) of Agbo-Oba (Ilorin) to engage slaves in agricultural and industrial production. Baikie reports that the Nupe Etsu Zubairu Jiya (1765-1785) built slave towns in the late eighteenth century to engage slaves in agricultural and industrial production[23]. Thus, before the seventeenth century, it is evident that many slaves acquired in this area were engaged for domestic purposes. Indeed, by the mid nineteenth century, there were several slaves' hamlets, plantations or settlements in the Bida area. Many of these ex-slave hamlets remain till date. Most of the slaves were adopted or absorbed into the domestic economies of the states either in the army or as domestic servants[24]. Quite a few of the slaves were sold or exported to the north in exchange for European goods such as muskets, cloth, and others. In Nupe, Igala, as well as Ilorin, slavery and slave trade transformed the states to complex and heterogeneous societies.

The State and Slavery

From the evidence, it is clear that what existed in the communities of this area before the growth of the export slave trade were small number of clients (*bara*) in the household of kings and nobles. The evidence gives the picture the institution of indigenous slavery as linked to the development of aristocratic institutions in the society. The export slave trade appears to have stimulated the militarisation of the Nupe, Igala and Oyo states from the period of the trans-Saharan trade when slaves were exchanged for Arabian and Mediterranean products such as swords, books, caps, etc., and for European trans-Atlantic trade guns, metal wares and spirits. The rise of militaristic states in the area and the dominance of a military class ensured the participation of the states in the export slave trade and their extensive slave use in plantations hamlets (*tunga*) in the area.

It is, however, particularly note worthy that the historical evidence shows that there was no large scale slave producing and slave selling communities in this area before the expansion of the export trade in slaves from the fifteenth century. The emergence of the principal states in this area was directly linked with the export trade in slaves. The communities came under intense pressure in external demands for slaves from European slavers at the coast and the Western arc of the Sokoto caliphate, leading to increased social tensions, a worsening of the integrative status of indigenous slavery, depopulation and economic backwardness of the area.

External Dimensions of Slavery and Slave Trade

Lovejoy reports that the trans-Atlantic slave trade acted as a stimulus to slave trade among African states and that slavery in Africa developed under the influence of external forces. He also claimed that trade slave marketing at the confluence area was as much as between 10,000 to 15,000 annually by the mid nineteenth century[25]. Mason has equally argued elsewhere that the Atlantic slave trade dislocated the trading economies of the states in central Nigeria; Oyo, Nupe, Igala, Kebbi with resultant conflict that created disequilibrium between the states. Slaves were derived by the states in this area from within and without. There is clear evidence to show that the Nupe kings sourced for slaves from the area of north east Yoruba, to areas below the confluence and Afenmai. It is possible that the area of northeast Yoruba and Afenmai were some sort of slave reservoir for raiding Nupe armies. Similarly the Igala kingdom derived slaves from neighbouring areas and the hinterland. From 1820s, the emirate of Ilorin was in a position to acquire slaves from a wide area of north and central Yoruba. Many of the slaves from these areas were tributes to the Sokoto caliphate or were sold to merchants from the south[26]. That the trans-Atlantic slave trade was responsible for the dramatic and ruthless nature of slavery and slave trade in this area cannot be doubted. Events from the eighteenth century were characterised by new policies of imperialism and expanded trade. In the process, several peoples were enslaved and many settlements destroyed.

People living around the Niger River were captured and transported from markets to the coast and sold at European trading ports in exchange for guns and gun powder, cloth and other European wares[27].

What is not known is the actual number of slaves imported into and exported from this area. The preference of ruling classes undoubtedly dictated that certain peoples were best employed at home and others best exported. Even in the nineteenth century, not all slaves crossed the Atlantic as Oldfield erroneously reported[28]. Mason calculates that between 200 and 300 slaves were exported from the area daily; but this was probably conservative. Sigismund Koelle's inventory of slaves in Sierra Leone in the mid-nineteenth century showed a significant proportion of peoples of this area among the enslaved. Koelle, for instance, identified 163 to 303 Nupe in an inventory carried out between 1848 and 1850 out of a total population of 13,273 slaves. By the mid-nineteenth century, it is possible that a significant number of the peoples of this area had been enslaved within the Nigerian area especially in the principal emirates of the Sokoto caliphate and across the Atlantic to the Americas. In fact, there is a significant presence of the peoples of this area, Nupe, Igala and Yoruba, in Trinidad and Tobago, Bahia in Brazil, Cuba, and the USA. Between 1781 and 1790, the Nupe were already represented as slaves in the Island of St. Dominique.

Judging from the number of slaves for sale at the Bida market in 1862, the number of slaves exported could have been high. Slaves with valuable skills such as cloth weavers and smiths were definitely retained for local production. Of the exported slaves, large numbers went to Gwandu from Nupe and Ilorin, the state which oversaw the affairs of the Western Emirates of the Sokoto caliphate in the nineteenth century. Aside slaves, Gwandu also collected tribute of guns, bought from the British by the Nupe, and textiles[29]. Slaves were also exported to Kano markets from this area in exchange for horses[30].

Southern towns and Lagos in particular were equally represented in the slave markets of this area. Emissaries of Madam Tinubu, the merchant queen of Lagos and one of the most successful of the mid nineteenth century Yoruba slave dealers, were seen by Baikie at Bida in 1859, trying to win the favour and business of the Etsu and Habiba, the Etsu's influential sister[31]. In fact, the Madam Tinubu connection to slavery in this area was to create disagreements between Etsu Masaba and his sister, who was friend to Madam Tinubu. While Masaba favoured a policy of settling slaves on farm hamlets (*tungazi*) for agricultural production, his sister was in favour of disposing slaves for sale to Madam Tinubu, her friend[32].

Very little is known of the mechanism of slave importation into this area. The British merchant, William Simpson reported in 1871 that states in this area exchanged guns for slaves from the north[33]. Many migrants into the states of this area from the north were also likely to be clients (*bara*) in search of fortune. Some had taken up farming in several locations in the area. Slaves were also detained through raiding to satisfy the demands of the trans-Atlantic slave trade and in doing this, many principal states of the area formed alliances to benefit from the slave trade. Rev. Crowther reported that the Nupe Etsu Majigi's campaign against the Ebira of Okene was an attempt to capture slaves. Indeed:

> ...King Umaru's Nupe and Hausa forces collected and large armies of his allies from Ilorin and Ibadan were united to strengthen his own ... who went, not so much for fighting as to frighten and catch plenty of slaves[34].

There is evidence to suggest that many of the captured slaves were more often settled than sold abroad, which suggests a turning point in the development of the economy of the states. For Oyo and the Ilorin area, Samuel Johnson wrote that:

> Excepting under especially pressing circumstances the chiefs do not now sell their slaves or rather captives of war excepting the old and infirm[35].

The missionary Paul also noted that:

> Slaves in the farms are not generally sold, unless they have committed some grave offence, or when their masters are hard pressed by taxation to meet the wants of the sultan of Gwandu[36].

These accounts suggest that by the mid-nineteenth century, slaves may have been more valuable as a means of production within the states than as commodity for trade. The labour of slaves and clients was essential to the economy of the states of this region. The slaves produced the food and the fodder which sustained the large and often unproductive population of the urban centres — it's rulers and their dependents, the courtiers, the middle men, the traders and the private armies of the nobles. Slaves also produced textiles, glass and copper wares, mats, vegetable oil and shea butter oil which became the staple trade goods in the commerce with the British which developed in the Niger area from the mid 1860s[37].

Due to the nature of slavery, where slave from the same ethnic groups were quartered together in contiguous farming settlements, the problem of slave rebellion seemed never to have arisen. This was in part due to the ethnic heterogeneity of the slave lands. It may also have been due to the fact that there was more security in slave lands than in other free areas. It should also be noted that the treatment of slaves was not substantially different from that of freemen; indeed, economic opportunities for slaves may have been better than those for freemen else where. Thus, there is no evidence of slave rebellion in the communities of this area. Neither were there instances of the creation of a caste system as a result of slavery. What can be remembered or recollected, however, are names and ethnic origin of peoples of slavery ancestry.

Comments made regarding the role of external factors in the nature of slave trade in the area, delineates the position of slaves and clients in the societies, and the effects of the extensive population transfer on the ethnic demography of the area. By the nineteenth century, population transfers resulted in the abandonment of settlements and the depopulation of many others[38]. But it was not all an outflow of people. The explorer, Henrich Barth, wrote that slaves from Kano were carried by small caravans to Nupe and that:

> ...the best of slaves now go to Niffee (Nupe)... slaves are sent from Zinder (Niger Republic) to Niffee[39].

Slave trading to a considerable extent, transformed the societies and economies of our region; especially because of the policies of the ruling classes. One writer has attributed:

The expansionist policies of African rulers both in the sense that wars are launched in the specific purpose of capturing slaves for sale to Europeans and in the sense that the rulers sought to expand in order to secure the control of trade routes, either to guarantee access to commercial opportunities or to levy taxes on mechants[40].

Slaves as trade commodities became vital in the accumulation of wealth by the elite. It As one scholar noted, during this period, "wealth consisted in the possession of slaves rather than the accumulation of land"[41].

At the onset of British colonial rule of this area, Lokoja in particular, became the centre of refuge for slaves. With the British declaration of Lokoja as being under British protection, many slaves from this area, in particular slaves from Bida, escaped there and many ex-slaves largely drawn from other Nigerian communities settled in the Lokoja area.

The Slave Routes

Slave trade routes transversed the entire area of the Nigeria. The Niger River was a principal route for the movement of slaves either northwards or southwards. Many of the slaves sold or captured were brought to the banks of the Niger River for transportation to the coast. Lokoja was an important transit camp for slaves; so also were Kotonkarfe, Rabba and Eggan, Shonga, Bida, Idah, etc. Many European travellers such as the Landers, Baikie and others actually saw slaves being exported through the Niger River to the sea coast[42].

There were several other slave routes transversing the area. Nadel suggests an age long transit route through the area from the north to the south. One route was from Sokoto through Birnin Kebbi and Kontagora to Mokwa. The route crossed the Niger at Jebba and ended up in old Oyo. Another route branches off at Mokwa going east through the kolanut town of Labozhi, Sakpe, Gbara to Muregi where it crosses the River Niger to Kabba, Ikare and Benin. One other route took off from Kontagora to Dabban and Kutigi to Mokwa and went through old Oyo to Gwanja. One final route in the western part of this area was the route that crossed the Niger at Eggan to North East Yoruba and down the Niger to Lokoja, Idah and Onitsha[43].

Relics, Sites and Monuments

There are incidences of the discovery of relics such as chains; clubs and other tools associated with slavery in this area, but the precise location of some of the tools of suppression are yet to be determined with certainty. The popular Tsoede Chain (Egba Tsoede) which came up river from the Portuguese but through Nupe merchants located at the coast in about the sixteenth century is yet to be located[44]. The chain was probably used to chain slaves to prevent them from running away. Some of these relics of slavery were seized or said to have been carted away by the British especially in the Benue valley area[45]. It is, however important to note that in the era of indigenous slavery, these items were hardly used; they came to be common features of slave control in the era of the trans-Atlantic slave trade. The only notable "tool" of coercion commonly used in these communities to control slaves was the popular or common horse hide known in local parlance as whip, *bulala* or *koboko*.

Evidences of relics and sites can be located in the Nupe, Ebira, Ilorin and Gbagyi speaking areas especially where slave markets existed. Rabba, Gudu i.e. Yoruba Ogudu, Kulfo and other towns were important slave markets in Nupe. Lander noted that Rabba was an open slave market and Clapperton reported seeing slaves put up for sale in the markets of Rabba and Kulfo[46]. In Ilorin, the popular Gambari market was an important slave market. Slaves came to the market from the routes linking Ilorin to Oyo and Nupe and Bariba areas[47]. An important slave house and market was the Asunara market also called Ile-Nla located in the Balogun Fulani compound, in the centre of Ilorin. Within Kwara State at Odo-Owa, there is a slave rock shelter called *Imolegboja*, which was probably a war camp where slaves were kept in transit. Other relics and monuments such as slave dwellings, or quarters, clothes worn by slave palace officials, can be located in the palaces of kings and chiefs in the area. These include slave regalia in Nupe palaces, clay walled buildings housing slaves in Igala-land, and markets often adjoining the palaces and whips used to flog slaves in the palace of the Etsu and the Attah. The important historical town of Adamugu was a prominent slave market below Idah as well as the trading town of Kiri further south. The town of Igbobe opposite Lokoja was renowned as a slave town and market in the nineteenth century as reported by African and European travelers[48].

Several slave farm settlements or hamlets are still visible in the area today. For instance, several *tunga* in the Bida area have emerged as settlements containing peoples of disparate origins. In Lokoja, the famous rod of liberty associated with the slave trade, can still be found in the early church established by the Reverend Samuel Ajayi Crowther. According to reports, all slaves who were able to escape from their owners flocked to the church and once they touched the rod, they were automatically set free. There are said to be two rods associated with the slave trade and they can still be located in Lokoja[49]. The rod or iron of liberty is an important relic of the slave trade and it's preservation will go a long way in tourist attraction in the country. It should be noted that most settlements along the banks of the River Niger are slave sites. They are significant relics of the slave trade.

Contemporary Slavery

Today, thousands of children from the area of study suffer child abuse. They are forced to live lives akin to slavery. Young girls in particular are sent to work in households across Nigeria, and housemaids are often abused sexually and physically. There is compelling evidence to suggest that a considerable percentage of parents from this area send their daughters especially to towns far away from them as house helps or maid. The boys are made to hawk or sell wares on behalf of their mothers. Although this type of exploitation is hidden under the guise of housemaid or house help, and is often not called slavery, the conditions are the same. These children are sold like objects, forced to work for little or no pay, and are at the "mercy" of their "employers" and also at the "mercy" of others in the neigbourhood.

Synopsis

There has never been any episode in human history as sad, as degrading and as tragic as slavery and slave trade. The slave trade in whatever form, indigenous, trans-Saharan or trans-Atlantic, was cruel, brutal and devaluing of humans. The evidence portends that while slavery had existed in our area of study for centuries; it's nature was in contra-distinction to what occurred later in the era of trans-Atlantic slave trade.

There is little doubt that social stratification formed the basis of the origin of indigenous slavery in the area, where the people were at the mercy of the ruling elite, who took advantage of the structure of the society to exploit defenseless people. But whatever conclusions are drawn, the slavery in the area, its origins, course and maturation, were at the instance of the influence of external forces who saw an opportunity to exploit the people as commodity or property. Unfortunately, the traditional ruling elite, who probably were never fully aware of the consequences of their actions, joined in the ruthless exploitation, abuse and degradation of their people. That the people were drained of their human capital, treated as chattels, abused, dehumanised and degraded without lawful repercussions to the perpetrators is the greatest injustice in the annals of the history of mankind.

Notes and References

[1] See especially, Nadel, S. F. A Black Byzantium: *The Kingdom of Nupe in Nigeria.* (London 1942). Boston, J. S., *The Igala Kingdom;* Mason, M., *The Foundations of the Bida Kingdom.* (A.B.U, Press).

[2] CMSCA 2/931 4 March 1857, see also cited by. Ade Ajayi, J. F *Christian Missions in Nigeria* (London. 1965), p.105.

[3] See, P. among others, Lovejoy, P., *Transformations in Slavery* 1989. J. Rawley, *The Trans-Atlantic Slave Trade: A History* (New York 1981). Klein, H., *The Middle Passage: Comparative Studies in the Atlantic Slave Trade* (Princeton 1978).

[4] M. K. Asante, "The Ideological Origins of Chattel Slavery in the British World". National Museum, Liverpool (2008), p.5

[5] See for Instance, J.D. Fage, *Slavery and the Slave Trade in the Context of West African History* Journal of African History (X, 3 1969); S. Miers and I. Kopytoff (eds), *Slavery in Africa* (Madison 1977); Lovejoy (ed) *The Ideology of Slavery* (London, 1981), also

his *Transformations in Slavery* (Cambridge, 1983); Grace, J., *Domestic Slavery in West Africa* (London 1975).
6   J.D. Fage, p. 394.
7   For Nupe, see S. F. Nadel, A Black Byzantiu:, pp 284. For the Igala and others, see J. S. Boston, *The Igala Kingdom; for the Ilorin*, see Johnson, History of the Yoruba.
8   Asante, *The Ideological Origins of Chattel Slavery*, p.2.
9   T, Allen, *The Invention of the White Race* (New York 1997), pp8-22. See also Andrew Smedley, "Race in North America, Origin and Evolution of a World View (Westview, 1999).
10 For Further details, see M. Mason, *Captive and Client Labour and the Economy, of the Bida Emirate 1857-1901*, JAH 14, 3, (1973) pp 453-471.
11 H. Palmer, *Sudanese Memoirs* (Lagos 1928), p 111, 102.
12 Oral Accounts, Fatima Idris, and Dr. M. Filaba, A.B.U, Zaria
13 D. Ndera, *Evidence of Slavery among the Tiv from early times to the 20th Century*. Paper Presented at the International Conference on Arts in the Benue Vealley. Institute of African Studies, University of Ibadan, 2002, p.2.
14 *Ibid*, p 2.
15 *Oral Account*. Sule, I. D. Department of Sociology A.B.U, Zaria.
16 M. Laird and A C Oldfield, *Narrative of an Expedition into the Interior of Africa by the River Niger in 1832, 1833, 1834* (London 1837), p.420.
17 See F.O 97/434 Baikie to Russell, 13 March 1862.
18 Richard and John Lander, *Narrative of an Expedition to Explore the River Niger* (London 1966), Vol. 1, p 90
19 Lander, R. and J.??? *Narrative of an Exploring*, Vol. 1. (p.90).
20 Traditions Recalled the Settlement of Groups such as the Nupe, Igala, Yoruba,(i.e. Yagba, Bunu, Akoko Igabomina) Afenmai (Kukuruku) Ebira, Gbagyi, Bassa, Kambari, Hausa, Fulani Kanuri in this general area as a result of slavery and slave trade.
21 For Nupe, See Frobenius, L. *The Voice of Africa* (London 1913). Vol. p 213, Vol.2 p 603, For Igala, see Boston, The Igala Kingdom.
22 S. Johnson, *History of the Yoruba*, pp. 18, 113.
23 Baikie, *Journal of a Journey from Bida in Nupe to Kano in Huasa'*

in 1864, JRGS, p. 105.
24 Mason, *Captive and Client Labour*, pp 456-459.
25 Lovejoy, *Transformations in Slavery, A History of Slavery in Africa* (Cambridge 1983).
26 Mason, *The Nupe Kingdom in the Nineteenth Contary; A Political History*. Unpublished Ph. D. Thesis, University of Birmingham, 1970, p. 76. See also his *The Jihad in the South: An Outline of Nineteenth Century Nupe Hegemony in North Eastern Yorubaland and Afenimai*, JHSN, 5,2 (1970).
27 Mason, *Captive and Client Labour*, p 459.
28 Liard M and Oldfield RAC, *Narrative of an Expedition*, p 85.
29 CMSCA3, Ozi John T.C. *A Report of the Lokoja Station, 1873*.
30 *Ibid*, F.O 2/32 Baikie to Russell 2 Sept 1859.
31 W. B. Baikie, *Narrative of an Exploring Voyage*, pp20-298; R. Lander, *Records of Captain Claperton's Last Expedition to Africa* (London 1966).
32 See Jimada, S. I. The Nupe and the Origins and Evolution of the Yoruba. ASC (2005), p. 125-6
33 F.O 84/1351 Simpson to Granville 21 Nov. 1891, *Report of the Niger Expedition, 1871*, Enclosure, 3.
34 CMSCA3 M, Annual Report of Bishop Crowther, 1875.
35 Cited in E.A. Oroge, *The Institution of Slavery in Yorubaland with Particular Reference to the Nineteenth Century*, Ph.D Thesis, Birmingham (1971). Also CA2/649 (a) Hinderer to Venn 26 Oct 1855.
36 CMSCA3 028, Rev C. Paul, *Journal for the Year 1878*.
37 M. Mason "Captive and Client Labour", p. 46.
38 See, W.B, *Baikie Narrative of an Exploring Voyage* (London 1967); Liard M. and Oldfield, *Narrative of an Expedition*; Crowther A and Schon, J. F., *Up the Niger 1814* (London, 1966)
39 H. Barth, *Travels in North and Central Africa*. 2. Vols, Vo.2, p 132.
40 R. C. Law, *The Oyo Empire, 1600-1836: A West Africa Imperialism in the Era of the Atlantic Slave Trade* (Oxford 1976), p.235.

41. A. G Hopkins, *Economic imperialism in West Africa. A Rejoiner*, Economic History Review, 25 (1972). p. 309.
42. W. B. Baikie, *Narrative of an Exploring Voyage*, Landers, Journal of an Expedition.
43. S. F. Nadel, *A Black Byzyentium*, pp 319-320.
44. Pictures exist of the Chain in S.F. Nadel, *A Black Byzantium*. The Chain is said by tradition to be located in one of the Ledu villages along the banks of the Niger. See also Nadel, *Nupe Religion* (London 1955), p210
45. Ndera, *Evidence of Slavery*, p 6. The writer mentioned Dikpo Hilltop Settlement as a major relic of slavery in the area. See also his *A Preliminary Archaeological Survey of Dikpo Hill Settlement in Benue State*, M. Sc. Thesis, University of Ibadan (1996).
46. Landers, *Journal of an Expedition*, Vol. 2, p. 313; Clapperton, Journal of a Second Expedition, pp. 40-41 and pp. 135-8, 190.
47. *Report of the Research on Indigenous Slavery in Nigeria: A Case Study of Kogi and Kwara States.*
48. See Back Liard, and R. Oilield above; see also A Crowther and J. F. Schon, *Journals of the Reverend James Schon and M. Samuel Crowther Who Accompanied the Expedition up the Niger in 1841* (London, 1966); also W. Allen and T. Thomson, *Narratives of an Expedition up the Niger* (London 1966).
49. *Report of the Research on Indigenous Slavery.*

Chapter 6

INDIGENOUS SLAVERY AND SLAVE TRADE IN THE CROSS RIVER REGION

Okon Edet Uya
Professor of History, Department of History and International Studies, University of Uyo, Uyo

Introduction

THE centrality of slavery and slave trade, both internal and external, in the pre-colonial history of Africa, especially between the fifteenth and nineteenth centuries, has been widely acknowledged. As late Professor Adiele Afigbo, one of the foremost historians on the subject, declared in 2007:

> Without fear of contradiction, one can say that no theme, not even that of evolution of states, big and small, in the early history of Africa, can contest for the position of first importance in the history of any region of Africa or of the continent as a whole with the slave trade and its abolition[1].

Throughout most of West Africa, another historian has stressed, "it was slaves rather than land that constituted the only form of private property" that could generate income sanctioned by law and custom. Consequently, slave holding, buying, and selling constituted important activities that affected every aspect of social, political, and economic life of West African societies in those years. However, despite their acknowledged centrality, understanding the nature and status of slaves in African societies; the transition from domestic slavery and slave trading to the export slave trade; the organisation and the overall impact of the trade and its abolition; as well as the slave trade in the context of globalisation has remained contentious and controversial. Two reasons for this have been the tendency to generalise findings from one region or sub-region to the entire continent and ignoring the inevitable changes in a dynamic institution that lasted for over four hundred years. This study of slavery and slave trade in the Cross River region, part of the Bight of Biafra of European records, a conspicuous participant in slavery and slave trade, should help clarify some of these issues.

Cross River Region

Historically speaking, the Cross River region of Nigeria covered the present states of Akwa Ibom, Cross River, parts of Abia and Ebonyi, Imo, lower Benue and parts of Southern Cameroon. A major feature of the area is the multiplicity of ethnic groups varying in sizes, living in non-centralised village communities, of which the equally small-sized city states of Old Calabar, Opobo, Bonny and Elem Kalabari (New Calabar) were the only exceptions. The principal occupations of the people have been peasant farming, fishing, crafts making and trading along the many rivers, riverlets and creeks. Despite the diversity of cultures and people, the Cross, Kwa Iboe, and Imo Rivers and their many tributaries facilitated contact and interaction between the people. By the time of the slave trade, the Efik language and *Ekpe* Secret Society had emerged as major unifying institutions for the entire area, to such an extent that the area is sometimes referred to as "Efik Cultural Zone" (see map 6.1). With her principal ports at Old Calabar, Bonny, Elem Kalabari (New Calabar) and Ikot Abasi (Opobo) and a vast hinterland stretching from the Atlantic coast through the Ejagham, Ogoja, Southern Cameroon, Benue Valley, Ibibio, Annang, Oron, and Cross River Igbo hinterlands, this region was to play an important role in the export slave trade. The extremely informative Voyages Database contains records of nearly 35,000 slaving voyages which emanated from the area between 1514 and 1866. Mohammed S. Bashir has stated that:

> More than 64 per cent of the enslaved people from within the boundaries of Nigeria were shipped out from the eastern parts of the region. Between 1651 and 1725, the dominant slave ports were at Bonny, Old Calabar and New Calabar. Initially most slaves left from

Old Calabar but by 1726, Bonny took over as the leading slave exporting port until it was replaced by Lagos in the closing decades of the transatlantic trade[2].

Indeed, it has been estimated that 1,329,100 slaves that left the Nigerian shores (89 per cent) between 1651 and 1865 were shipped from the ports of Old Calabar, New Calabar and Bonny. The estimated departures of slaves from the Bight of Biafra ports between 1650 and 1850 are given in Table 6.1 below.

Table 6.1: Estimated Departures of Slaves (in thousands) from Ports in the Bight of Biafra, 1650-1865

Bonny	New Calabar	Old Calabar	Cameroon	Gabon/Corisco	Others		Total
1651-1675	1.0	31.7	25.8	0	0	0	58.5
1676-1700	2.8	15.5	33.2	0	0	0	51.5
1701-1725	4.2	4.7	34.4	0	1.3	1.4	45.9
1726.1750	93.2	3.3	66.8	0	2.1	1.3	166.8
1751-1775	193.0	29.0	103.8	17.7	9.5	0.9	354.0
1776-1800	207.9	37.8	82.5	16.6	11.3	2.6	358.7
1801-1825	161.8	17.7	41.8	17.6	9.3	9.2	257.4
1826-1850	82.6	5.4	49.2	12.3	21.4	27.4	198.2
1851-1865	746.5	145.1	437.5	64.2	54.9	42.8	1491.0

Source: Bashir, 466

How the peoples of the region organised themselves to meet the challenges of the European demand for slaves and the overall impact of these activities on them socially, politically and economically are the main focus of this chapter.

Domestic Slavery in the Akwa-Cross Region

Until recently, it was fashionable to argue that the existence of both domestic slavery and slave trading in the pre-European period accounted for the effective take off of the Atlantic Slave Trade. This "reservour theory", popularised in the works of John Fage, Philip Curtin and others, despite the commendable efforts of Walter Rodney,

Basil Davidson, Claude Meillassoux and others to deflate it, persists in the literature. In his otherwise informative study, *The Rise and Fall of Black Slavery*, C. Duncan Rice, for example, wrote:

> It is not true that African nations were peaceful and uniformly prosperous until they felt the impact of the Atlantic slave trade. With a few exceptions, too, slaving was not a new enterprise for them.

For our region of focus, one of the most important English slave traders in the region, John Hawkins, asserted in the 1550's that "apart from being very good merchandise, stores of Negroes might easily be had upon the coast of Guinea". And writing about the Old Calabar region, Jean Barbot noted that:

> All the vast number of slaves which the Calabar Blacks sell to all European nations are not their prisoners of war; the greatest part of them being bought by those people from their inland neighbours.

In the 18th century, other European slave traders like Robert Morris and Archibald Dalzel explained the rapid development of the Atlantic slave trade and the African response to it as arising from "the pre-existence of slavery and slave trading" and concluded that the Atlantic slave trade provided a "safety valve to better life for the enslaved Africans who would have become victims of human sacrifice". John Fage was to conclude later that the institution of slavery was endemic in, and a natural feature of indigenous West African society, so that when foreigners arrived with a demand for slaves, West Africans were able immediately to organise an export trade in slaves on ever increasing scale. In contrast to the above views, historians Walter Rodney, Claude Meillassoux and Basil Davidson have insisted that the direct linkage of domestic slave trade and slavery to the rapid development of the Atlantic slave trade is not only stretched but largely inaccurate. In their view, the Atlantic slave trade would have developed the way it did, with or without the pre-existence of the two institutions in Africa[3]. Our study of the Cross River region appears to suggest that the reality in the above controversy lies somewhere in between the two contesting views.

From the oral evidences in the field and careful examination of the proverbs and other literary expressions of the many different communities in the region, there is little doubt that varying forms of human degradation, subordination and pawnship associated with sedentary living and the challenges posed by concentration of populations and expanding economy, existed in our area of study. In the Akwa Ibom area, informants freely admit the existence of human subordination and use, especially by the nobility. According to one informant, they were used by the well-to-do in a variety of ways including domestic service, farm work and trading. The chiefs also kept some for domestic service and as concubines. However, they were quick to add that these persons were considered part of the extended family and treated as family members. Various forms of human subordination existed in other communities of our study area. Interviews in the Ogoja hinterland, understood to refer to the present Central and Northern Senatorial Districts of Cross River State as well as the Abakiliki and Afikpo areas of Ebonyi State, confirm that even before the development of the Atlantic slave trade, people of subordinate status in thralldom and pawnship were found in such diverse occupations as farm work, trading, running of errands and potterage. Having them was also regarded as an index of social prestige. Some were used for human sacrifice, especially when they had to "escort their masters to the world beyond". This practice was widespread throughout the Cross River region. A large number were used by their families to redeem debts they owed. Evidence from S. W. Koelle's *Polyglotta Africana* refers to at least three former "slaves" in Sierra Leone from the area: one named Obe or Saly Thomas of Wellington claimed to have been sold by her relatives because of "threatening economic hardship"; another, one Obi or William Renner of Freetown was sold for his inability to pay the debt he owed; the third, one Oga or John Tailor of Freetown had offered himself to be enslaved in place of his son who had accidentally killed another person's slave[4]. Social misfits were also sold. There is even an interesting case of a woman, one Madam Ukonghmer Ogar, who was rich enough to buy some slaves for herself and her brothers, most of them engaged in farm work. A man, one Ukpang, is remembered in the oral traditions as buying slaves for his father to restore his dignity as a warrior and community leader and elder.

There are also words in the languages of the area of reasonable antiquity that refer to people in servitude.

However, in all cases in our study area, such persons were treated, more or less, as members of the extended family, enjoying peculiums which varied from one area to another, depending on the circumstances of their patrons. Such peculiums ("bundle of social and economic goods recognized as belonging to the slave"), included the access to communal land to farm and build his own house; the right to marry and have his wife and children recognised and accorded some measure of respect; the right to change patrons if dissatisfied; the right to accumulate his own wealth as distinct from the patron's; and the right of limited participation in the affairs of the community, consistent with his "outsider"status[5].

From available records and studies, it is reasonable to conclude that the practice of pawning individuals as collateral for debts is ancient in the Cross River region. There is no doubt that human pawnship in Old Calabar and environs existed before the middle of the 18th century. Pawnship, a system of taking humans as collateral or "hostages" for loans, arose from "a value system where people are more highly valued than territory" and was used to expand the number of one's dependents, power, wealth and influence. From available evidence, it was used in the earliest transactions between the Calabar kings, chiefs and the Europeans before the 1760's. John Ashley, a British merchant, in his testimony before a Parliamentary Selected Committee in the 1790's claimed that it was "the way trade was carried on in Calabar, Del Rey, and the Cross River estuary." As pointed out by Lovejoy and Richardson "it was the local institution of debt pawnship that was appropriated and adapted by both the British and Old Calabar traders for their trading purposes before 1807"[6].

It is clear that various forms of human subordination and gradations of "unfreedoms" existed in our area of study before the development and maturation of the trans-Atlantic system. Some prominent individuals held people in subordinate status, but their numbers were rather few. Kinship lineage, whether defined by genealogy or the occupation of a common territory or "fictive", was the most dominant ideology of social and political life in these societies.

It was lineage that protected and defined a person's rights, obligations and responsibilities. People in subordinate status in traditional societies, often referred to as "slaves", were those who were unprotected by lineage and therefore "outsiders" in the societies in which they found themselves. As we have indicated elsewhere:

> The slave in traditional Africa was a person who, finding himself destitute of kin through certain circumstances, pledges or is forced to pledge, his labour temporarily to another person in return for protection or sustenance[7].

Labour recruited outside the traditional community protected by the common or defining charter of that community, and therefore, kinless, living on the margins of the society, formed the bulk of subordinated persons in our area of study. Their numbers tended to expand under conditions of "large-scale" farming, as was the case in much of the central and upper Cross River and Akwa Ibom hinterlands, or long distance trade, as was the case in the coastal communities of our study area. The extensive cultivation of yams in the Igbo areas of our study area created such demands, especially in the nineteenth century[8].

To what extent these local practices in our study area approximated classical slavery in the Western world associated with the Atlantic slave trade is debatable. As we have explained elsewhere, Western slavery was:

> A cruel, unjust, exploitative and oppressive system which rested on the principle of property-in-man, that is, one man's appropriation of another person as well as the fruits of his labour. The slave was regarded, at least theoretically, as a chattel, a thing, the possession of another, the mere extension of the master's will, a legal non-person, a socially dead person. Slavery was thus an institution of coerced labour, a relation of domination, a brutal system of exploitation and human degradation and a special form of human parasitism[9].

Clearly, this picture does not apply in most respects to our study area. Monday Noah was thus generally correct when he wrote:

> If the so-called slaves in traditional African society were free to marry, own and till their own soil, move about freely and live normal lives, is this not the very opposite of what it was to be a slave? The fact of the

matter is that slavery in the Western sense did not exist in Old Calabar before the Atlantic slave trade[10].

Indeed, Simon Newman is right on the mark when he observes that:

> West African social organisation meant that individuals did not always enjoy complete control over their wealth. Before the arrival of European traders, slavery was not as fundamental an institution in West Africa as it was elsewhere in the continent, and the status of slaves was relatively fluid[11].

And the Atlantic Slave Trade Came

There is little doubt that the coming of the Atlantic slave trade to our region played a defining role in transforming the existing system and relations between the major slave ports of the region and the hinterland communities, on the one hand, and between them and the Europeans, on the other. It is clear from the extant records and studies that Old Calabar, Bonny, Elem Kalabari, and Ikot Abasi, the principal ports of the region, drew most of their slaves from the densely populated Ibibio and Igbo peoples to the west of the Cross River and the relatively thinly populated and ethno-liguistically diverse peoples, loosely referred to as Ogoja, Ekoi or Atam east of the river. The import of the emerging, expanding and often changing relationship between the ports and their hinterlands is of great interest in this study. On the European side, Lovejoy and Richardson captured the essence of the relationship succinctly when they wrote:

> As a region, the Bight of Biafra was on the margin of the emergent Atlantic economy. During the hundred years or so after 1740, however, it became a major supplier of slaves to the Americas and, in the early nineteenth century, a primary source of palm oil, a vital ingredient in some branches of British industry[12].

Trade between Old Calabar and the Europeans, principally British, concludes another historian "brought about cultural contacts, ethnic mingling and exchange of ideas which resulted in political complications, conflict and change"[13]. We examine these developments below.

European trade in the Bight of Biafra, in general, and Old

Calabar, in particular, is often traced back to the Portuguese and Spanish period. The European traders mentioned in this period include Ruy de Sequeira (1474), Fernando (1472), Pinteado (1490 and 1530), Diego Cam (1490), and Alfonso D'Aviero (1530). However, from more reliable records, it is obvious that the slave trade in old Calabar in appreciable terms began in the seventeenth century. In 1668, the English sailor, John Watts, spent several months in Old Calabar to buy slaves bound for Barbados. John Elliot of the ship ironically called *Welcome*, shipped 210 slaves from Calabar to Barbados in 1679. The following year, Captain Branfill landed 278 slaves in Jamaica, most from Old Calabar. Other ships, principally English, from Bristol, Liverpool and London, followed in quick succession, which, according to current estimates, "probably took eighty percent of all Biafran slaves (including those from Old Calabar) between 1662 and 1807"[14]. The early phase of this British trading enterprise was dominated by the Royal African Company which enjoyed a monopoly over the trade in the region. The trade expanded substantially following the passage of the African Trade Act which not only broke the monopoly of the Royal African Company but opened the area to competition by individual traders and merchant houses. William Pettigrew has argued that:

> Though the company never entirely enforced its monopoly, its demise allowed more English men to become involved in the slave trade and ship more slaves. The separate traders traded faster, beat the company's ships across the Atlantic and in the century after 1660, the annual volume of the English slave trade increased[15].

Some of the ships that traded in Calabar were *Dragon* which in 1618 carried 212 slaves made up of 102 men, 53 women, 43 boys and 14 girls; the *Eagle Galley* of London that took a cargo of 400 slaves in 1704; *the Edgar, Peach Tree, Nancy, Jupiter, Indian Queen, Duke of York, Fortune, Oxford* and many others [16]. The pressures — the arrivals and departures — these vessels demanding slave cargoes exerted on the rising number of slave exports are indicated below.

Table 6.2: African Slave Exports from the Bight of Biafra

Period	Number of slaves	Proportion of total trade
1701-1710	10,807	3.4 per cent
1711-1720	21,956	5.5 per cent
1731-1740	34,069	6.6 per cent
1741-1750	99,870	18.5 per cent
1751-1760	97,968	15.7 per cent
1761-1770	152,076	18.2 per cent
1771-1780	119,005	16.3 per cent
1781-1790	175,428	20.4 per cent
1791-1800	151,365	19.6 per cent
1801-1810	100,567	14.7 per cent

Source: David Eltis, David Richardson, Stephen D. Bechren and Robert Klein, *The Atlantic Slave Trade, 1527-1807: A Database.* Cambridge, 1999.

Organisation of the Slave Trade in the Cross River Region

Rise of Old Calabar

From all available records, almost all the slaves sold in the coastal ports of Old Calabar, Bonny, Ikot Abasi and Elem Kalabari came from the hinterland and were acquired therefrom. Despite the considerable confusion created by the common use of the terms "Calabars", or "Moko" or "Agbisherea" to designate them in the Americas, we are able to identify some specific ethnic groups from which the slaves came. In the days of the Old Calabar diarist, Antera Duke (1785-1787), most of the slaves were obtained from Orroup or Ododop, a people about 30 miles east of Calabar who secured slaves from the Cameroon Grasslands; "Curcock" or Ekrikok referring to the Mbiabo Efik communities north west of Calabar; and Enyong about 30 miles up the Cross River. The agent of the African Association in Calabar in 1805 named the slaves that formed the bulk of those exported from Old Calabar as Ekrikok, Mbiabo (Efik), Tobac (Ibibio, Oron), Eiricock Boatswain (Umon), Eboe (Igbo), Brassy (Ijo), and Cameroon. These were obviously major centers of collection and bulking from the surrounding communities. It has been estimated, for example, that in the 1820s, 56 per cent of the slaves exported through Old Calabar were Igbo; 42 per cent were Ibibio; while the others mainly Ejagham, Cameroons, Igala, Nupe, Kakanda and Hausa constituted the remaining two per cent. It therefore appears that the prosperity, viability and fame that came to Old Calabar from the slave trade were dependent on her productive hinterland[16].

Several factors explain the emergence of Old Calabar as the principal port of the Cross River region from the middle of the 18th century. Old Calabar, a cluster of settlements off the Cross River estuary as it flows into the Atlantic Ocean, initially comprising the city states of Creek Town, Duke Town, Old Town (Obutong) and Henshaw Town, took advantage of her geographical location to fraternise with the European merchants and would eventually emerge as the middlemen, mediating the trade between the Europeans and the hinterland peoples. Important Efik families like the Ephraims of Duke Town, Mbo Otu or King Robin and the Eyos of Creek Town and prominent traders like Antera Duke, Eyo Nsa, Edem Effiom, Duke Ephraim, Duke Abashy, Ambo Robin John, Ekpenyong Offiong, Ephraim Robin John, Egbo Young, Eyamba, Edem Ekpo and Tommy Henshaw, emerged over time to take advantage of opportunities offered by the European presence. This geographical location also ensured that from the seventeenth century onwards, Calabar would emerge as a major cosmopolitan crossroads in trade, religion, culture and "civilisation", exerting tremendous pull on all the societies of the Cross River Region[17].

Apart from the accident of geography, other factors combined to catapult Calabar into the dominant port since the slave trade era. Among these were the acknowledged ingenuity of the Efik traders and their ability to manipulate their geographical location for economic gain. As earlier observed by late Professor J. C. Anene:

> The Efik of the estuary exploited the opportunities afforded by their location to achieve extensive economic and political power. Economic power carried considerable political and cultural significance[18].

All contemporary accounts confirm that the Efik were indeed astute traders, establishing and maintaining a monopoly of direct trade with the Europeans. They stoutly and generally successfully resisted any direct contact between the Europeans and the hinterland peoples and, as was the case with the Okoyong and Aguagune up river, were ready to go to war to protect their monopoly. Latham was thus right when he observed that Efik dominance of the coastal trade of the Cross River basin was because "they excluded all other peoples from direct access to the Europeans, establishing and maintaining a position as monopolistic middlemen." They were also able to adapt their existing institutions, such as human pawnship, to the needs of the trade.

Besides, in response to the increasing demands of the trade, the government of the city states underwent some transformation. David Northrup has shown that the Efik embarked on a process of political centralisation that effectively catapulted Duke Town, especially under King Duke Ephraim, to the position of virtual dominance to the near exclusion of the other Efik polities like Old Town and Creek Town. By holding both the offices of King (Obong) and the highest *Ekpe* title of Eyamba, which was critical to negotiate terms of trade and collect debts, an important feature of trade in the region, Duke Ephraim was able to virtually freeze out other Efik competitors in the trade and establish a single quasi absolute rulership over the city states. This fitted the natural desire of European captains to want to gather an entire ship cargo from a single port. Duke Ephraim was indeed, as observed by many scholars of the region, a "man of tremendous imagination, energy and determination under whom the energies of the lineage units in Duke Town were directed toward commercial purposes leading to a degree of economic specialisation heretofore unknown in the area." Under him also, the *Ekpe* Society and the *Etuboms* (trade captains) became more and more important in Efik politics. Indeed, so obvious were the trade advantages of Ekpe especially in the collection of trade debts by the imposition of sanctions, that many European traders purchased membership in it[19].

Since the Efik coastal traders possessed neither the military force nor the ritual power to compel uninterrupted flow of trade from the hinterland, they devised ingenious and intricate systems of alliances based on a network of friends, relatives, trading agents and in-laws with the hinterland communities to serve as hosts and escorts in the routes. From Antera Duke's diary, it is clear that there were Efik trading agents in such places as Itu, Uruan, Ibaka (Bakassey), Ikot Offiong, Ibeno, Agwagune and the Cameroons which were to reach full maturity in the days of the palm oil trade. The *Ekpe* Society, which apparently had originated in the upper Cross River, spread to other areas of the region and acquired new significance during the Slave trade era and after, establishing in the process what one scholar has referred to as an "Ekpe imperium." For, as Northrup has observed, "although each community had its own totally independent branch, membership in a common society appears to have greatly facilitated trade between Old Calabar and those other communities". Similarly, an intricate web of marriage alliances and friendships cultivated through gift exchanges ensured the free flow of trade from the interior. One of the many wives of King Eyo Honesty II of Creek Town, for example, was the daughter of the wealthiest man in Umon; another was the daughter of the Chief of Ikot Offiong, and so on. These alliances protected the trade of the hinterland as they set up a complex set of reciprocal obligations between the contracting families.

Of equal importance was the ability of the Efik traders and rulers to establish mutually beneficial relationships with the off-shore European traders in the Atlantic web. These off-shore British merchants, David Imbua has recently concluded that:

> Provided the enabling environment for greater intercourse between Calabar and Britain. More than any other community on the Bight of Biafra, Old Calabar used its trade with the British and more specifically access to their capital to move from the margins of the Atlantic economy to a much more prominent position[20].

The existing institution of "canoe-men" was quickly adopted to meet the needs of the Europeans, carrying goods between the ships and the shore. The institution of debt bondage or pawnship was modified to meet the needs of the new trade. The efficacy of the trust system on which much of the trade depended relied on the personal interaction and friendships between the British traders and the Efik middlemen. Confidence was built on both sides by the use of terms and expressions of endearment and familiarity to settle disputes as well as the many dinners hosted by the Efik in their homes and the Europeans on their ships.

An important factor in the emerging mutual respect between the trading parties was that even before the maturity of the slave trade, the Efik had acquired and developed both language and accounting skills that stood them well in their relations with the English traders. As reported by John Adams, in the last part of the eighteenth century, even before the missionaries established schools in Calabar, "the natives of Old Calabar write English, an art first acquired by some traders sons who had visited England and which they had the sagacity to retain up the present period." Thus, the leading traders in Old Calabar were literate and relatively fluent in English (pidgin version) as early as the 1750's[21]. This knowledge gave the Calabar merchants considerable advantage as they could and did communicate across the Atlantic through letters, and record their trade transactions. The emergence of old Calabar as the major port of our region is thus not surprising, given all the above factors.

Recruiting Slaves for the Market

The relative role of warfare vis-à-vis other methods of recruitment has been a subject of debate since the publication of Ajayi and Smith's book on Yoruba warfare in the nineteenth century. For our region of study, Toyin Falola has recently observed that since there were no centralised polities in the area, slaves were not procured through war as was generally the case in the Bight of Benin. He writes:

> Enslavement in the Bight of Biafra was much more commonly the result of judicial rulings, orders of oracles and above all kidnapping[22].

Available contemporary records, oral evidences and extant scholarly studies on the subject confirm that old Calabar obtained her slaves from the hinterland through a variety of means. These included: *panyarring* or the act of taking free persons when they were offered passage between ports by Europeans; boating, a very dangerous system in which some Europeans were killed by those they tried to forcefully steal from their boats; kidnapping, which probably accounted for the largest number of slaves shipped from the region; raiding for slaves by both European and African merchants; theft of children; buying and selling by slave agents, both European and African along the waterways and markets in the region; child abandonment and sale; self enslavement; punishment for crimes, especially crimes against social norms that threatened the wellbeing of the community; the manipulation of the many oracles and shrines that existed in the area, especially the Aro Long Juju of European records, known by the Igbo as *Ibini Ukpabi* and and the Ibibio as *Ibritam Inokon.*

Oral evidences collected among the Ibibio and Annang of Akwa Ibom State insist that "wrongdoers sold by rightful authorities" were the mainstay of the slave trade in the area. An old man in Mbiatok Itam, Itu Local Government Area and a member of the Ekpo society, maintained that those sold as slaves were people "with bad behaviour" which was against the ethics and values of society. Among these were: women who commited adultery and were sold by their husbands; thieves sold by their families; those who committed "crimes of revenge" like destroying peoples' crops or arson; witches; women who gave birth to twin children, and so on. In the Igbo area, "abnormal children", that is, those whose upper teeth appeared before the lower, who walked and talked sooner than expected; who had supernumerary fingers or toes or any other deformity, were sold. Similar practices obtained in Ibibioland. A woman who menstruated before attaining the proper age or climbed trees was also sold[23].

In addition, slave merchants, both African and European, acquired slaves through robbery and slave catching expeditions. An account given by Thomas Clarkson in the 1770's confirms this thus:

> I had two opportunities of seeing how slaves were procured in the River of Old Calabar. I resided with the king of New Town for months, and he allowed me to go up the river with him to trade for slaves. In the day time we called at the villages as we passed, and purchased our slaves fairly; but in the night we made several excursions to the bank of the river. The canoes were usually left with an armed force; the rest when landed broke into villages, and rushing into the huts of

the inhabitants, seized men, women and children promiscuously. We obtained fifty Negroes in this manner[24].

Similar incidences were recorded by Isaac Parker of the ship Latham, in 1765. King Eyo Honesty of Creek Town informed Hope Waddell that the slaves he sold:

> come from different countries and were sold for different reasons- some as prisoners of war; some for debt; some for breaking their country's laws and some by great men who hated them. The king of a town sells whom he dislikes or fears; his wives and children are sold by his successors in return[25].

Inter-communal conflicts and raids were source of slaves. These conflicts have been a feature of the societies of the middle and upper Cross River and Southern Cameroon, and led to the capture of slaves. East and West of the lower Kwa Iboe River, there are numerous traditions of slave raids carried out mainly by the Aro and the Abam, especially in the Bende area. In Ikot Akpe Ntek area of Akwa Ibom, there is a report to the effect that the village chief usually sponsored men to murder some other village men. Once that was done, the chief would send to the dead man's compound to seize all the property, including wives and children, whom he sold as slaves. It is further reported that during the raids, some categories of persons were captured and sold. These included: those who had suffered small pox before and therefore had acquired immunity; men and women between the ages of twenty and twenty five "with bodily perfection"; able bodied young men and women between the ages of twelve and twenty.

The Role of the Aro

The Aro loom large in any reconstruction of slave recruitment in our region of study. They have been the subject of intense studies precisely because of their dominance in the slave trade in the Bight of Biafra hinterland by Kenneth Dike and Felicia Ekejuba, Adiele Afigbo, David Northrup, G. I. Jones and others[26]. From these studies, it is clear that most of the Igbo, Ibibio, Annang and Upper Cross River slaves sold in Calabar and Bonny were recruited by the Aro from the hinterland. Aro success in this regard has been credited to a number of factors, among them their raids, kidnapping, direct purchase in interior slave markets, trade fairs, and, above all, the manipulation of their *Ibini Ukpabi*. Commenting on the role of the Aro in the trade of the area in the nineteenth century, Mcfarlan wrote:

> For over a hundred miles on the right bank of the Cross River, (Aro) influence was supreme and they were known and feared as far as the Niger. They used the Akunakuna [sic] people as their agents. To the South, the Enyong River was an Aro waterway down which thousands passed in chains to the big slave market at Itu[27].

Similarly, writing in the *Ladder or Bones*, Ellen Thorp had this to say on Aro influence:

> If measured by the yardstick of time and power, the long juju may well be counted among the great oracles of the world. For, over a period of hundreds of years, it has attained immense power, and was the supreme court of appeal to more than millions of Negroes who believed that the great goddess, *Ibini Ukpabi*, spoke through the oracle. Aro priests of the oracle were to be found living in most of the principal places and exercising a most baneful influence[28].

Appropriately described by David Northrup as "the God-men of the Slave Trade", the Aro used the extensive influence earned them within the non-centralised communities of the region and their trading connections and acumen to become easily the greatest suppliers of slaves to Old Calabar. Aro agents frequented the Ukanafun and the Ubium hinterlands. Aro permanent settlements which served as major agencies for slave recruitment were found in the Nsit Ibom area where prototypes of the Aro oracle are still found[29]. So prevalent and wide spread was Aro impact in recruiting slaves that it has been captured in the rather popular Ibibio saying "*Ibritam ete ino owo afo udoho owo*" (*Ibritam* wants human being, are you not one?). Some people in the hinterland sold out some of their family members to the Aro out of greed for money and guns. Unredeemed children pledged as settlement for debt were also sold. Some important personages in the hinterland sold some of their victims to get resources to buy higher grades in the Ekpo, Ekpe and Idiong societies. Children left in the Annang area unattended at play were kidnapped by the Aro. Other oracles with limited influences also existed in the region that complemented the Aro Oracle. The best known of these was the Akpa Aya shrine in Ikot Abasi.

Slave Trade Routes and Hinterland Markets

However recruited in the interior by the agents, slaves had to be transported to the coastal markets for sale to the Europeans. A network of routes and markets emerged to serve this purpose. Slaves passed from hand to hand in a relay fashion, through many villages and markets in the interior to the coast. Even before the coming of the Europeans, the hinterland people had traded with the coast and exchanged such food items as yams for fish and salt which came mainly from the coast. These rather imprecise routes were to develop into slave trade routes. The journey from the interior to the coast was long and lasted several days or weeks or even months. The middlemen and agents sometimes moved from one interior gathering point to another. There were frequent breaks on the routes and since major markets and selling points were few and far between, several collecting points were established on the routes, the village squares and other important buildings serving such purposes.

Waterways were the major arteries between communities. The Cross River with its many tributaries played a crucial part in the lower Cross River region in this regard. Several entrepots early developed along the routes notably at Ikom, Umon Island and Itu. The eventual boom in the slave trade increased the volume of trade and expanded the trade routes. Numerous Igbo, Ekoi and other slaves were thus brought down mainly through Umon market to Itu where mostly Efik traders purchased them for sale to European slavers at Calabar. Other trade goods from the upper Cross River region included yams, livestock, palm oil, ivory, wild rubber, canoes and pots which found their way mainly through the Umon market to major Akwa Ibom markets like Asang, Itu, Use Ikot Oku, Ikpa, Ikot Obong and Oron. Efik became the *lingua franca* or trade language widely spoken by the communities on the routes. Indeed, by the 19th century, Efik had formally established itself as "the trading language of all the markets up to the Aro country".

In the hinterland, slave routes were footpaths meandering in a fashion that the people took through villages and markets. As the trade grew, more road networks came into existence. Much of the footpath network of trade routes created in the period was incorporated into the early colonial road system. Some important river beaches which were used as routes to convey slaves from the interior to the coastal markets were: the Essene Beach in Ikot Abasi; Ikot Obio Nko in Asutan Ekpe; Ndiya in Nsit; Ekpene Ukpa in Iman; and Eyiesana Beach in Nsit. Other routes were the Awa river-Ibeno through Effiat, and Ikot Ebong Beach. Slaves from Annang land, Enyong, Ibiono Ibom, and Ikpa Uruan reached Old Calabar port through Itu. In the Ikot Abasi axis, King Jaja, known locally as jojo, used Opokalama and Iwoma on the Imo River where slaves were shipped to Opobo. Another route passed through Uta Ewa, which, in 1919, was expanded as a trading post and a harbor built to evacuate goods to Europe. Footpaths like the one connecting Essene Town with Jaja creek were used.

For the slaves in Itu axis, waterways were used to move them from Itu to Calabar. A footpath linking Mbiatok Itam to Ekoi Itam and to Mbiaya to Ikpa Uruan Beach still exists. The central slave collecting centre and market was at Ikpa Beach. Some bush tracks used in moving slaves from Ikpa market to the port in Calabar are still existing at Ikot Abasi Oku in Ikpa Uruan called *"afaha Usung Adep"*, meaning "narrow path of no return". Another route passed through Etak Ikot in Ibiono Ibom, where the slave market was situated. This was the route taken by the Aro expedition to Etak Ikot. Slaves were taken from there through Enyong Creek to Calabar. Routes existed from Arochukwu to Enyong Creek, from Umon Island to Enyong Creek, and from there to Calabar through the waterways.

The people of Ikot Abasi recall the central role of slave trading among them. Many collecting points served as centres for slave business. Elders and cult members of Ekpo, Okonko, Idiong and Inam served as collectors. Shrines like the Akpa Aya played a role in the trade. Mkpasa shrine at Uta Ewa served the purpose for King Jaja of Opobo's raids and trading activities. Essene Beach served a similar purpose. These centres at Ikot Abasi linked them with the coastal ports of Opobo and Bonny through the Imo River. Itu served as a central collecting point coordinating the movement of the slaves from the interior. Indeed, the Itu central market became famous as a major collecting point for slaves bound for Calabar down the Cross River.

Apart from Ikot Abasi and Itu axes, there were other places where slave trading occurred. Slave trading in Annang territories was dominated mainly by the Aro. The Abam and Aro dominated the main trade routes between Arochukwu and Annang land. Odoro Ikpe and Ikot Nkon markets were places where the trade flourished and were connected to Ibakesi, Ndinya Mfia, Nung Ukim, Ediene, Itak and to Ifiayong in Uruan. Obo Anang market in Ukana was famous for goods and slaves. Agwagune, Umon, and Umon Island were other collection centers for slaves from Arochukwu. The slaves from Aro, Ohafia, Itu and parts of Enyong creek, Aguagune and Umon were also moved to Old Calabar through waterways in these villages and communities. As E. A. Ayandele has observed:

> Starting from Old Calabar, the ethnic groups of Efiks [sic], Enyong, Umon and Akunakuna [sic] were monopolistic in their commercial activities. One tribe along the river would not allow the other to pass through its territory for the purpose of trade. The tradition was that the Akunakuna [sic] must sell to the Umon, the Umon to the Enyong and the later to the Efik[29].

By the early 19th century when the slave trade had reached maturity, a well established route ran from Bende east to the Cross and Benue Rivers. A route extended from the upper and middle Benue down to Calabar. An overland route linked Calabar to Ikom through which Nde Ekoi (Boki) slaves were brought to Calabar. The longest route east of the river ran overland from the Cameroon grasslands to the Ododop foothills ending in Calabar. The principal stopping places on the routes were Mamfe and Anyang. Many slaves exported from Cameroon and North-eastern Nigeria through Calabar came through this route. An important slave route regularly used by the Aro ran from Uzuakoli through Ena, Edda and Biakpan down the Cross River to Calabar. This criss-crossing, complex and meandering network of routes is captured in Maps 6.2 and 6.3.

Although the hinterland routes and markets were dominated by the Aro, oral evidences insist that some important indigenous traders emerged in the Akwa Ibom area. Among these was one Chief Akpanowo of Ibekwe who apparently bought and kept slaves in Bonny town for trading purposes. There was one Akpan Ude who bought and sold slaves at Ikot Ekong Beach. The acknowledged "supreme slave trader" in the Ukanafun area was one Chief Udodong, whose magnificent but aged two storey building still stands as testimony to his conspicuous role in the trade. His man-size iron pot used to control very violent slaves is still in the custody of his family. One Chief Aman Udo Udo was a major slave trader in the Ibesikpo area[30].

Slave Trade Currencies

From the rather scanty information available, the prices of slaves in Old Calabar, as elsewhere, fluctuated, depending on the market conditions of demand and supply. In 1787, for example, the master of the vessel, *Pearl*, reported that he had trouble getting slaves from Old Calabar, complaining that the prices demanded for slaves were "very high". However, between 1787 and 1792, slaves in Calabar sold for between twelve and fourteen pounds, the cheapest range on the coast of West Africa. Be that at it may, slaves were bartered for goods in Calabar, as elsewhere. The major goods/currencies in Old Calabar were beads, mirrors, East Indian and English textiles, bar iron, hardware, arms, gun powder, liquor, pewter basins, knives, locks, belts, swords, tankards, imported fancy clocks, paintings, organs, fabricated wood and cast-iron houses, beer in kegs, copper rods, copper brass wristlets (manillas), copper wires and cowries. Copper rod (manillas) was a general purposes money throughout the Cross River region all the way into Tiv land while iron bars, because of their rather high value, were of limited use. Brass manilla was the general purpose money in the south-central part of the hinterland (see figure 6.1). These were the goods for which the most precious resource of our area, our youth, were exchanged.

Quartering Slaves at the Coast

However acquired in the hinterland, the slaves, when brought, were warehoused at the coast. Baracoons, warehouses and depots were thus established at the coast. A sunk steamer ship was used at Uta Ewa in the Ikot Abasi axis by Jaja of Opobo and would later become the Old UAC warehouse. Ship sinking platforms served as depots for slaves in the Enyong and Ikpa Uruan areas of Akwa Ibom State. In Calabar, the Offiong Square in Duke Town, the Afia Obom Beach popularly called Fort Stuart, the Matilda Beaches and so on, served as slave depots. These were to develop into major trading depots for the incoming European merchant firms like UAC and Elder Dempster of the oil palm and other commodities era. Indeed, the transition from slave trade to trade in other commodities represented no major break in the patterns of relationships between the Old Calabar middlemen and the Europeans, on the one hand, and between them and the hinterland communities, on the other. If anything, the cultivation and processing of the new commodities resulted in the expansion of slave holdings in Calabar, especially in the Akpabuyo plantations. Here also, the slaves developed a culture of solidarity expressed in blood oaths with which they bound themselves together against the cruel practices of their owners.

Slave Trade Relics, Artifacts, Routes and Cultural Tourism

The most important relics which have survived from the slave trade are: trade currencies (see figure 6.1); forts and baracoons along the coast; imported pre-fabricated buildings, especially in Old Calabar; diaries and other memorials; squares, compounds and beaches where slaves were quartered; clocks; paintings, the Cumber Beach presented by Sir John Tobin in 1826 and King Eyamba's iron palace. The Arochukwu *Ibini Ukpabi,* Akwa *Agballa,* Ikot Abasi *Akpa Aya* and other shrines that played important roles in slave recruitment are still there. Some of the important Efik families that participated in the trade are still available and carry some memories of the trade and its import for their families. Above all, the trade routes (see maps 6.2 and 6.3) that traversed the region can be integrated into a major tourism circuit and thus restore the image of the organisation of the trade which bound together present day Ebonyi, Abia, Rivers, Akwa-Ibom, Cross River and lower Benue. As the Slave History Museum established by the Cross River State government on the old site of Matilda Beach has shown, this can be an important source of foreign currency earning for the states of the region, especially in this era of "back-to-roots" cultural tourism and the rising importance of the "museums of conscience" around the world. Fortunately, some of the relics and artifacts have been collected and custodied in the National Museum, Old Residency, Calabar, the National Museum, Uyo, but most importantly, in the Slave History Museum, Calabar. The possibility of using the memories from the slave trade era for musical compositions and drama has also been demonstrated by the hymn, *Amazing Grace*, written by the notorious slave trader turned abolishment, John Newton in Calabar, and the film, *Amazing Grace*, produced by the Cross River State Government for tourism purposes.

Impact of Slave Trade in the Cross River Region

From our analysis above, it is clear that the Atlantic slave trade had profound impacts, some positive, but others mainly negative, on the societies and peoples of the Cross River Region. We have already noted the emergence of Efik noble middlemen who would dominate the sale of slaves to Europeans and the enormous economic benefits they derived there from. The liaisons and friendships they established with the English merchants principally from Liverpool, Bristol and London, were to serve them well and catapult them into agents of British activities: the so-called "legitimate commerce" that eventually and gradually replaced the slave trade towards the end of the nineteenth century; British missionary enterprise of the Church of Scotland Mission, the Primitive and Wesleyan Methodists and later Roman Catholics in the entire region; as well as political agents in the early colonial period. It was indeed from those families that the early local teachers of the region emerged. So positively important had the slave trade become to the economic wellbeing and statue of the Efik middlemen that they would oppose the abolitionist movement of the period[31]. Equally benefiting economically, socially and politically were the Aro, the principal slave recruiters in the hinterlands of the region. There is no question that the Aro grossed profits from the slave trade approximating those of the Efik middlemen. It is for the above reason that we can appreciate the recent calls for the Efik and Aro to pay reparations for their roles in the slave trade. Their gains, however, represented "private gains", with little impact on the common people of the region. The enormous economic and social benefits of the slave trade to the European traders from Bristol, London and Liverpool which doubtless qualify them as "gainers" in current parlance of the debate on the subject falls outside the concern of this chapter.

Although a few traders emerged in the hinterlands and took advantage of the economic pool coming from Calabar, Bonny and Opobo, the vast majority of the hinterland populations were victims or "losers" in the trade. It was from them that the virile young men and women, "the flower of their society", were extracted. They bore the brunt of the considerable insecurity of life and property that accompanied slave raids. In some cases as in Ibibio land, they were compelled to construct fences and walls to protect themselves from the Abam and Aro raiders, especially in the Ikono, Ini, and Ikpe Clan areas adjacent to Arockukwu[32]. It is doubtful, even in the present state of our knowledge, that the overall economic impact on these communities was anything but negative. As we have observed elsewhere:

Some of the goods for which slaves were exchanged in the Cross River Region were frivolous and worthless; others such as strong drinks and fire arms were destructive; yet others, especially manufactured hardware undermined traditional industries and led to retardation in existing techniques of production[33].

Be that as it may, we are on firmer grounds regarding the demographic impact brought about by population movements associated with the slave trade, both internally and externally. Assessing the full significance of the population loss on the region has been problematic, especially against the backdrop of the paradox that areas like Akwa Ibom and Igboland that lost the most people to the trade are still today the areas with the highest population concentrations in Black Africa. This debate as to whether or not large scale emigration, involuntary as it was in the case, was an economic handicap in circumstances such as ours, should not detain us here. It is important to note, however, that the overall picture at the macro-level assumes greater significance at the micro-level of families that lost populations to the trade. Such losses were no doubt devastating for the welfare and wellbeing of such families in these labour demanding farming and fishing communities.

We are on firmer grounds, however, when we examine the outward migration of populations from the hinterlands to the coastal regions which had become new frontiers of opportunity during the slave trade era and beyond. There is little doubt, for example, that the slave trade was largely responsible for the dispersal of Akwa Ibom populations and cultures to the Niger Delta, city states of Old Calabar and beyond to the Americas. It was mainly slaves from the Ibibio and Igbo hinterlands that worked the plantations that brought prosperity to the kings and chiefs of Old Calabar in the nineteenth century. The descendants of those slaves still constitute an important ratio of the population in the Akpabuyo area of Cross River State. Similarly, the descendants of slaves quartered by Chief Akpanowo of Ibekwe in the Bonny area of Rivers State are reportedly still there. Conversely, it was during the era of the slave trade that Igbo elements, especially those of the Aro and Abam, were introduced into present Akwa Ibom State. The presence of Igbo names for villages and persons especially in Ukanafun and the areas bordering Arochukwu testifies to this development. Even more obvious, major trade settlements were established by the Efik of Old Calabar in such paces as Uruan, Ibeno, Itu, Ikpa, Ifiayong, Ibaka and Idua Oron which expanded under the impact of the trade in produce and form important elements in Akwa Ibom State population today. It was indeed the slave trade that tied present Akwa Ibom communities rather closely into the Efik commercial, cultural and social orbits which have compounded the problem of boundary demarcation between present Akwa Ibom and Cross River States. As far as the Lower Cross River is concerned, history seems to show that the river united rather than divided the people on its east and west bank estuary[34].

Equally interesting in this regard is the question of what happened to the cultures of people of the Cross River Region which the slaves carried across the Atlantic to the Americas and the Caribbean. It is now increasingly becoming accepted that, contrary to earlier views, the "Middle Passage" or Atlantic crossing, was not "a historical discontinuity, one in which Africans lost their identities and life ways." Indeed, as we have insisted in our book, *African Diaspora and the Black Experience in New World Slavery*, the middle passage, though unquestionably a most "jarring and brutal experience" both physically and emotionally for the slaves, was "clearly a bridge through which the enslaved Africans transported their cultures to the New World." Indeed, the researches of Bruce Connell and Ivor Miller challenge us to identify and relate to "Calabar" or "Moko" or "Agbisherea" cultures in such places as Jamaica, Cuba and other Caribbean Islands. Connell, in his work on the Abakua or Ekpe in Cuba has stated clearly that:

> Africans enslaved by the Efik from the surrounding regions who became assimilated by learning Efik and becoming low level members of Ekpe, were likely important to the creation of Abakua in Cuba.

He hypothesises further that since the Efik proper were very few in the Caribbean slave population, "Efik influence in the Caribbean was promoted by non-Efik peoples from the region, principally the Ibibio." Further work on Abakua by Ivor Miller has also shown that of the five dominant cabildos (Ekpe Lodges) that have survived in Cuban *Ekpe*, two, namely *Bibi* and *Oru* obviously derived from present Akwa Ibom State while the remaining three, namely *Efi*, *Efo* and *Suama* are from present Cross River State. Besides, researches in Jamaica have shown the prevalence of Ibibio derived cultures in the Island. Similarly Lorena S. Walsh, with some hesitation has admitted in her rather fascinating study, *From Calabar to Carter's Grove*, the persistence of African cultures shown in such areas as food preferences, names, the kinship idiom of association, clothing and family organisation in the Virginia Slave Communities especially up to the late 18th Century [35]. This important cultural extension of Akwa Ibom and Cross River to the Americas challenges us to interconnect with these populations, especially in this era of globalisation and inter-cultural connectivity.

Conclusion

In this chapter, we have attempted to reconstruct the patterns of indigenous slavery and slave trade in the Cross River region. We have shown that many of the generalisations concerning the nature of indigenous slavery, the organisation and general impact of the slave trade, and the transition from slave to commodities trade need serious revision. The Cross River Region was indeed one of the most important in shaping the character of the Atlantic slave trade and clearly demonstrates the interplay between the European traders, the coastal middlemen and the vast producing hinterland communities. The slave trade bound these three together and had consequences that outlived the trade.

Notes and References

1. *Africa and the Abolition of the Slave Trade*, key-note address, Conference on the Consequences of the First Governmental Effort to Abolish the Atlantic Slave Trade, Accra, Ghana. August 8, 2007.
2. "The Atlantic Slave Trade and the Impact on the Nigerian Hinterland, 1500-1900" in Akinwuni Ogundiran ed. *Pre-Colonial Nigeria: Essays in Honour of Toyin Falola* (Tenton: African World Press, 2005), pp 447-470.
3. For detailed discussion of this controversy, see Okon E. Uya, *African Diaspora and the Black Experience in New World Slavery* (New York: Third Press, 1992), pp. 56-65.
4. See *Polyglotta Africana* (London: Church Missionary House, 1853), pp 18-19.
5. These traditions are reproduced in Joseph Akwa Ushie's, *Images of the Slave and Slavery in the Oral Traditions of the Bette-Bendi, 1500-1700*. Unpublished Paper. University of Uyo, 2009.
6. *Trust, Pawnship and Atlantic History. The Institutional Foundations of the Old Calabar Slave Trade*. The American Historical Review, Vol. 104, No. 2 (1999), pp. 333-355. See also

Randy Sparks, *The Two Princes of Calabar*. (Cambridge: Harvard University Press, 2000).

7   Uya, African Diaspora, p.59.

8   For details, see Paul Lovejoy, *Ideology of Slavery in Africa*. (Beverly Hills, Cal., 1982) and Susan Meiers and I. Kopytoff eds., *Slavery in Africa*. (Madison: University of Wisconsin Press, 1997).

9   See Okon Uya, *Contemporary Issues on Slavery and the Black World*. Calabar: (Cats Publishers, 2003) and, with others, editors. *Slave Trade and Slavery in Africa: The Akwa Ibom State Experience*. (Uyo: Ministry of Culture and Tourism, 2006). See also Orlando Patterson, *Slavery as Social Death*. (Cambridge: Harvard University Press, 1982).

10 *Old Calabar: The City States and the Europeans, 1800-1885*. (Uyo: Scholars Press, 1980).

11 *Labour and Race: Working the Slave Trade in the British Atlantic World*. Workshop Paper, Africa, Europe and the Americas, 1500-1700. Accra, Ghana, July 12-26, 2009.

12 *Trade, Pawnship and Atlantic History*, p 353.

13 A.J.H. Latham, *Old Calabar, 1600-1891*. (London: Clarendon Press, 1973), p. 14.

14 Matt D. Childs "Review of Randy J. Sparks' The Two Princes of Old Calabar." *www.common-place.org*. vol.51 no I October 2004.

15 See Pettigrew, *Free to Enslave: Politics and the Escalation of Britain's Transatlantic Slave Trade, 1688-1714*, William and Mary Quarterly, (LXIV,1, 2007), pp3-38.

16 For details, see Uya, *Slave Routes of the Lower Cross River Region*; Northrup, *Trade Without Rulers, and Africa's Discovery of Europe 1450-1850*. (New York: Oxford UP, 2009); and Kalu Ume, *The Rise of British Colonization in Southern Nigeria, 1700-1900* (New York: Exposition Press, 1980).

17 See Okon E. Uya, Effiong U. Aye, Emmanuel Nsan and Ekpenyong Ndiyo, eds., *The Efik and their Neighbours* (Calabar. Cats Publishers, 2006).

18 *The International Boundaries of Nigeria, 1885-1960* (London, 1960).

19 For details see Latham, *Old Calabar* and Northrup, *Trade Without*

Rulers, p.110. See also Asuquo Anwana *Ekpe Imperium in South-eastern Nigeria* (Calabar: University of Calabar Press, 2009).

20. See David Imbua, *The Off-shore British Community and Old Calabar 1650-1700*, unpublished, 2009 and his excellent Ph.D Thesis, *Intercourse and Cross Currents in the Atlantic World: Calabar-British Experience, 1650-1960*, University of Calabar Ph.D Thesis, 2009.

21. See Lovejoy and Richardson, *Trade and Pawnship*; also Robin Hallet (ed.), *Records of the African Association, 1788-1831* (London: Thomas Nelson and Sons, 1964).

22. *A History of Nigeria* (Cambridge University Press, 2008), p. 56.

23. For details, see Uya *et al*, *Slave Trade and Slavery in Africa: Akwa Ibom State Experience*, pp. 14-15.

24. Quoted in Northrup, *Trade Without Rulers*, p.66.

25. Quoted in Monday Noah, "Social and Political Development: The Lower Cross River Region, 1600-1910", in *A History of the Cross River Region of Nigeria*, edited by Monday Abasiattai (Enugu: Harris Publishers, 1990), pp. 90-108.

26. See Dike and Ekejuba, *The Aro of South-eastern Nigeria*, (Ibadan: University Press 1980); Afigbo, *Ropes of Sand: Studies in Igbo History and Culture* (Ibadan: Ibadan University Press, 1981), *Pre-Colonial Trade Links between South-eastern Nigeria and the Benue Valley*, Journal of African Studies (Vol. 4 No2); Northrup, *Trade Without Rulers* and Jones, *The Trading States of the Oil Rivers* (London, 1963).

27. Calabar: *The Church of Scotland Mission* (London: 1846) p.105.

28. Thorp, *Ladder or Bones* (Fontana Books, 1986), 203.

29. E. A. Ayandele. *The Missionary Impact on Modern Nigeria, 1842-1914* (London, 1966), p. 111 and M. B. Abasiattai, *Akwa Ibom and Cross River States: The Land, The People and Their Culture.* Calabar (Wusen Press, 1987), pp. 58-59.

30. Much of the reconstruction of these trade routes and hinterland markets is taken from Uya, *et al*, *Slave Trade and Slavery in Africa: Akwa Ibom State Experience* and Uya, *Slave Routes of the Lower Cross River Basin*.

31. For details, see Ralph Austen and Woodruff D. Smith, *Images of Africa and British Slave Trade Abolition: the Transition to an*

Imperialist Ideology, 1787-1807, African Historical Studies, (Vol. 2, (1969), pp. 69-83; Okon E. Uya, *Slave Trade and Slavery Abolition: An Afro-Centric Perspective* (Calabar: Cats Publishers, 2007); Adiele Afigbo, *Britain and the Hydra in the Bight of Biafra*, African Economic History, 31 (2003), pp. 1-18; and Christopher Brown, *Moral Capital: Foundations of British Abolitionism* (Chapel Hill: University of North Carolina Press, 2006).

32 For details see Northrup, *Trade Without Rulers*, pp 118-120. This is also confirmed in the oral evidences collected in the area.

33 Uya, *Trade Routes of the Lower Cross River Basin*, pp. 11-12. See also Ini Udoka, *The Atlantic Slave Trade and its impact on Akwa Ibom area*, Ibom Journal of History and International Studies (No. 17).

34 For details, see G. Ugo Nwokeji, *The Atlantic Slave Trade and Population Density: A Historical Geography of the Biafran Hinterland*, Canadian Journal of Africa Studies, (Vol 34, No3 (2000), pp. 616-651

35 See Ivor L. Miller, *The Formation of African Identities in the Americas. Spiritual Ethnicity*, Contours (Fall, 2004, Vol. 2 No. 2), pp. 193-221. Okon E. Uya, *African Dimensions of America Cultures* (Calabar: University of Calabar Press, 1994). See also Lorena S. Walsh, *From Calabar to Carter's Grove: The History of a Virginia Slave Community* (Charlottesville: University Press of Virginia, 1997) and Stephanie E. Smallwood, *Saltwater Slavery: A Middle Passage from Africa to American Diaspora* (Cambridge: Harvard University Press, 2008).

Field Work

The oral interviews and collecting of relics for Akwa Ibom State were conducted under the auspices of the State Ministry of Culture and Tourism by the Slave Trade Route Committee between 2005 and 2006. The Research Team comprised:

Professor Okon E. Uya	Coordinator and Supervisor
Professor Monday B. Abasiattai	Member
Mr. Peter Odey	Member
Mr. Victor Akpan	Member
Mr. Emmanuel Etta	Member

Mr. Edet O. Okuette   Member
Miss Nsima C. Edem   Member

The Calabar based activities were co-ordinated by the National Museum, Old Residency, Calabar, under the leadership of its then Curator, Mr. Mayo Adediran and the Calabar Museum Society. Mr. G. N. Ufot, Director of Culture, Federal Ministry of Tourism, Culture and National Orientation supervised the Abuja based activities.

Map 6.1: Depicting the Slave Trade in Cross River Region
Redrawn by Keith Scurr, School of Geography, University of Hull, after a map in Kannan K. Nair, *Politics and Society in South Eastern Nigeria. 1841-1906: A Study of Power, Diplomacy and Commerce in Old Calabar* (London, 1972).

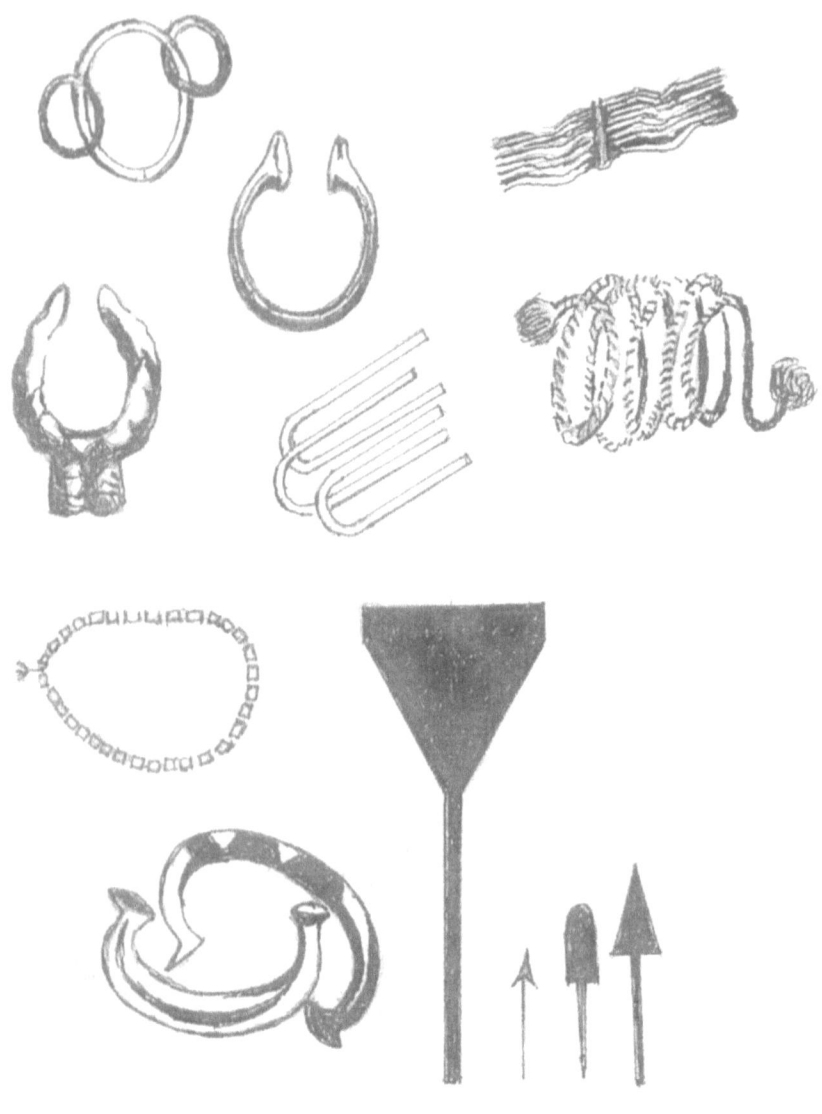

Figure 6.2: Some Currencies used in Exchange for Slaves

Chapter 7

SLAVERY AND SLAVE TRADE IN NIGER DELTA AND ITS HINTERLANDS

Abi A. Derefaka
Professor of Archaelogy, Department of History and Diplomatic Studies, University of Port Harcourt, Port Harcourt

Introduction

IN a keynote address at the inauguration of the Professor Bassey Andah Memorial Foundation at Calabar on 22nd January, 2004, Professor E. J. Alagoa summarised the genesis of the Slave Routes Project in the following words:

> The slave routes project is the result of the recent clamour by black scholars and leaders across the world for the western beneficiaries of the Atlantic Slave Trade to pay reparation to the core victims of the trade in black Africa and Africans in diaspora in the Americas and the Caribbean. Eventually taken by the Organisation of African Unity to the United Nations, the project was designed by UNESCO, the expert in constructing perfect projects which can only be realised in part, or not at all. It was adopted by UNESCO in 1993, and launched in Ouidah/Whydah, the slave Port of Benin Republic in 1994. UNESCO set the 23rd day of August each year as International Day for the Remembrance of the Slave Trade and its Abolition, from the day in 1791 when a great revolt against slavery began in the Caribbean Island of of Santa Domingo. Member nations of UNESCO were required to organise activities to observe the ten year period 1999-2004 as International Decade for the Commemoration of the Struggle Against Slavery and its Abolition. This year, 2004, was proposed as he Struggle Against Slavery and its Abolition... In the heirachy of UNESCO projects, the Slave Route Project is given top billing as "an interdisciplinary flagship project".

It is also E. J. Alagoa (1986: 125-135) who has aptly provided a synthesis of the positions taken on the subject matter by scholars such as K. O. Dike (1956), G. I. Jones (1963), R. Horton (1969), A. F. C. Ryder (1959), and P. C. Lloyd (1963). Alagoa had earlier (1972) discussed the issue of the slave trade among other matters.

Slavery

There is no doubt now that slavery predated the trans-Atlantic slave trade era in the Niger Delta communities as well as in those of their hinterland neighbours. Horton (1954: 311-336) for example, reported the nature of slavery in the village-group of Nike, a northern Igbo village-group. He has discussed the position of Nike in relation to three important trade routes in Igboland (Horton, 1954:311-312). In discussing the origin of the *Ohu* system, he makes a distinction between the slaves living within the *free-born* villages and those "forming discrete village communities of slave status". He also discusses the rights and functions of *Ohu*. These include their "rights in land", legal status, marriage rules, their use of labour, ritual functions, and religious (prophetic and divination) functions.

Lovejoy (1983: 1-8) has also defined slavery. He says:

> Slavery was one form of exploitation. Its special characteristics included the idea that slaves were property; that they were outsiders who were alien by origin who had been denied their heritage through judicial or other sanctions; that coercion could be used at will; that their labour power was at the complete disposal of a master; that they did not have the right to their own sexuality and, by extension, to their reproductive capacities; and that the slave status was inherited unless provision was made to ameliorate that status.

These characteristics were present in the forms of slavery, which existed in the Niger Delta and its hinterland. Indeed, slavery as a means of social differentiation and a strategy for economic production existed both in the hinterland communities such as among the Igbo, where one word for slave was *Ohu*, as well as among the Niger Delta communities such as the Ijo, where one word for slave was *Omoni*. There is ample evidence that the advent of the trans-Atlantic slave trade benefited from slavery that featured in the socio-economic organisation of the local communities of present day Rivers and Bayelsa States.

Nature of the Institution of Slavery

The nature of domestic slavery among the Okrika Ijo, for example, shows that the people did not subscribe to Aristotle's view that, "certain people are naturally free, others are naturally slaves. For the latter slavery is both just and expedient." Once adopted, slavery became an important institution in the socio-economic structure of the society. The basic reason for the acquisition of slaves was *for increasing the population of the compound and the 'house'*. Polygyny was one way of achieving this objective but a faster means of achieving the same objective was the acquisition of already grown males and females as slaves. Consequently, upon acquisition of new slaves, the master assigned them to live *with his wives who became the mothers* of the slaves. The master also considered them to be his children if they were well behaved. The hair on the heads of the new slaves would be shaved and new local names assigned to each of them. The process of *enculturation* had begun. It was mandatory for each slave to learn and speak only the local language (*Kirike*) and never to communicate in his/her original language. The master's wives treated the slaves as their own children. The extent to which the male slaves became proficient, in competence and performance, in the local language and demonstrated understanding of Okrika customs, traditions, taboos and worldview, determined their qualification for admission into *Sekeni Ogbo*. This socio-political organisation played a key role in the pre-colonial political system of the Okrika. The same criteria were used by female socio-cultural institutions to determine suitability for *admission of female slaves* into their ranks. Such assimilated slaves were fully integrated into the family and the *house* (both for trading and for war) in the host community. In the *house* system both freeborn and slave belonged to a closely knit socio-political and economic institution and the slave was afforded the opportunity to demonstrate his intelligence and industry and acquire wealth which would improve his status in society.

When fully assimilated, the social differences between slaves and freeborn become hardly evident as a servile past or ancestry did not prevent a hardworking and intelligent man from attaining the highest social and political positions in the society. Indeed, at the death of the master, *slaves* could inherit his property along with his biological children. Domestic slaves in Okrika society became so integrated that it became an offence punishable by fine for anyone to be called a slave. When Christianity and Western education came, it was the offspring of slaves that were first sent to test the usefulness of the new introductions as the wealthy merchants did not want their children taught strange religious doctrines or flogged by teachers. However, the slaves still had mostly psychological handicaps as members of the host community. For example, the stigma of slavery was so strong that marriage of a slave man to a freeborn woman was rare. However, marriage of slave women to freeborn men was more common. Sometimes, the master and his male siblings and their male children as well as male slaves who had become successful traders, married slave women and their daughters.

In a typical household with slaves there were both newly arrived slaves who were not yet part of the family and those already successfully assimilated. From among the new *arrivals some could be resold or chosen for sacrifice* and some would serve as porters if the master was a long distance trader. It was also from this category of slaves the master could pledge some as surety for advances obtained from trading partners. However, a well-behaved and hardworking slave in this category who was successfully acculturated and socialised could be fully integrated into the family, *house* and community. Some slaves could before assimilation, visit their original homes occasionally and return or eventually buy their freedom and return home. Most slaves were assimilated and even when their masters sent them on trading expeditions to the hinterland, where their original homes were, they preferred to remain loyal to their masters and return to the coast where economic prospects were brighter and opportunities for significant political achievement were more available.

The Atlantic Trade

The period from the 15th to 19th century is best remembered in Nigerian history as the period of the Atlantic trade between the supercargoes from Europe and the Nigerian coastal kingdoms and city-states. The Portuguese were dominant in the 15th and 16th centuries; the Dutch in the 17th century, while the 18th century saw the French and English becoming the most influential. For the Niger Delta Region, the period saw the rapid transformation and re-direction of the pre-existing city-states and their commercial network to meet the demands of the Atlantic trade. The Atlantic commerce itself took the form of a trade, mainly in human cargoes, while from the middle of the 19th century, it metamorphosed into what came to be known as the legitimate trade in agricultural resources, especially palm produce.

The Slave Trade Routes into and in The Niger Delta

Generally, slave trade routes linked markets to export outlets. There were two types of routes, namely, land routes and water routes. It is inevitable that in tracing slave trade routes for the Niger Delta region, one has to begin by identifying the main collection points in the Delta. Thereafter, the markets in the hinterland that supplied the human cargo can be identified and then the route followed from minor markets to major markets and from these markets to the coast can be traced. This was how the routes in the map that follows were reconstructed. In the Niger Delta, the city-states of the eastern Delta, namely, Kalabari, Bonny, Okrika and Nembe played prominent roles in the slave trade. The Andoni, Ogoni, Ikwerre and Ndoki were also involved.

However, all told, there is no gainsaying the fact that the kingdom of Bonny was quite prominent in slave trade and indeed all forms of trade from the sixteenth century to the twenty-first century. Ibani traders followed a route along the Bonny River and then behind the Okrika settlement, Ogu to Ogoniland. They reached Ndokiland following different branches of the Azumini or Imo River. Opuoko in Ogoniland was an important place on this route. The Ogoni are reported to have been hostile to the traders from Bonny and so the latter moved along the Essene Creek to Otuomo near Egwanga close to Opobo. Early Ibani contacts with the Ndoki were very close and some traditions suggest that the former had moved through the territory of the latter in the final stages of their migration to their present location. Ibani traders also went eastwards through Andoni territory to Ogoniland and to the Ndoki markets.

Located to the north of Bonny (Okoloama) was Elem Kalabari in the same estuary of the Rio Real that was the combined estuary of the Bonny and New Calabar Rivers. It understandably became a major commercial rival of Bonny both in the bid to establish control over hinterland markets and trade with Europeans. For the trade with the hinterland Elem Kalabari had greater proximity to Ikwerreland, for example, and therefore had the advantage of direct contact.

The Okrika are also located to the north of Bonny off the Bonny River. They had direct access to Ikwerre Eleme (Mboli), Ogoni, and Akwete/Ndoki markets. Consequently, conflict with the Kalabari over control of some of these markets and fishing grounds was inevitable. However, surprisingly, there was never a bilateral war between the Okrika and Ibani kingdoms.

Like Okrika, the kingdom of Nembe to the east of Elem Kalabari never fought bilaterally against Bonny. Indeed in the nineteenth century, Nembe is reported to have fought the Kalabari in alliance with Bonny.

Our major concern here is slave trade. We have, therefore, focused our searchlight on the communities of the Niger Delta city states of present day Bayelsa and Rivers States and their immediate and distant hinterlands, which played significant roles in the slave-trading network. Historians working on the Niger Delta have divided the region into three sub-regions: the Western Delta, the Central Delta and the Eastern Delta. The Western Delta produced only one major city-state, the Itsekiri city state. The Central Delta, which is in Bayelsa State also had only one city-state, the Nembe (Brass) City State. The Eastern Delta, which is in Rivers State, had three city-states: the Elem Kalabari (New Calabar), Okrika and Bonny (Ibani) city-states. In the second half of the 19th century, Bonny was broken into two,

Table 7.1 : The Atlantic Slave Trade Route of Niger Delta and its Hinterland

S/N	City State	Immediate Hinterland	Distant Hinterland
1.	Nembe (Brass) (Nembe: Ogbolomabiri and Bassambiri) Odual -Saka	Akassa Twon - Brass Angiama Amassoma Kaiama	Igala-land Aboh Onitsha Oguta-land
2.	Elem Kalabari (New Calabar) (Elem Ama)	Ikwerreland Iwofe Choba Beach) Ibaa Isiokpo Ogbakiri Emohua Ndele Epkeyeland Ogbahland Omoku Kreigani Abualand Bille	Akwa Oguta (kalabari Owerri
3.	Okrika (Okrika Island)	Eleme (Mboli) Mbaise Western Ogboniland Ikwerreland Diobu Rumukurushe Etche-land Omuma Abuloma PHC	Umuahia
4.	Ibani (Bonny) (Bonny town) and Opobo	Ogboni-land Opu - Oku Kala - Oko Andoniland Dony Town Opobo Town	Nkwerreland Amaigbo Town Ndoki - land Ohambele Akwete Umugbai

with the smaller though, equally influential group, moving into the Andoni area to establish the independent city-state of Opobo. Each of these city-states was able to establish special commercial and sometimes social and political ties with communities in their immediate and distant hinterland from which they derived the products they traded on. The trade routes, markets etc., shown on figure 7.1 illustrate this. Also, the details of the communities within their commercial orbit are shown in table 7.1.

The leading slave port in the Eastern Niger Delta was Elem Kalabari between the 15th and 17th centuries AD while Bonny predominated as a centre for the transatlantic slave trade in the area from about 1699 to the nineteenth century. (See Figure 7.1: Slave Trade Routes Map). As Alagoa (1986:126) rightly points out, the sequence of attempts by the British to sign treaties to abolish the slave trade indicates the varying importance of the various Niger Delta city-states in the slave trade during the nineteenth century. He says (Alagoa: 126-127):

> The first treaty of its type was signed with the kingdom of Bonny on 11 March 1839, a second on 20 August 1841, and a third on 21 November 1848. Compensation for loss of trade to the value of $2,000-$10,000 a year were agreed to be paid to the rulers. The treaty with Elem Kalabari was signed 8 August 1851 and with Nembe (Brass) on 17 November 1856...But between the desire for the fees, the activities of the British preventive squadron, and the growing profitability of the trade in palm oil, the overseas slave trade gradually disappeared in the middle of the nineteenth century.

> The slaves sold at the ports of the Eastern Niger Delta came predominantly from the Igbo country. Nembe (Brass) also received slaves from beyond the Igbo country down the Niger, from the Igala, and other Northern Nigerian peoples. In the western delta, some western Igbo passed through Itsekiri middlemen, as well as Urhobo, Isoko and other groups from the region under Benin influence. Some riverine Yoruba also came through the lagoon trade into the western delta. Thus Osifekunde, an Ijebu, had been captured by Ijo pirates (Lloyd 1967)....The traders of the delta, then did not themselves raid for the slaves they sold to ships but procured them from the communities adjoining the delta or through the Aro and other trading communities of the hinterland.

It is useful to note, however, that Alagoa (1986:130-131) indicates (relying on the oral traditions of smaller communities and the siting of their settlements away from the major river courses) that slave traders in the delta sometimes raided weaker communities in the delta to obtain slaves. This helps to explain how small numbers of Niger Delta people were sold along with slaves from the hinterland to the European traders. The study by Williamson, Smith and Robertson of Berbice Dutch spoken in Guiana, which shows an unusually large vocabulary contributed by the eastern Ijo dialects of Okrika, Kalabari, Ibani and Nembe confirms the presence of slaves of Niger Delta origin in the New World. Also, although the European traders do not seem to have raided for slaves in the Niger Delta, there were, nevertheless, rumours of their impending raids on some parts of the Delta. Such rumours were the basis for drastic measures such as the one undertaken by the Kabo to dam their portion of the Forcados River and divert its course, which led to their loss of control of the slave trade in the area to the Mein.

However, there is no gainsaying the fact that slave raids provided many of the slaves available to the city states in Rivers and Bayelsa States of today. It is also important to note that Alagoa (1986:132) is right when he says:

> The states tried to keep the level of slave raids to a minimum. Many accounts of wars undertaken by the states relate to punishments against unruly communities along the trade routes. This violence along the trade routes and the competition between the various states and within states between...Wari (Houses) became one reason for retaining more and more slaves to increase the force of war-canoe hands... The names of two important "houses" among the Kalabari are considered to be related to the practice of building slave stores or barracoons (barrikos) in a section of the delta ports for the security of slaves. The lineages of Biriomoni (Omoni), meaning, literally, slave quarter, and Barboy, apparently derived from barracoon boy, demonstrate the connection between the trade and these "houses"....The conditions created by the slave trade in the Niger Delta apparently obliged smaller communities to seek protection of the more powerful ones.

Some Lessons From The Atlantic Slave Trade Experience

What were the material gains that the coastal middlemen in the slave trade derived from the trade? The guns they procured seemed to be useful for protection of their communities but in reality they were instruments of death and insecurity. The shackles, chains and other materials paraphernalia of the abominable trade are likely to have been acquired from the blacksmiths in the hinterland such as the Awka Igbo. In the period of "legitimate trade", these could have been useful for maintaining discipline and preventing escape of slaves. The prefabricated houses imported from Europe, for which the area is well known, came mostly from the proceeds of the palm produce trade. When western education came, with teachers flogging the pupils, the Delta merchants and rulers sent their slaves' children to school and protected their children from such "suffering".

The result during the colonial and post-colonial era was the paradoxical situation, which one can describe as the tail wagging the dog. Those who marginalised slaves during the slave trade became marginalised during the colonial and post-colonial period when western educational qualification became the requirement for social mobility and the measure of achievement and success. The liberal system, which made it possible for people of servile background, like Jaja of Opobo, to aspire to and attain the position in the land, began to backfire. Animosities that can be traced to the slave trade era have continued to sour inter-group relations to this day within Delta communities and between them and their neighbours. How much monetary compensation can be sufficient to recompense the people for the psychological, economic and demographic dislocations resulting from the slave trade? Indeed, whatever is eventually paid will only be a token. With regard to the payment of reparations, the necessity for such payment has been raised and continues to be discussed. The material and psychological devastation effects of the slave trade on the communities of the Niger Delta and their hinterland neighbours necessitate the payment of reparations by the western world.

Yet another lesson learnt from the consequences of the slave trade is the palpable collective amnesia about the horrible event in the memory of otherwise very historically conscious peoples of the area of study whose oral traditions are replete with evidence of detailed recording of events in the past. Alagoa (1986: 129-130) states that Niger Delta oral traditions "provide little information on the trade, which may reflect the role assigned to the slave trade in the historical consciousness of the people, or it may merely represent the neglect of the slave trade theme in research." Clark, J. P. (2000:45) ponders the question thus:

> ...The slave trade in Africa, first plied by the Arabs in East and Central Africa, then characteristically capitalised in both the East and Western coasts by the Europeans, is by all measures the most devastating historic event to have happened to African people in this millennium now about to close with storm clouds again breaking all over the continent. Why then do we as a people have no common memory of this event? What accounts for this collective amnesia? How is it no collective unconsciousness arose from this all prevalent event in Africa south of the Sahara in some large areas well before the present millennium, and manifested itself in idea, images and memories among the many people who lived through it for centuries?

As Clark rightly points out, even accounts of slaves in the new world displayed this selective amnesia as his example of Olaudah Equiano or Olu-Uda Ekwuno or Gustavus Vassa aptly illustrates. He says:

> Equiano hardly uses any personal names for the family members or proper names for the many places at home that he misses so much in his narrative. He gives no name of his father, obviously a prominent figure in both family and town circles, and certainly one who even in a polygamous setup, although he does not seem to have practiced it, must have made an early indelible impression on his son often. He does not disclose the name of his loving mother, a character in the narrative as dear to him as his sister with whom he is twice taken into captivity.

Alagoa (1986: 134) had also said:

> Those (slaves who escaped shipment across the Atlantic) left in the Delta were incorporated into the communities under circumstances that did not encourage remembrance of a slave past of identity. Among

communities that suffered slave raids, also, there has been no eagerness to remember.

Obviously, there is need for more detailed and widespread research into this and other aspects to reconstruct the *dramatis personae* in the slave trade. In this contribution an attempt has been made to provide a tentative table showing the trading centres in parts of the Delta and their catchment areas in the hinterland. Further research under the slave route project should elucidate the information and identify individuals and families involved in the trade. How else would we be able to identify the ration of sharing of the anticipated reparations if and when they are paid?

Enugu State

The origin of slavery in the communities of Enugu State is difficult to trace. According to oral traditions, it existed many decades before the trans-Atlantic slave trade era. When the Europeans became interested in the slave trade, the Aro merchants were the intermediaries between the producers of the slaves and the coastal middlemen, who then sold the slaves to the Europeans traders. It was the Aro who stimulated the trade in slaves in the communities of Uzuakoli in Abia State and Nkanu and Nike in Enugu State. How did people become slaves? People became slaves through different means. Some of these are:

Pawnship (Poverty)

Some poor families pledged, handed over or pawned some of their children to wealthy people in exchange for money, food, or protection.

Captives

People captured during inter-communal wars were used as domestic slaves. Some of them were later sold to the Aro, who in turn sold them to the coastal middlemen.

Criminals

Social miscreants such as thieves, vagabonds and other criminals were sold into slavery. According to Mr. Nwanze Agu (Permanent Secretary, Enugu State Ministry of Culture and Tourism), thieves were handed over to those whose property they stole to serve them as slaves.

Stubborn and Unruly Children

Children who were troublesome stood the risk of being sold into slavery so as to remove their bad influence on the well-behaved children and protect the family name from being dragged into the mud.

Restitution

Sometimes a *freeborn* is killed accidentally during a hunting expedition or a traditional ceremony. The penalty for this offence is death or banishment. In order to avoid this penanlty the offender could offer his child to the family of the deceased as restitution.

Protection

Weaker members of a community who are afraid that their farmlands and even their lives are in danger willingly seek the protection of powerful individuals. Such people became slaves of their protectors.

Ransom

Wealthy men could pay for the ransom of criminals who had been condemned to death and prevent their being buried alive. Those who were saved in this manner became the slaves of the wealthy men who had paid their ransom.

The Nature and Role of Slaves In Enugu State Communities

Provision of security for their owners

According to Nwanze Agu, slaves lived at the periphery of the compounds of their owners in order to help protect them from enemy attack or invasion especially during inter-communal wars. They were used as a human shield against surprise attacks.

Farm Hands

Slaves provided manpower for wealthy farmers in these basically agrarian communities.

Shrine Keepers

In the Nkanu area of Enugu State freeborn (*amadi*) cannot be priests of some deities. They have to be served by the slaves (*ohu*) now euphemistically referred to as *ndiobia*. However, freeborn, who breach or break taboos are dedicated to such gods and serve them on behalf of the community. With the advent of slave trade, some of such unfortunate individuals were sold to Aro slave traders.

Communal Work

Slave labour was used for road maintenance and other menial chores such as basket making, mat weaving, pottery, palmwine tapping, and other domestic chores for the community and their owners.

The two prominent communities in Enugu State that participated in indigenous slavery were Nkanu and Nike. Large numbers of slaves were brought to the Nike slave market by Igalla warriors from present day Benue State and Abakaliki people in present day Ebonyi State. Such slaves were either sold to Aro slave traders or moved to the neighbouring Nkanu transit market. Both Nwanze Agu and Sir Ferdinand Anikwe are agreed on this account. According to His Royal Highness, Igwe J. Onovo of Akegbe Ugwu (Chairman Traditional Rulers Council, Enugu State), all the wealthy members of his community, including elders and chiefs, participated actively in the trade. The other participants in the slave trade apart from the *Ndichie* (titled men) were the itinerant Aro who camped near the host communities to source for and buy slaves to sell to the coastal middlemen.

There are no communal archives on slavery and slave trade in the communities studied in Enugu State. According to HRH Igwe J. Onovo, the absence of communal archives was deliberate as the people wanted to wipe out the ugly and sad memory of the inhuman trade. It is also important to note that at the height of the slave trade, the articles for which slaves were exchanged included European spirits (rum, whisky, gin etc.), guns, gun flints and gun powder, cloth, chains, iron bars, salt, manilas, cowries etc. There are also no physical vestiges of slavery. However, the undercurrents of tension in the relationship between the former slave masters or their descendants and the former slaves or their descendants have remained quite palpable even if such tension has not manifested in open hostility. Occasionally, animosities based on such subdued tension manifest during the struggle for land ownership, especially farmland.

It is important to indicate that, according to Sir Ferdinand Anikwe (a native of Nkanu), from 1933 when the colonial administrative officer, Richard Chadwick, separated the former slaves from the former slave-owning communities, slavery and internal slave trade officially ended in what is now Enugu State. The freed slaves settled in Akwu Uke, Ihuokpara, and Ugwuaji communities of the state, serve as a painful reminder of the era of the obnoxious trade. Even in communities such as Uruku, and Ugboka, where the separation was not effected, the former slave owners and their descendants and the former slaves and their descendants have lived in harmony and have developed mutual respect for one another.

There are also no structures or relics of slavery and slave trade found in the two communities studied in Enugu State. The once thriving slave markets and active routes have been taken over by modern houses and roads. At Nike (in Enugu), the former slave market is now part of the area occupied by the 82nd Division of the Nigerian Army. HRH Igwe Julius Nnaji narrated, to the research team, how the first person to build a storey building at the site of the market was driven away by ghosts. Thereafter, nobody lived there until the land was donated to the Nigerian Army.

Concerning the issue of how slavery and slave trade had affected intergroup relations or relations with other ethnic groups, Igwe Onovo had this to say, "social relations were very cordial in the former slave trading communities of Enugu State. However, in traditional and other social ceremonies, kola nuts, as a matter of convention, must be broken by the former warrior class (slave merchants)." On the other hand, the socio-economic impacts of slavery and the transatlantic slave trade on the communities studied are still felt to this day. These include:

1. The Economic Impact

The aftermath of slavery and slave trade has generated rivalry between the descendants of former slaves and the descendants of *freeborn*, especially in the areas of business and building of impressive and high quality houses in the community. This has raised the general standard of living and quality of life in the community. However, within the former slave trading commu-nities, the relationship between the *freeborn* and former slaves have been cordial. There is no evidence of the existence of a slave-based caste system in either of the communities studied. According to Igwe Onovo, "these days, emphasis has shifted from aristocracy of birth to aristocracy of intelligence." This helps to explain why currently the descendants of former slaves are occupying the commanding heights of the socio-economic and political sectors in Enugu State.

2. Emergence of classes of *haves* and *have nots*

It is ironic but true that most of those who made material progress, after the abolition of the slave trade and the local freeing of slaves, were the descendants of ex-slaves. However, the families that had been actively involved in slavery and had large numbers of slaves, had more farmlands and yam barns secured through slave labour than families that did not have slaves. The resultant inequality in wealth distribution in the largely rural communities studied subsists till now.

3. Establishment of Diaspora settlements by the Aro
When slavery and slave trade were abolished in the communities in present day Enugu State, the Arochukwu slave traders remained in many parts of the state and were integrated into their host communities. The result was the establishment of Aro diaspora settlements in different parts of the state.

4. Social Isolation of Ex-slaves
Most of the *freeborn* and their descendants do not approve of contracting marriages with the ex-slaves or their descendants. However, this barrier is breaking down increasingly in all the communities with the influence of Christianity and western education and civilisation.

Slave Trade Routes

Two distinct slave routes are discernible in Enugu State. The first was from Igalaland in present day Benue State to the Nike slave market in present day Enugu State. The second was from the Nike Slave market to Nkanu and thence to Uzuakoli and Arochukwu in present day Abia State; from where the slaves were moved to the coast for sale to the Europeans by the coastal middlemen. It is also important to note that some of the slaves from Abakaliki regional markets such as the Eke Imoha market also ended up at Nike and Nkanu slave depots. The movement of slaves could also be in the reverse direction depending on where the demand for slaves was higher.

Ebonyi State

In the area covered by present day Ebonyi State, the oral traditions about the origin of slavery are similar to what has been recorded for Enugu State. It was the Arochukwu slave traders that instigated the trade in slaves, having come through Afikpo and Uzuakoli. In order to satisfy their demand, people were enslaved by various means including:
1. Conversion of convicted criminals to slaves and selling them to protect the image of their families and the community.

2. Acquisition by wealthy individuals of criminals condemned to be buried alive and making them their slaves.
3. Making war captives slaves.
4. Kidnapping both children and adults and selling them as slaves. One *Egbudu Ugo Mgbo* is said to have specialised in this aspect of the trade.
5. Purchase of slaves from Udi, Nike and Nkanu.
6. Sale of troublesome children and social miscreants as slaves.
7. Purchase of slaves at Ekelinoha market in present day Ezza East LGA and Uburu market in Onicha LGA.
8. Sale of children of slaves especially in Kings' palaces.
9. Sale of children into slavery as a result of famine or poverty.
10. Sale of people presented to deities into slavery by priests.
11. Impulsive decision by some wicked rulers to sell some of their subjects as slaves.

The duties of the domestic slaves in Ebonyi State were similar to those described for Enugu State. Domestic slavery no longer exists in any community of Ebonyi State. Former slave owners and their descendants and ex-slaves and their descendants in these communities live in harmony and have mutual respect for each other.

The relics and monuments still in existence in Ebonyi State include:
1. *Mkpamkpa Ogbu* and *Amagu Ugwuengu* extant settlements with standing *Ogbu* trees.
2. Slave chain in *Izi Okoche* village.
3. *Aha Ogbonja* (sacred Iroko tree), place of traditional sacrifice.
4. *Odudukaekwa* (a type of iron bar), ivory ornaments and elephant tusks.

Communities of Afikpo, Ezza, Izzi, Ikwo, Onicha (Uburn) and Izhia practiced slavery and later participated actively in the slave trade dealing with the Aro slave traders. Wealthy men and the *Ndichie* (titled men) in these communities were involved and their trading partners were the Arochukwu slave traders. No communal slave archives have been put together but there are materials in private holdings. There are no physical structures from the slave trade era remaining in the communities but the descendants of ex-slaves, who have now been fully integrated, are there. Also, inter community relations are very cordial among the former slave trading communities. However, in intra-community relations, only *freeborn* can break kola nuts during social gatherings. The discrimination is not subtle.

The socio-economic consequences of slavery and the slave trade on these communities have remained to this day. They include the following:

1. The Arochukwu slave traders and their descendants have settled in many parts of Ezza, Ikwo, Izi, etc. They have become part of the host communities.
2. The intermarriage between ex-slaves and their descendants on one hand and the *freeborn* and their descendants on the other hand is still unacceptable to some of the *freeborn*.
3. Perhaps as a reaction to the stigma of slavery, the ex-slaves and their descendants worked hard and now occupy the commanding heights of the education, commerce and government sectors because of the skills and training they received from their forebears.

There is no visible slave-based caste system. This is not to say that there is no discrimination based on slave ancestry. The slave routes identified in Ebonyi State are as follows: Ezhia (Ezzangbo) to Izzii to Ezza (Ekee Imoha regional market) to Afikpo to Uburn (Salt lake) to Uzuakoli to Arochukwu.

The significant sites identified are in Ezza, Izzi, Afikpo and Uburn. They could be developed for cultural tourism. For instance, *Amagu cave* has three groves about five kilometers long and each capable of holding 25 to 30 slaves. The slaves were sold to Aro buyers and the stock continuously replenished. In Ezza, the famous *Imoha* regional slave market still retains much of its original structure as the sacred *Ogbu tree* where slaves were displayed for sale still stands. Also, the *Uburu* salt lake where the Aro traders stopped over still exists. Here large scale buying and selling of slaves took place. This could also be an attractive tourist centre, especially for Africans in diaspora, if properly developed.

Edo and Delta States

In Edo and Delta States, recent research focused on Benin City, Koko, Agbor and Aboh. The palaces of the Oba of Benin, Asagba of Asaba and Dein of Agbor were noted as relevant traditional socio-political institutions to the object of study. An attempt was also made to rediscover the slave routes and identify relevant relics and sites in this part of Nigeria. The Edo State Commissioner for Arts, Culture and Tourism, Dr. Patrick Ojebuoboh, exemplifies the tendency to forget or deny the existence of slavery and slave trade in the past among the Edo. He holds the view that the Kingdom of Benin was never involved in slavery and slave trade. He rejects the view that the Benin moat can be seen as evidence of the existence of slavery in Benin. He says, "the moat was developed to aid Benin kingdom protect and preserve itself against external aggressors." He, however, admitted that the Benin kingdom was strong militarily and had the desire to expand but that this also had nothing to do with slavery or slave trade. There is no documentation of slave routes in the Edo State Ministry of Arts, Culture and Tourism. It will be recalled that by the late fifteenth century (1472 or 1486), the Portuguese were in Benin. Crowder, M (19:50) has it that during the second half of the 15th century, the Portuguese built a factory at Ughoton for the pepper trade and to purchase slaves. When the French slave trader, Landolphe, could not cross the bar with his cargo of slaves, both the Oba of Benin and the Olu of Itsekiri invited him to their towns. His ship was towed to Warri by Iyastere Okorodudu who was revenue collector between 1780 and 1785. The diverse nature of French trade in the Benin/Warri area is shown by the fact that Captain Landolphe had wanted to establish a salt factory at Gborodo in Itsekiriland in 1783 but was also engaged in the slave trade in Ughoton, the Benin port. It is also useful to note that Bakie (1856:317) indicated that slaves were commonly purchased with salt at Aboh and other slave markets.

The Curator of the National Museum in Benin told the research team that slavery existed in the Benin kingdom before the beginning of the trans-Atlantic slave trade. He also said that the famous Benin moat was constructed and maintained using slave labour provided by slaves captured during Benin invasion of neighbouring communities or even indigenes who became slaves through various circumstances. With regard to relics and sites related to slavery and the slave trade, the curator directed the research team to Koko in Warri North LGA in Delta State and Gelegele, an Ijo area of Edo State. He also indicated that there is a canal between Benin city and Koko junction which linked up with the Benin River on the shore on which Koko is located. This waterway is said to have been used during the slave trade era. The waterway is visible at Ologbo village along the Benin-Warri expressway. The curator is also of the view that a new form of slavery and slave trade still exists in Edo State. He describes trafficking of girls for prostitution abroad and child labour as new faces of slave trade and slavery.

The research team also reports that a lecturer in the Department of Fine and Applied Arts at the University of Benin, Rev. Ebigbo Chris, confirmed that Benin kingdom was fully involved in the slave trade and that slavery within the kingdom was a common practice among the affluent families. There were domestic slaves. He also confirmed that the Benin moat was developed with slave labour.

The research team visited Chief Nana's palace in Koko, which is presently in Warri North LGA of Delta State. It was the grandson of Chief Nana who conducted the research team round the palace and its environs. He is the caretaker of the palace and its grounds. He said the palace was built after Chief Nana returned from Ghana after ten years of exile on which the British had sent him. It was in Ebrohimi that slave trade is said to have taken place. Nana's grandson confirmed that both local slavery and the trans-Atlantic slave trade took place in and from Ebrohimi. He was also of the view that the existence of child labour and the exodus of young girls to Europe indicate that there is still modern day slavery and slave trade. In order to provide an escape route for himself in Koko as a result of aggression from neighbours and foreigners, Chief Nana constructed a canal linking the palace grounds with Edo (Benin) river and the hinterland using slave labour (500 slaves). There are still some relics and monuments that attest to the fact that Chief Nana was a great merchant. Also, the Benin river, which is opposite Nana's palace has served as a waterway to Badagry. The research team reports that there are photographs from Koko.

Two members of staff of the Delta State Council for Arts and Culture were interviewed by the research team. Both could not throw any light on the origins of slavery and slave trade in Delta State. They said that slavery existed in places like Agbor, Asaba and Aboh in Ndokwa East LGA before the advent of the trans-Atlantic slave trade. Some slaves were captured as prisoners of war while others were kidnapped. They were domestic slaves to start with. Other ways by which slaves were acquired included the use of human beings as pawns as well as voluntary submission of self to powerful individuals or shrines for the purpose of obtaining protection. Slaves from these places were exported during the era of the trans-Atlantic slave trade through Calabar or Badagry slave ports.

Bakie, W.B. (1856: 317) says:

> At Abo a great medium of barter is salt, which is brought up from Numbe and from Bini, and is always in demand. Slaves are almost always purchased with salt, the prices varying somewhat according to the condition of the market. The average price of a stout male slave is from ten to twelve bags of salt, or from 60,000 to 70,000 cowries, and for a good-looking young female, eight to ten bags of salt, or from 45,000 to 50,000 cowries.

The increased demand for slaves as a result of the trans-Atlantic slave trade led to inter community conflicts which in turn led to wars. The informants confirmed that there were two main evacuation points for slaves in present day Delta State, namely, Aboh in Ndokwa East LGA and Koko in Warri North LGA. There are relics of the slave trade in Aboh.

Slave trade was on a relatively small scale in all the communities discussed in this contribution until the demand for slaves to satisfy the requirements of the trans-Atlantic slave trade increased the scale. Slavery was, however, a familiar concept and was practiced in these communities before the beginning of the trans-Atlantic slave trade.

Figure 7.1: Uncompleted Palace of Obi Obodo of Abor, the son of the great merchant

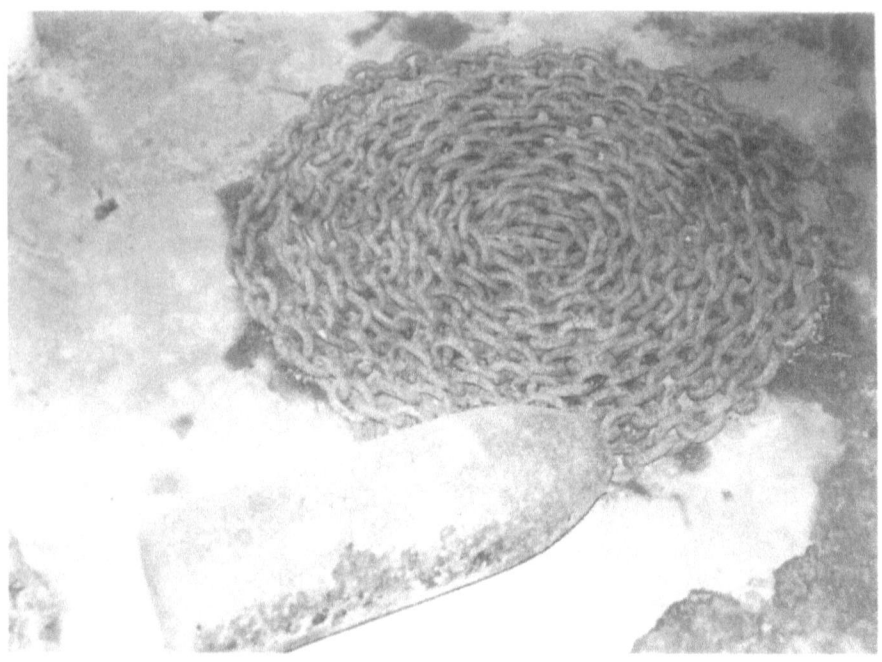

Figure 7.2: Chains used during the Slave Trade Era in Aboh

Figure 7.3: Cannons used during the Slave Trade and in Wars with Aboh's Neighbours

Notes and References

E. J. Alagoa, "The slave trade in Niger Delta Oral Tradition and History" in Lovejoy P. E. (ed.), *Africans in Bondage*, 125-135 (Madison, University of Wisconsin Press, 1986).

E. J. Alagoa, *A History of the Niger Delta: An Historical Interpretation of Ijo Oral Tradition* (Ibadan: Ibadan University Press, 1962).

Okon E. Uya et al, for Akwa Ibom State Ministry of Culture and Tourism, *Slave Trade and Slavery in Africa: Akwa Ibom State Experience* (Calabar: CATS Publishers 2006).

W. B. Bakie, *Narrative of an Exploring Voyage up the Rivers Kwora and Binue commonly known as the Niger and Tsadda in 1854 1856*.

J. P. Clark, "A Peculiar Faculty" in Banjo, A. (ed.) *Humanity in Context* (Ibadan: Occassional Publications of the Nigerian Academy of Letters, 2000).

K. O. Dike, *Trade and Politics in the Niger Delta, 1830-1885: An Introduction to the Economic and Political History of Nigeria* (Oxford, 1956).

W. R. G. Horton, *The Ohu system of Slavery in a Northern Ibo Village-Group*, AFRICA Journal of the International African Inst. Vol. XXIV No. 4 (1954).

Robin Horton, (1969), "From Fishing Village to City-state: A Social History of New Calabar" in M. Douglas and P.M. Kaberry, (eds.), *Man in Africa* (London, 1969), pp. 37-58.

J. Inikori, (ed.) (1982), *Forced Migration: The Impact of the Export Slave Trade on African Societies* (London: Hutchison University Library, 1982).

G. I. Jones, *The Trading States of the Oil Rivers: A Study of Political Development in Eastern Nigeria* (London, 1963)

P.C. Lloyd, (1963). *The Itsekiri in the 19th Century: An Outline Social History*, Journal of African History, Vol. 4 No. 2: (1963) pp. 207-231.

P. E. Lovejoy, *Transformations in Slavery. A History of Slavery in Africa* (Cambridge, Cambridge University Press, 1983).

M. Noah, *Old Calabar: The City States and the Europeans* (Uyo: Scholars Press, 1980).

D. Northrop, *Trade Without Rulers* (Oxford University Press, 1978).

A. F. C. Ryder, *An Early Portuguese trading voyage to the Forcados*

River, Journal of the Historical Society of Nigeria , Vol. 1 No. 4 (1959), 294-321.
R. L. Sparks, *The Two Princes of Calabar: An Eighteenth Century Atlantic Odyssey* (Cambridge, Massachusetts: Harvard University Press, 2004).
Okon E. Uya, *Black Brotherhood: Afro-Americans and Africa* (Boston: D. C. Heath and Company, 1971).
African Diaspora and the Black Experience in New World Slavery (New York, Third Press, 1992).
Slave Routes of the Lower Cross River Region. Calabar National Museum, Old Residency., 2006.
Contemporary Issues on Slavery and the Black World (Cats Publishers and Department of History, University of Ibadan, 2003)

Unpublished Reports

Keshi, E. Q., N.U.B. Anamah, and O.O. Ashiru (2008), *Report on the Research on Slave Route in Edo and Delta States,* February 2008.
Report on Research on Indigenous Slavery in Enugu and Ebonyi States from 9-14 March, 2008.

Chapter 8

SLAVERY AND THE TRANS-ATLANTIC SLAVE TRADE IN SOUTHWESTERN NIGERIA

Akin Alao
Associate Professor, Department of History, Obafemi Awolowo University, Ile-Ife

Introduction

THE Yoruba as an ethnic and cultural group is one of the most researched ethnic groups in the world. A Yoruba civilisation with a set of ideas, values, practices, philosophical thought, beliefs, traditions, institutions, material goods and technologies is well established and never in doubt. Concrete historical realities show that the Yoruba possess a rich civilisation that is comparable to other civilisations of the world. The major aspects of this culture are expressed in visible attributes and in sublime values. The material culture is exhibited in commerce, manufacturing technology, arts and crafts and, of course, as well in music and dance. Yoruba values are best seen in respect for elders and constituted authorities, honesty, integrity, diligence and a profound religious belief system[1,2].

The Yoruba Homeland

The Yoruba country lies roughly between latitudes 60 and 90 N and longitudes 20 30' and 60 30' East with a total land area of about 181,300 sq kilometers in what is now known as Southwestern Nigeria. The Yoruba culture area is, however, not coterminous with this geographical delimitation as it spreads from the present Edo

State in Nigeria, over the whole of the southwest and across to the Republics of Benin and Togo on the West African coast. Significant aspects of Yoruba culture are also found in such places as Sierra Leone, the Gambia, Brazil, Cuba, Trinidad, Puerto-Rico and the United States of America[3]. Worldwide, it is estimated that they have a population of over twenty million. The major sub-ethnic groups include the: Oyo, Ibarapa, Ife, Ijesa, Igbomina, Egba, Egbado, Awori, Egun, Ijebu, Ekiti, Ilaje, Ikale, Owo, Akoko, Ondo, Yagba, Owe, Bunu, Idaisa, Ajase, Ketu and Sabe.

The Yoruba speak a standard Yoruba language that is mutually intelligible to all in spite of the dialectal variations noticeable among the sub-groups. The historical consciousness of the Yoruba started at Ile-Ife, the cradle of the Yoruba race and civilisation. The Yoruba claim descent from Oduduwa, who, according to traditions, is the eponymous father and culture hero of all Yoruba.

Geographically, the Yoruba country rises gradually from the low-lying swampy regions with thick undergrowth to the forest belt and finally semi- or derived Savannah. A large part of the Yoruba homeland consists of low flat plateau with only a range of hills, running from east to west. Annual rainfall ranges from 254cm to 101cm. Consequently, the climate, rainfall pattern and soil fertility make the environment conducive to human settlement and development.

Two major factors are important in the crystallisation of the salient aspects of Yoruba civilisation. The first is the fact that virtually all the indigenous inhabitants of Yorubaland belonged to the same linguistic stock. In fact, it is generally agreed that language is the first basic element of Yoruba civilisation. The second factor is the environment, which, to a large extent, influenced the historical development of Yoruba people. The geographical features of the Yoruba country made it well suited for agriculture, metal technology, industry and commerce. Each of these factors is essential for urbanisation and arising from this, the Yoruba developed an urban culture, being one of the most urbanised ethnic groups in sub-Saharan Africa.

Going by substantial linguistic evidence based in part on the works of J.H. Greenberg, R.G. Armstrong and S. Koelle, it is convenient to conclude that Yoruba emerged as a distinct language group from the Kwa group between about 2,000 BC and 1,000BC. Ile-Ife was the first Yoruba settlement to become prominent soon after the people acquired distinctiveness and self-awareness as a separate language group. Oral traditions point to Ile-Ife as the spiritual and ancestral home of the Yoruba. From Ile-Ife, they dispersed into different directions led by the children of Oduduwa to found new kingdoms, which more or less constitute the present Yoruba sub-groups.

The process of state formation in Yorubaland started at Ile-Ife where Oduduwa instituted a centralised system of civil administration centred on the monarch or Oba. The structures of government were put in place, and according to Adediran, the Oduduwa political ingenuity became the archetype for all Yoruba kingdoms that derived from Ile-Ife. The success of the Oduduwa experiment encouraged his princes to spread out in different directions, seizing political power from pre-existing groups and enforcing their own supremacy by establishing flourishing states with allegiance to Ile-Ife, which was regarded as *orirun*, the source. The kingdoms of Owu, Oyo, Popo, Sabe, Ila (Igbomina), Ondo, Ijesha, Ekiti, Akure, Owo, Ijebu, Egba, Ketu and Idaisa emerged at different times to constitute the Yoruba complex of states. Many other states are today claiming direct dynastic relationship with Oduduwa to legitimise their claims on the beaded crown, which is considered the most symbolic gift of Oduduwa to his children[4].

Between 1500 and 1800, Yoruba history centred on the perfection and expansion of the Yoruba state system with all the attendant socio-political, economic and cultural trappings. The distinctiveness of the culture became visible and a strong pan Yoruba identity emerged. All indices of Yoruba culture had crystallised and the sacredness of Ile-Ife as the cradle and birthplace of a new civilisation was kept inviolate.

By the beginning of the 19th century, it was evident that this peace would be disturbed as Yorubaland came under severe internal disabilities and external pressures throughout the period. The 19th century was one of inter-group warfare which led to monstrous political, economic, demographic and social consequences. At the risk of offering a monocausal explanation for an historical development, the war that started all the wars, was a result of the violation of the sacredness of Ile-Ife, the ancestral home. According to Akinjogbin, there was an unwritten Yoruba tradition that forbade any kingdom or Oba that obtained the beaded crown from Ile-Ife to raise his sword against Ile-Ife or any territory under its jurisdiction[5]. In 1813, Owu kingdom did, and this was enough to start the first conflagration in Yorubaland. Owu faced a coalition of Ife, Ijebu and Oyo armies and within a period of five years, Owu an erstwhile flourishing kingdom, had been completely destroyed and an interdict was placed on its rebuilding. It became a curse for anybody in Yorubaland to rebuild Owu. The people were displaced and forced to live as refugees in other kingdoms[6].

The destruction of Owu and the sack of Oyo by the Fulani jihadists from Northern Nigeria, radically transformed the political character of Yorubaland[7]. Oyo had the best form of government with an elaborate mechanism of checks and balance. It was the destruction of this edifice that led to the rise of Ibadan in 1829 as the first military state in Yorubaland. Ibadan later played very important role in Yorubaland, fighting many wars and starting a new political experiment. The new military class in Ibadan considered the monarchical system as unprogressive and rather anachronistic in view of the changing realities of the 19th century. Bashorun Oluyole was suspicious and in fact opposed to the demands and exertions of hereditary royalty. He consistently warned against recourse to traditional institutions, which were capable of destroying self expression, self actualisation and personal sense of success. Oluyole believed that leadership should be a function of what the individual possessed as advantage over those who could favorably compete with him and that leadership should be earned and not ascribed. By the time Oluyole died in 1847, Ibadan's hold on Yorubaland was virtually total. The republican institutions and practices had already been put in place and militarism successfully established as a career. The military chiefs and their ever restless war boys who stood to benefit from the Oluyole experiment resolutely defended the system. The advantages of the new system were very obvious and within a short time, Ibadan became haven to many progressive elements all over Yorubaland who had become disillusioned of the hereditary monarchy. A system that was based on birth right was unimpressive to a new class of leaders who became lords as a result of personal accomplishments. Ibadan wars were fought with a view to establishing the new order that would acknowledge and reward personal valor, industry and ability to stand and be counted when the tough gets going[7].

In spite of the wars and the efforts at reconfiguring Yoruba political system, the essentials of the culture remained. In fact Ibadan was committed to the defense of Yorubaland more than any other state. Fulani ambition for complete Islamisation of Yorubaland was frustrated by Ibadan at the battle of Osogbo in 1844. The Ibadan war chiefs recognised tradition and paid adequate respect to the legacy of Yoruba ancestors. Despite the wrangling and disaffection created by Ibadan imperialism in Ijesha, Ekiti, Akoko, Igbomina and Ibolo Kingdoms, the ideals of Yoruba culture were never affected. The instability of the 19th century mixed the population and created new centres of political power and influence. For instance, Ibadan established a military republican state[8], while Abeokuta came up with a federal arrangement to accommodate the peculiarities of its component groups. Oyo relapsed to the background, and for all practical purposes, Ile-Ife became more or less a religious sanctuary for all Yoruba.

Slavery as Social Institution: Status, Rights and Privileges of Slaves

Before the contact with Europe and the Arabs, slavery was more or less a social institution in Yorubaland which could be best appreciated if examined within the context of the sociology of the people. In traditional Yoruba society, the interdependence of one on the other emphasised the prominence of the group. As rightly observed by Gardiol van Niekerk, the preservation of the group was a fundamental principle which directed social, political and legal ordering in society. In the period before the introduction and use of currency, slavery did not play any significant role in indigenous Yoruba mode of production, pattern of distribution and exchange. Slaves in traditional Yorubaland did not in any sense whatsoever constitute the most important labour force or come close to what obtained in other especially Western and Indian societies. The institution of slavery was, at best, the result of a natural process and forms which could be regarded as a part of the history of the Yoruba.

However, with the emergence of city states and kingdoms in Yorubaland, the institution of slavery and slave holding assumed new dimensions. The Yoruba group became larger and it produced its own complications leading to the emergence of a multiplicity of groups and their differentiation into various sizes, roles and orientation. As from the 12th century AD, Yoruba sociology witnessed a redefinition which invariably affected the pattern of social relations. The emergence of privileged groups and their domination of the social, political and economic order introduced a structure that was based on ranking. The new relations of power created its own order and privileged certain groups at the expense of others. The sophistication of the economy, which was characterised by unequal access to resources, created a new subaltern class of the under privileged[9].

The kingdom of Oyo which became the best known in terms of elaborate political and administrative structures provided the best example of the changing definition of slavery and the impact of structural readjustment on the institution of slavery in Yorubaland. It was in Oyo, for instance, that the state system became well developed for administrative efficiency at both the metropolitan city as well as the provinces. Persons of slave *origin became involved in wholly political, administrative and religious matters* at the state level where they served as agents of daily administration of the Alafin's immediate estate.

Slaves in Administrative and Religious Duties

The saying *"Oba lo nile"* means that "king (Alaafin) is the overall landlord of the land in his territory". As a result of this privilege, all inhabitants in the king's territory are his subjects, who were obliged to feed him out of the farm produce they harvested on the land annually. The king's share of the produce is called *Isakole* meaning, the act of hoeing the ground. This *isakole* means "compensation for the king by those who farm on his land" and this shows that farming has been the major occupation of the Yoruba since their existence as a race.

Isakole for Alaafin could also be in form of free services to repair the king's palace by towns and villages under the Alafin's sphere of political influence. Any contrary action by any provincial head was considered an act of disloyalty which must be punished by punitive wars of plunder, forced labour or payment of heavy fines to the royal purse. As the power and influence of Alafin increased, these vassal towns and villages were under royal obligation to send men, women and provender to the imperial court of the Alaafin in Oyo[10].

It was against state policy and in some instances a disregard of the authority of the Alafin for anybody or group under the political umbrella of the Alafin to beat, abuse or even decline to carry out an *order issued by the Alafin but delivered through any of his slaves*. This was regarded and treated as an assault on the person and power of the owner of the slave, the Alafin. Disobedience to the person of the king himself was high treason often punished by the pains of death. For the Yoruba in imperial times, the fear of the Alafin was the beginning of wisdom.

Progressively, the position of the slaves became better recognised in the palace and slaves started having influential status in the palace and administration of the city, towns and villages. *Aare Apeka* and *Olori eru Alaafin* (head of Alaafin's slaves) were slaves who occupied high administrative positions in Oyo. *Olori eru* represented his compound *Ile olori eru* and whoever came from that family would become the head of the palace slaves. The *Olori eru* did not sleep in the palace like lesser slaves. He could go home at the close of the business of the day and return in the morning to ensure that palace activities went on without hitch. He took orders only from the Alafin.

Though second in overall influence to the *Olori Eru*, *Kudefu* was the most popular resident slave of the Alafin. He was the closest slave to the king and the custodian and repository of royal rites and history respectively. He was also a member of the Alafin's kitchen cabinet whose voice was respected within the royal chamber. As the principal custodian of palace traditions, *Kudefu* was responsible for keeping palace records and ensuring continuity of practice. He lived his entire life in the palace having no other home apart from the royal domain.

Other titled slaves were *Olokun Esin* who was in charge of the royal stable of horses. Since he accompanied the king to all ceremonies, he often appeared like an important personality. Having enjoyed all royal privileges and perquisites of office with his master the Alafin, the *Olokun Esin* was traditionally required to die with his master; hence his appellation, *Arojubobaku,* one who took pains to die with the king.

There were also *Osi Efa, Otun Efa, Ona Efa, Obalolu, Obakayeja, Obagbori, Olu-o-bunu-n-toba-o-je, Opayakata, Iludero, Mogaji, Obagbayi, Obalagba* and *Ilupemika*[11]. All these slaves turned chiefs represented various compounds in Oyo and they received salaries and compensations for their work. Palace administration in Oyo did not allow for indolence and every palace attendant had a role to play in administration. Oyo royal slaves who managed the machinery of traditional administration enjoyed special privileges which stood them out as special. They had access through the generosity of the Alafin to *Isakole,* other gifts received by Alaafin and fines from minor cases settled in the palace. According to the head of slaves *Eru tiwa kii se atoroje* (royal slaves do not beg to eat). The family compounds of the slaves or palace attendants mentioned above were located around Alafin's palace. There were still other such compounds located very near the popular Akesan market but not too far from the palace. One of them was Aroja compound. Aroja was one of Alaafin's slaves in charge of the market affairs. He went to the market to collect commodities from the traders *Eni ti n re oja* "one who picks commodities".

The status of slaves in the Alafin's palace was such that conferred special privileges to the extent that not many people knew that the principal slaves could be anything like slaves in view of their life styles, privileges and influence.

A seru ni kudefu
A seru ni' lusinmi
A serujaye
Eru Oyo ni n o se

Kudefu is a slave
Ilusinmi is a slave

Offspring of one who enjoys being slaves
I prefer to be a slave of Oyo

Generally, slaves in the palace were kept to serve the Alafin and to oil the machinery of administration in the palace and at the same time ensuring that vassal towns and villages remained loyal to the Alafin.

In many Yoruba states, slaves played leading roles as religious officers, attendants at shrines and even assistants to priests. The involvement of slaves in religious matters could have been a result of the belief that some of them in fact possessed extra sensory and psychic powers. For instance Ifa Ogunda Meji said:

Gbinrin biiti
Biiti gbinrin
O difa fun Orunmila
Ni ojo ti yoo ra
Osanyin leru
Ewe aje re e
E wo ni n ro nbe
Gbinrin biiti
Biiti gbinrin
Ewe omo re e
E wo ni n ro nbe
Gbirin biiti
Biiti gbinrin[12]

Biiti gbinrin
Divined for Orunmila
When he bought Osanyin as slave
This leaf is for financial success
Which should I mow?
Gbinrin biiti
Biiti gbinrin
This leaf is cure for barrenness
Which should I mow?
Gbirin biiti
Biiti gbinrin

Orunmila, the repository of knowledge and Ifa's creative genius[13] once had an encounter with his slave, Osanyin. Orunmila had instructed Osanyin to prepare a parcel of land for cultivation. Osanyin did not clear the land and when asked he told his master that he was confused not knowing which plant to cut and which ones to spare. He explained the medicinal or spiritual importance of each plant and concluded that all of them could be useful for one thing or the other. Orunmila therefore made him a priest and consultant on herbs despite being a slave.

Following the Orunmila example, slaves, especially female ones, performed religious and ritual duties depending, however, on the social responsibilities of their masters. In many palaces, slaves were engaged as shrine officials to perform rituals of appeasement and collective security.

Slaves as Executioner or *Abenilori*

The Yoruba of Southwestern Nigeria established efficient machinery of state administration. The judiciary at the state level operated as a paramount agency of social control, moral check and justice. This public policy direction is confirmed by a study of the system of judicial administration in the leading states of Oyo, Ife, Ibadan and Abeokuta. It is conclusive that the level of legal and judicial administration in a state is indicative of the level of its political and administrative sophistication. Judicial tribunals in these states operated on the basis of highly developed and advanced body of legal principles and jurisprudential thoughts. They equally became involved in the resolution of matters with major consequences for state policy. The application of legal principles in the identified political systems was visible and therefore amenable to historical analysis. The coordinated relationship of the executive and the judiciary among the Yoruba is best demonstrated by the existence of well-defined and well-known machinery for the enforcement of judgments and other judicial decisions. The Yoruba made distinctions between civil and criminal law and also between law and custom. The public policy direction of the system of judicial administration in Yorubaland was never in doubt especially in states with central authority[14]. Certain slaves with necessary physical features were often procured and trained for state assignments such as the execution of condemned criminals. Oyo, Ife, Ondo, Abeokuta and Ibadan became notable in the use of people of slave origin as state executioners.

The 19th Century Civil Wars and Slave Trade

The disintegration of Old Oyo and the eventual collapse of its central authority system could not be divorced from the insensitivity of its constitution and the intensity of intra-class conflict amongst members of the ruling class. It would seem that the participation of Oyo elite, including members of the ruling class, in the slave trade diverted state attention from using the military to ensure and maintain internal security of persons and protecting the territorial integrity of the state against all forms of external aggression. Indeed, it has been said that the declaration of independence by Dahomey, Borgu and Nupe was in [15]fact consequences of the parlous and near rustic state of the army in Oyo during this period. The slave trade was an ill wind; it destroyed the mythical invincibility of Oyo, opened areas under her sphere of influence to reckless plundering by slave raiders and made participation in other economic activities extremely hazardous. By 1835, it was obvious that the Oyo edifice was at its end, and Ibadan one of the three successor states, had consolidated its hold on power in Yorubaland Ibadan became known for the efficiency and capability of its military organisation, the vision of its leaders as state builders and the ascendancy of its political system. By 1840, it was evident that Ibadan was the most viable state to succeed Oyo and to protect the territorial integrity of Yorubaland against every form of external aggression, including the Fulani attack.

Bashorun Oluyole emerged as the ideologue/warrior of Ibadan at a crucial stage of creating and sustaining an identity for the Ibadan system. His ambition for the state of Ibadan, his personal accomplishments as a consummate military tactician especially during the Eleduwe war, and his thoughts on the progressive system of government were obvious[16].

Consequently, Yorubaland in the 19th century, witnessed a vigorous demographic readjustment and shifts with attendant consequences on socio-cultural interconnections and interpenetrations, development of new centres of political power and the establishment of a new class of power brokers who had found a career in militarism. The combination of these three important developments necessarily affected the political geography of Yorubaland in a most profound way. The new centres of power i.e. Ibadan, Abeokuta and Oyo Atiba dominated socio, political as well as the economic system of Yorubaland up to the time of British colonial rule and subjugation in the closing years of the 19th century[17].

As observed, the Yoruba did not take part in the trans-Atlantic slave trade on any appreciable scale until toward the close of the 18th century when the old Oyo Empire had started to show signs of imminent political instability and systemic collapse. The inter state wars of the 19th century in Yorubaland eventually opened up the country for brutal plundering and the slave trade became a major economic activity, with peculiar nature and character.

Ibadan Wars and the Trans-Atlantic Slave Trade in Yorubaland

The notoriety of the port of Lagos as an exit point could be ascribed to the massive flow of slaves from the Yoruba hinterland which was then the theatre of many wars. After succeeding to the mantle of leadership vacated by Oyo, Ibadan was engaged in many wars for various reasons. In 1840, the Ibadan army checkmated the Fulani jihadists at the battle of Osogbo winning a decisive victory which completely shattered the jihadists ambition of dipping the Quoran into the sea in Lagos. This success, however, introduced Ibadan to other parts of Yorubaland in the Ibolo, Igbomina, Ijesa, Ife, Ekiti and Akoko areas[18]. The attempt to impose imperial domination over erstwhile independent societies and build a far flung Ibadan empire of what Bolanle Awe called military republicanism led to many wars in Yorubaland. By 1855, it was obvious that the peace of Yorubaland had been seriously disturbed, necessitating a call for truce and understanding. One of the major resolutions of the Alabaja conference was the proclamation that forbade the sale of Yoruba men and women, a proclamation that could not be executed due largely to the outbreak of the famous Kurunmi war between Ibadan and Ijaiye in March 1860. It is estimated that this war produced the largest number of slaves from any single theatre of war. When Are Kurunmi, the maximum ruler of Ijaiye, died in 1862, the enemies and friends of Ijaiye plundered the kingdom, moved its remaining inhabitants into exile and left the capital city in ruins. Yorubaland entered a new phase of rapacious military campaigns which produced a great haul of Yoruba slaves for the trans-Atlantic slave trade.

Slave Trade Routes and Markets

Trade routes in Yorubaland could be divided into three major arteries, all flowing from the north to the south and passing through what could be described as nodal points which eventually became markets for the buying and selling of human and other commodities. The well known and documented western routes originated from the Northern fringes of the old Oyo Empire and were in fact made popular by Oyo's trading activities from earliest time. The routes passed through Ekun Osi or western part of the upper Ogun River to the lower grassland area of Borgu and then to the coastal centres of Whydah, Allada Abomey and Porto Novo. Routes originating from Oyo speaking areas through the Yewa area became popular after Dahomey had secured its independence from Oyo in the closing years of the 18th century[19]. The routes eventually terminated at the port of Badagry which assumed relative importance as a result of the volume of Yoruba slaves it exported. The central region routes originated in the Ibolo areas south of Ilorin, passed through Ede, Apomu Ijebu, Epe and finally Lagos. It was this route that carried the largest number of slaves captured and sold as a result of the Ibadan wars of empire building and imperial domination. Finally, the eastern route from Yagba, Ijumu and Owe areas passed through, Ekiti, Akoko, Akure, Ode Ondo, Ikale and Ilaje before terminating in Mahin where other routes from Izon area of the Niger Delta complex joined it. The coastline connected the mouths of the five great slave rivers, forming as it were, an interesting system of slave collection before eventual and final movement to the exit point in Lagos.

Along the routes were important markets which provided

opportunities for the exchange of services and goods, including slaves. Individual slave dealers visited the markets either to sell their slaves or to buy more either for export or for internal trade. The existence of markets on the routes made the movement of slaves less hazardous and risky because of the dangers associated with moving reluctant captives in the prime of life over a long distance and the possibility of running into other slave raids. It is however important to note that not all slaves captured, sold and bought during the era of the slave trade in Yorubaland ended as human cargoes for the trans-Atlantic slave trade. Important markets included Ijanna, Ilaro, Ede, Apomu, Ejinrin, Epe, Igo-Omi, Madagbayu, Mahin.

Slave Ports and Exit Points: Porto Novo, Whydah, Badagry and Lagos

As noted above, Porto Novo and Whydah used to be the main ports for the export of slaves from the old Oyo Empire whose political sphere of influence extended to present day republics of Togo and Benin. As noted by Akinjogbin and Adediran, Oyo's hold over these provinces was never in doubt as there are shreds of evidence to confirm that the Alafin had station officers and representatives in many of these towns and villages. Indeed, the traditional ruler of Whydah is said to have been one of Alafin's imperial agents in this area and that the Onikoyi, in present day Benin Republic, represented the interest of the Alafin at this slave port. The decline in the power of Oyo to maintain the fact of its hegemony over these areas led to a shift to a new port east of Whydah[20].

The port of Badagry as an exit point during the era of the trans-Atlantic slave trade was made popular by a Portuguese slave trader and sailor, Freman Gomez who was better known to the indigenes as Huntokonu. He was responsible for the development of the little beach at Gberefu to serve as the stage for embankment into the slave ships. The "point of no return" was therefore located on this erstwhile peaceful and serene peninsular. Vlekete in Badagry soon became a very important slave market and as from 1502 had been involved in the buying and selling of human beings as slaves for the trans-Atlantic slave trade. Vlekete eventually grew to become the largest slave market on the West coast and, at the height of the slave trade, it was responsible for the sale of about 900 slaves per week[21]. It was also responsible for the export of about 550,000 African slaves to plantations in the United States of America in addition to those enslaved to serve in Europe, South America and the Caribbean. Badagry served as exit point for slaves procured from Oyo, Benin, Togo and the Northern parts of Nigeria.

What went on between African slave traders and their European and American counterparts at the slave market of Vlekete should compel us to interrogate further the treachery and deceit associated with the slave trade on the part of the foreigners. It would seem that the slave traders deceived their African collaborators about the condition and nature of servitude in Europe and America. They probably did not disclose to the African dealers that a slave on the other side of the Atlantic was no more than a chattel which could be variously treated and abused. They probably did not let the African traders know that slavery in Africa was far more humane than what obtained on the American plantations for instance. This deceit must have been responsible for what they paid in exchange for human beings. For example in Badagry, a cannon meant only for warfare and destruction exchanged for 100 able bodied Africans and a useless bottle of gin with no known nutritional value attracted two African slaves. The commodities that were exchanged for human beings had no value for African development, but were mere articles of ostentation popularided by the Europeans themselves. Such articles as umbrellas, socks, mirrors, gin, pipes, dane guns and gun powder were alien to African culture and the African would never have dreamt of indulging in their use. Islam and African Traditional Religion, the two dominant religions in the era of the slave trade, forbade the use of alcohol yet the Europeans sold the idea of indulgence in alcohol to Africans, to the extent that they traded human beings for it. Again, Africans in the era of the slave trade had to opportunity of knowing the conditions of exported slaves. They no doubt relied on information volunteered by the slave traders which in most cases would have been variously manipulated to sustain the trade. Trade secrets no doubt owe their origin to the era of the slave trade when Africans were kept in the dark, manipulated and exploited.

The port of Lagos assumed importance as the busiest slave port on the eve of the abolition of the slave trade[22]. The Yoruba inter state wars of the 19th century and the continued participation of the Benin monarch in the slave trade jointly led to the phenomenal growth of activities in Lagos. The ease of getting slaves to Lagos from the nodal points through the eastern coastline, the participation of the Lagos monarchy and the burgeoning interest of Ijebu traders and their other hinterland counterparts in the slave trade transformed Lagos into both a slave market and a port of exit. By the middle of the 19th century and despite its late participation in the trade, Lagos had become one of the important slave ports in West Africa and station home to many slave traders. By the end of the slave trade, the city of Lagos had to contend with the problems associated with internal or domestic slavery more than any other exit point in West Africa[23].

Impact of The Slave Trade

There is no doubt that the slave trade was an ill wind that blew across Southwestern Nigeria leaving in its trail "sorrows, tears and blood". The slave trade was responsible for the political decline and the constitutional crisis that eventually destroyed the Yoruba political edifice of old Oyo Empire. As noted earlier, because of their participation in the slave trade, successive Alafin of Oyo neglected the army and failed to secure the territorial integrity and imperial hegemony of Oyo over vassal states. The weakness of the army led to multiple defeats in battle and the declaration of independence by erstwhile vassal states. The loss of revenue soon encouraged intra class acrimony and conflicts among members of the ruling class in Oyo which soon degenerated into complete breakdown of Oyo's central authority and hold over the Yoruba area. Indeed, the Yoruba inter state wars of the 19th century were provoked by the inordinate ambitions of a number of successor states which wanted to fill the power vacuum created by the fall of Oyo. The slave wars of the 19th century destroyed people's capacity to engage in other forms of economic activity which were in fact more productive than the slave trade. The incessant raids and kidnapping, the growing population of restless war boys and chiefs and the rise of militarism generally made participation in other economic ventures very dangerous and hazardous. The slave trade was responsible for the vicissitudes of the monarchy in Lagos when the British played one ruling house against the other and using the instability that they introduced as excuse to bombard Lagos in 1851 and annex as it Crown colony in 1861.

While it lasted, the slave trade equally created a pseudo class of economic elite in Southwestern Nigeria. The kings, chiefs and notable traders who participated in the slave trade became more powerful than others because of the access they had to European arms, fire arms and other articles of ostentation. No African principal participant in the slave trade left any enduring legacy. They all failed to make monumental contributions to their respective societies and many of them died uncelebrated and even unsung.

Trans-Atlantic Slave Trade and Human Sacrifice

Arguably, the slave trade was in part responsible for the return to and the escalation of human sacrifice in Yoruba societies. Before this period, human sacrifice, though a part of Yoruba religious belief, was not as widespread as it turned out to be in the era of the slave trade and shortly after. Before the slave trade specifically, sacrifices of human beings were made to the *orisa* at certain times of the year to propitiate and appease the gods on behalf of the society or certain individuals whose life had significant implications for the health and survival of the society. The number of sacrificial victims was small and limited to complete strangers, condemned criminals and vagabonds. The Yoruba saying that *a kii fi omo ore bo ore* ("you do not offer as sacrifice a member of a society to the god of that society"), is a fitting summary of the Yoruba attitude to sacrifice. However, with the slave trade, the inhumanity of man to man became commonplace and the value placed on human life was almost lost. In some societies, it became fashionable to offer slaves as sacrifice at the funeral of wealthy individuals. Some of them even became rich enough to buy slaves for sacrifice at the funeral of their not too wealthy relations. The abolition of the slave trade and the activities of the anti slavery squadron of the British Navy on the Atlantic Ocean led to what could be regarded as glut in the slave market. It became fashionable for individuals to buy slaves and keep them for various purposes at home. It is said that such individuals as Madam Tinubu of Lagos, later Abeokuta, had a large pool of slaves for sale and for internal or domestic use. Madam Efunsetan Aniwura of Ibadan had about five hundred male slaves and almost the same number of female slaves at the time of her death in 1877. In Ondo kingdom where human sacrifice assumed unmatchable notoriety, two 19th century individuals, Oba Arilekolasi and High Chief Edun Kolidoye had 380 and 800 slaves respectively[24]. At the funeral of High Chief Edun in 1880, about seventeen slaves were killed, two of whom were reported to have been buried alive. In 1882, six male and four female slaves were killed at the burial of High Chief Adaja and again, in 1885 when Lurowo died, five slaves were killed[25]. The elite of the 19th century indulged in this obnoxious practice because they believed that it was the best demonstration of wealth and power. Stopping this practice even after the abolition of the slave trade and in the era of legitimate commerce became a hard nut for the colonial authorities to crack.

Deconstructing Slave Trade Literature In Yorubaland

It is necessary to attempt a deconstruction of the slave trade literature in Yorubaland. In spite of the vigorous effort to trace the path of the trans-Saharan slave trade in Yorubaland, no concrete evidence could be given for the wholesome participation of the Yoruba in this trade. While it is possible that certain Yoruba elements became victims of the slave trade, participation comparable to what obtained in the era of the trans-Atlantic slave trade might be difficult if not impossible to establish at this stage of our knowledge. Every evidence points to the exchange of goods and commodities and not to human beings for the trans-Saharan trade. Such articles as krona (*tiro*), rock salt (*iyo obu*), indigo dye, swords, knives, horses and horse saddles were brought to Yorubaland through the agency of the trans-Saharan trade. It may be too hazy to report that the Yoruba participated in the trade as slave traders, but that some people of Yoruba origin were kidnapped and sold into slavery through the trans-Saharan routes is well established.

Again, the impression created by earlier writers on Yorubaland that *Iwofa* as a system of servitude compared favourably with slavery should be revised. Pre contact Yorubaland did not develop any form of servitude that could be compared to slavery on the other side of the Atlantic Ocean. The point has already been made in recent studies that *Iwofa* was a social security institution quite different from slavery[26]. An *Iwofa* was just an individual offering service to a creditor in lieu of interest on a loan facility advanced to him or a relation. *Iwofa* was different from a pawn which was usually in the strict English sense and understanding a good held but not used by the creditor as collateral on loan. *Iwofa* was a credit system that was developed to provide secured financial assistance, a form of apprenticeship in vocational training and even as a source of labour supply in predominantly agrarian and pre literate societies of Yorubaland. Unlike the situation under slavery, the *Iwofa* had certain rights including the right to life, modest lodging and boarding in the creditor's house[27]. He should be treated like a freeborn and must not be exposed to any form of danger. He would work for the creditor for certain number of days in the week and his labour for the other days could be quantified and paid for or accepted as payment for his freedom. This form of servitude actually pre dated the trans-Atlantic slave trade in Southwestern Nigeria and in fact outlived it. The introduction of currencies as legal tender for economic transactions, the intensity of the 19th century civil wars, and the attendant short supply of cowries as currency, created situations of poverty and want in Yorubaland that sustained the *Iwofa* system until the opening decades of the 20th century.

Relics of The Slave Trade

The Trans-Atlantic Experience and Global Yoruba Cultural Influence

The trans-Atlantic slave trade was in part responsible for the existence of the Yoruba diaspora in places where there are vestiges of Yoruba culture in the New World. The most enduring relic of the slave trade is in fact the existence of Yoruba cultural influences in such places as the United States of America, South America and the Caribbean. Yoruba religion is no doubt a major cultural influence in Africa and could be described as providing basis for new religious movements such as Santeria in Cuba and Puerto Rico and Candomble in Brazil[28]. Even in the United States of America, the acceptance of traditional Yoruba religion as a possible source of knowledge about man in relation to his physical and spiritual environment is fast becoming popular. The enslaved Yoruba took with them their belief systems which eventually came alive again where ever they found themselves[29]. Today, Yoruba deities like *Oya, Ifa Orunmila, Orisa Ibeji Osanyin, Osun, Yemoja, Olokun, Sango* and *Obatala* are better worshipped in the diaspora than in the Yoruba homeland which has been penetrated by the two religions of Islam and Christianity.

Tangible Relics of Slave Trade

Yoruba participants in the trans-Atlantic slave trade did not leave behind any significant monument or records of their participation that could be described as relics. Apart from the sacred *Iyalode* tree in Osogun, the birthplace of Bishop Ajayi Crowther, the slave dealers of Oyo, Ede, Apomu, Ibadan, Ilesa, Ondo and Ikaleland had nothing to show for their participation in the obnoxious trade. It could well be that these traders got converted, repented and actually destroyed what could be regarded as gentle reminders of their infamy.

The slave chains, shackles, cannons, baracoons, 17th century water cistern and umbrella, pottery gift items, the door of no return and a slave ship anchor were actually left by the foreign slave traders. Two families in Badagry, the Sunbu Mobee and Seriki Abbass, share the custody of these items in their family museums[30]. Curiously, there seems to be a studied silence on the trans-Atlantic slave trade even in Yoruba oral literature which for other historical occurrences could be regarded as a rich reservoir of information. The slave dance and narratives are recent developments of an age that is more interested in promoting tourism than in the documentation of history.

Conclusion

Coupled with colonial intervention in the affairs of Southwesetrn Nigeria, the trans-Atlantic slave trade could be regarded as the major limitation on the progress that was already underway in Yorubaland in the period before contact with Europe. Participation in the trans-

Atlantic slave trade destroyed the foundation of Yoruba indigenous economy, the political structures and patterns of social relations. The massive demographic readjustment compelled by the slave induced wars of the 19th century left its toll on the ability of each state to manage its affairs without interference from outside forces and interests. With the benefit of hindsight, it is not too far fetched to conclude that ignorance of what slavery was in the New World helped in no small measure to sustain the participation of African chiefs and kings in the trans-Atlantic slave trade. The present voluntary slavery which is taking Africans in droves to Europe and America is thriving because of the apparent lack of knowledge about the realities of living in these societies. Human trafficking, especially of young men and women is very popular because the financiers, agents, scouts and couriers of this illegal business will not disclose to their unsuspecting victims what they will be exposed to as soon as they leave their native land. There is, therefore, an urgent need to teach the history of the slave trade, its praxis, tactics, dehumanisation and contributions to the under development of African societies. Beyond tourism, efforts should be made to rehabilitate the historic sites of the slave trade in a way that will enable the victims of enslavement reconnect with their roots for meaningful re-engagement and spiritual rearmament. Research should be promoted in the study of African oral literature to further deepen understanding about slavery and extend the frontiers of knowledge about how Europe and America deceived Africa.

Notes and References

[1] For details of the Yoruba world and the development of its civilisation see, Samuel Johnson, *History of the Yorubas* (Lagos: CSS Bookshop, 1921); R.S. Smith, *Kingdoms of the Yoruba* (Mathuen, 1969), S.O. Biobaku, *The Origins of the Yoruba* (Lagos, 1955); N.A. Fadipe, *The Sociology of the Yoruba* (Ibadan: Ibadan University Press, 1970).

[2] Afolabi Ojo, *Yoruba Culture: A Geographical Analysis* (London: University of London Press, 1973), pp.17-20.

[3] For a summary of Yoruba traditions within the context of global black traditions, see Akin Alao, "Yoruba Traditions" in Molefi

Asante, *Encyclopedia of Black Studies* (USA: Sage Publishers, 2004).
4   Biodun Adediran, "Yorubaland up to the Emergence of the States" in Deji Ogunremi and Biodun Aadediran (eds.), *Culture and Society in Yorubaland* (Ibadan: Rex Charles Publications, 1998,), pp.1-11.
5   I.A. Akinjogbin, *Milestones and Concepts in Yoruba History and Culture* (Lagos: Joakin Publishers, 2003), pp.105-119.
6   Akin Alao, "Two New Owu Settlements" in Toyin Falola and Robin Law (eds.), *Warfare and Diplomacy in Pre-colonial Nigeria Essays in Honour of Robert Smith* (Wisconsin: University of Wisconsin Press), pp 73-77.
7   Toyin Falola, *The Political Economy of a Pre Colonial African State: Ibadan, 1830-1900* (Ile-Ife: University of Ife Press, 1984), pp. 15-20.
8   For details about the emergence of Ibadan in the 19th century, see Bolanle Awe, *The Rise of Ibadan as a Yoruba Power, 1851-1883*, D. Phil. Thesis Oxford, 1964.
9   N.A. Fadipe, *The Sociology of the Yoruba*.
10 For incisive discussion of the system of land ownership, acquisition and utilisation in Yorubaland, see N.A. Fadipe, *The Sociology of the Yoruba*; T.O Elias, *Nigerian Land Law and Custom* (London: Sweet and Maxwell, 1957).
11 J.A. Atanda, *The New Oyo Empire*.
12 Personal Communication: Baba Awo Dr. Biodun Agboola, 20th August 2009.
13 William Bosman described Ifa as the unwritten scriptures of the Yoruba,. See also, Wande Abimbola, *An Exposition of Ifa Literary Corpus* (Ibadan: Oxford University Press, 1976); M.O. Opeloye, "Evolution of Religious Culture among the Yoruba" in Deji Ogunremi and Biodun Adediran (eds.), *Culture and Society in Yorubaland*, p.139-148.
14 Akin Alao, *Oral Traditions and Indigenous Judicial System in Yorubaland*, presented at the Summit of Cultural Associations in Africa and the Diaspora, Yaoundé, Cameroon, 9th April 2009.
15 For details of the political ascendancy of Ibadan and the development of its institutions and structures, see G.O.

Ogunremi, *Ibadan: A Historical, Cultural and Socio-Economic Study of an African City* (Lagos: Oluyole Club, 2000).
16. Toyin Falola, *The Political Economy*, pp.25-29.
17. Akin Alao, *Tradition and Change in Africa: Ibadan-Oyo Relations in Historical Perspective, 1829-1939*, AAU African Studies Review, Vol. 3 (2004).
18. For details of Ibadan's military campaigns in Ibolo, Ijesa, Ife, Ekiti and Akoko areas of Yorubaland, see Banji Akintoye, *Revolution and Power Politics in Yorubaland* (Ibadan: Heinemann Publishers, 1976).
19. I.A. Akinjogbin, *Dahomey and Its Neighbours* (London, 1966).
20. *Ibid*.
21. These two works specifically examine the historical development of Badagry as an ancient settlement and slave market. G.O. Ogunremi, M.O. Opeloye and Siyan Oyeweso (eds.), *Badagry: A Study in History, Culture and Traditions of an Ancient City* (Ibadan: Rex Charles Publications, 1994); T Avoseh, *A Short History of Badagry*, (Lagos: Ife-Olu Printing Press, 1938).
22. A. Adefuye, *A History of the People of Lagos State*.
23. Ayodeji Olukoju, *The "Liverpool" of West Africa: Dynamics and Impact of Maritime Trade in Lagos, 1900-1950* (New Jersey: Africa World Press).
24. Olatunji Ojo, *Slavery and Human Sacrifice in Yorubaland, Ondo.c. 1870-1894*, Journal of African History, 46 (2005), pp.379-404.
25. *Ibid*, p.383.
26. For details see, Samuel Johnson, *The History of the Yoruba* p.126-130, E. Adeniyi Oroge, *Iwofa: An Historical Survey of the Yoruba Institution of Indenture*, African Economic History, No.14 (1985), pp.75-106.
27. *Ibid*.
28. Adenrele Alade, *The African Diaspora: The Yoruba Culture in the New World in Yoruba*, Vol.1 No.1 (2001), pp.38-48.
29. *Ibid*.
30. These two individuals were about the best known slave dealers whose families still keep these items in private museums. See, Alaba Simpson, *Some Reflections on Relics of the Trans Atlantic Slave Trade in the Historic Town of Badagry, Nigeria* at *http://www.diaspora.uiuc.edu/news0608.html*.

Chapter 9

SLAVERY, SLAVE TRADE AND THE STATE IN PRE-COLONIAL NIGERIA

Okon Edet Uya
Professor of History, Department of History and International Studies, University of Uyo, Uyo

Introduction

THIS book, *Slavery and Slave Trade in Nigeria* has examined, using primarily oral evidences supplemented by extant written records, the development, nature and character of indigenous use of people of subordinate status or unfree labour as well as the impact of the external slave trade, both trans-Saharan and trans-Atlantic and their abolition, in Nigeria. From the analyses of various sub-regions of Nigeria, it is clear, that slavery and slave trade played important roles, varying in intensity, in the history of the peoples of the region internally and externally, especially between the sixteenth and late nineteenth centuries. They were not only major institutions of social subordination and control, but also important labour source throughout the sub-regions. For much of the period under consideration, they influenced in substantial ways, the relations between the organised and centralising polities and their non-centralised ones, and, with the maturation of the external slave trade, dominated and shaped virtually all major social, economic and political relations between these polities. They were indeed major factors in the growth, development, decline and collapse of the centralised states in the Sahel, Savannah and Forest zones.

At the maturation of the trans-Atlantic trade and slavery in Europe, the Americas and the Caribbean, slave trade and slavery shaped economic, political and even cultural relations between the coastal polities of Nigeria and their hinterland neighbours as well as those between them and the Europeans. Black slavery played a very significant role in "the emergence, consolidation and ideological validation of Euro-American racism, a powerful force in world history since the eighteenth century, of which the Black world has remained perhaps the greatest victim." The campaign to eradicate slavery and slave trade from the late eighteenth century also significantly influenced the rationalisation and consolidation of European imperialism and colonisation in the Niger-Benue region, the Nigeria of our present day[1]. As has been shown in all the chapter contributions in this book, apart from its related cousin, state formation, slave trade and slavery were no doubt the central themes of the history of the Nigerian region between the fifteenth and early twentieth centuries.

North West and North East Nigeria

Beyond the above generalisation, however, our examination of the dynamics of slave trade and slavery has demonstrated that the institutions varied from sub-region to sub-region in their antiquity, emergence, organisation and overall significance for the peoples concerned. It is clear, for example, that both institutions were more ancient in the Sudan and Sahel zones than in the forest regions precisely because of the early emergence of centralised polities in that region. As the chapters on Sokoto, Kebbi, Gobir, Zamfara, Katsina, Kano, Zazzau, Daura, Kano and the Borno regions have shown, slavery and slave trading were important in the trans-Saharan trade between these areas and north Africa, Europe and the Middle East dating back to at least the tenth century AD. It should also be noted that Islam, which became the dominant religion in the area since the establishment of the western Sudanese, Hausa and Borno states, sanctioned enslavement, especially of war captives. As Toyin Falola and Matthew Heaton have concluded:

> The value and versatility of slaves had made them an important aspect of the trans-Saharan trade for centuries before the coming of Europeans and the establishment of the trans-Atlantic trade on the coast. Indeed, slaves had been particularly important commodity of the trans-Saharan trade at least since the establishment of the

kingdoms of the Savanna and their association with the Muslim states of North Africa from about the eleventh century if not earlier[2].

The use of slaves was to expand considerably during the campaigns for the establishment of the Sokoto Caliphate and the many inter-state wars that these unleashed in the region both for the defence of the boundaries of the state and territorial expansion. As shown by Adamu, Sa'ad Abubakar and Bawuro Barkindo, slavery and slave trading played important roles in the social, economic, political and military life of these states up to the end of the nineteenth century. As detailed by Mahdi Adamu, the many slaves used in various activities were recruited largely through wars, raids, kidnapping, condemnation through judicial processes, natural increase through births, etc. They were utilised in domestic service, as public officers, as farm lands, in metal works and leather goods industries, but most importantly, in the many military engagements of the period and for export. Also, though they were of subordinate status socially, some categories, especially those in the courts of the rulers, enjoyed privileges approximating those of some freemen in the society. Indeed, the slavery status was rather fluid, raging from extreme deprivation of the lowest slaves in the social hierarchy to positions of considerable influence and authority of those involved in the administration and the bureaucracy of the states. Some even served as overseers over other slaves, village heads and as provincial governors.

Professors Sa'ad Abubakar and Barkindo, in their analysis of slavery and slave trading in the North East region, have shown clearly that the institutions, in origins, organisations, status of slaves, ideology and impact were very similar to what obtained in the North-West areas of Sokoto, Kebbi. Sa'ad Abubakar's contribution is a comprehensive discussion of the two institutions in the entire North-East region, Barkindo, on the other hand, focuses specifically on Kanem-Bornu and the three emirates of the region and thus provides fascinating details that enriche our knowledge, especially of the chieftaincy titles that have their origins in slavery and the slave trade.

Among the many items of the trans-Saharan trade, such as gold, salt and textiles, slaves were not only self-transporting over the harsh Sahara desert, but were also needed as porters in the trade and as currency. Thus, as guesstimated by Paul Lovejoy, between 3,000 and 8,000 slaves per year were moved on each of the main routes across the Sahara. Slave trade and slavery were thus important aspects of the political economy of the Hausa States and Karem-Borno throughout their periods of territorial expansion and consolidation. It is also known that slaves captured in the many wars of Borno, especially during the reign of Mai Idris Aloma, were traded for horses, guns and musketeers with Tripoli and thus played decisive roles in the success of Borno military expeditions since it enabled them to access superior technology over their foes. The significance of slaves in the political economy of the Hausa States and Kanem-Borno is aptly captured by Falola and Heaton as follows:

> While much of the production and trade of the Hausa states was based on free labour and commodities such as gold, grain, livestock and leather goods, slaves were also an important aspect of the Hausa states economies. It is clear that during the sixteenth century, Kano's infrastructure developed enormously, largely because of an increase in the number of slaves used for the production of agricultural goods, as porters and guards on trade routes, as soldiers in the many military campaigns against neighbours, and, as in Borno, as export items used in purchase of goods from north Africa especially horses[3].

Significantly, the slaves tended to be integrated politically, socially, culturally and religiously, into the state institutions and structures, thus validating substantially the "absorptionist" theory of Susan Meiers and Igor Kopytoff[4]. The analysis also shows that though the vast majority of slaves in the region were exported to the north, a considerable number found their way through the trans-Atlantic trade into the West where they played significant role in slave revolts and the perpetuation of Islam[5].

The Middle Belt Zone

Inspite of their peripheral locations for both the northern bound trans-Saharan and the southern bound European slave trade and slavery, both institutions played significant roles in the socio-political economy of the Middle Belt region, especially in present day states of Niger, Kwara and Kogi. In his clearly "gap filling" attempt, Shaaba Jimadu, subjects both domestic slavery and the export slave trade among the Nupe, Igala, Yoruba (Ilorin and Offa), and the Gbagyi groups to careful analysis. He concludes that "indigenous slavery was a vital part of the social structure. Slave labour was an essential factor in the productive life of the people". Besides, the geographical location of the area at the centre of modern Nigeria exposed it to influences coming both from the north and south as the area served as major route and gateway to both.

Domestic slavery in the region, Jimadu claims, was more like "indentured servitude" which, though it bound the slave labourer to his owner, allowed him considerable latitude over his personal and domestic life, provided such did not interfere with his productivity. As elsewhere, the slaves tended to be assimilated into the society "since slaves could buy or obtain their freedom in a variety of ways." Clearly, the inter-state struggles and warfare to the north affected domestic slavery in the region as evidence confirms that as early as the sixteenth century "slaves were sold by the ruling elite of the states in the area in return for horses from Hausaland." Also, the slaves were recruited mainly from debtors, pawns, witches and wizards, miscreants, in exchange for food during famine, raiding and wars of expansion from the seventeenth century. Poverty, debt and inability to pay tributes and taxes forced families to sell some of their members. Slaves were also war captives who were sold in the towns on the river bank towns such as Bussa, Ilorin, Jebba, Mokwa, Rabba, Bida, Lokoja and Idah. These became important markets where slaves were sold and bought daily.

Apart from serving as trade goods in exchange for horses, slaves performed a number of domestic duties, such as rope making, barbing and tending horses. Some slaves performed important functions in the palaces in Nupe, Igala, Ilorin, and Idah with the principal palace slaves enjoying considerable political, administrative and military influence. Slaves were engaged in agriculture and industrial production especially in the *tunga* or harmlets established by the royalties in the nineteenth century. Jimada claims that by the mid-nineteenth centuries, there were over 200 slave towns in the area. A large number of slaves were sold to the northern states of Gwandu, the Sokoto Caliphate, Kano as well as down south to Lagos and Oyo areas from where they were exported into the trans-Atlantic trade. One significant impact of the presence of domestic slaves from various ethnic groups, Jimada points out, was the ethnic heterogenisation of the region. Jimada's account further confirms that domestic slavery in this region, as elsewhere, was vastly different in its ideology from the Western slavery resulting from the Atlantic slave trade.

South Western Nigeria

Indigenous slavery and slave trade were important factors in the political, social and economic life of the Yoruba of south western Nigeria, especially from the twelve to the nineteenth century, following the emergence of states and centralised polities. Before then, whatever social differentiation existed was minimal and those at the bottom of society formed part of an integral social structure, playing no overwhelmingly important role in the Yoruba mode of production nor constituting the most important labour force in the society. This, however, was to change radically with the rise of centralised states. As Alao explains:

> The emergence of privileged groups and their domination of the social, political and economic order introduced a structure that was based on ranking. The new relations of power created its own order and privileged certain groups at the expense of others. The sophistication of the economy, which was characterised by unequal access to resources created a new subaltern class of the under privileged.

Alao's point, and this is important, is that it was the processes of state formation, expansion, consolidation and administration that catapulted slavery and slave trading into important institutions in Yorubaland. In Old Oyo, for example, persons of slave origin became involved in political, administrative, and religious matters exercising, as did the *Aare Apeka, Olori eru Alaafin* and the *Kudefu* (all important palace head slaves) enormous influence in the administration of the state. These, along with other slaves-turned-chiefs, were made to represent various compounds in Oyo, paid salaries and compensations for their work, and enjoyed special privileges.

Beyond this, slaves played important roles as religious officers, shrine attendants and assistants to the priests of the many deities that dotted the Yoruba religious landscape. Some were trained and used for state assignments such as the execution of condemned criminals, especially in Oyo, Ife, Ondo, Abeokuta and Ibadan. Some female slaves were used to perform rituals of appeasement and collective security in the palaces. Indeed, three slave eunuchs were crucial in the successful palace administration of the Alaafin of Oyo. The *ona iwefa* (eunuch of the middle), *otun iwefa* (eunuch of the right) and *osi iwefa* (eunuch of the left) were the highest authority only next to the Alafin in judicial, religious and administrative matters, standing in as proxy for the Alafin in handing down legal rulings, in charge of the Sango cult which mystified the Alafin and collection of revenue, respectively. Indeed, as aptly stated by Falola and Heaton:

> That the office of the *alafin* did not crumble under the instability created by Bashorun Gaha and the Oyo Mesi is a testament to the organisation of the *alafin's* palace administration which rested heavily on slaves with positions of high authority and responsibility. It is clear that, from the reconquest of Oyo Ile in the late sixteenth century, slaves had performed integral duties within the palace administration, not only in the everyday affairs of running the palace, but also in ruling the city of Oyo Ile and the provinces of the Oyo empire[6].

As elsewhere in the Nigerian region, slaves in Yorubaland also performed other duties such as domestic work, agricultural work and food production, trained artisans, and in the military. Slavery and slave trading were thus central to the politics and economy of Old Oyo. Slaves captured in war as well as convicted criminals, along with European goods were traded to the Hausa sates in exchange for Hausa slaves and horses. Oyo also traded slaves to the coast, especially from the beginning of the seventeenth century in exchange for European luxury goods, cowry shells and firearms. Also, because of her strategic position between the forest zone and the savannah states, Oyo was able to impose heavy levies on traders from both sides. Slave trade was, indeed, one of Oyo's "most prosperous enterprises."

The role of slave trade and slavery in the collapse of Old Oyo and the Yoruba wars of the nineteenth century is also examined by

Alao. On the first, he asserts that "it would seem that the participation of Oyo elite, including members of the ruling class in slave trade diverted state attention from using the military to ensure and maintain internal security of persons and protecting the territorial integrity of the state." This, apparently, was responsible for the declaration of independence by the vassal states of Dahomey, Borgu and Nupe and the subsequent ascendery of Ibadan, Abeokuta and Oyo Atiba. The slave trade, Alao concludes, was an ill wind which destroyed "the mythical invincibility of Oyo, opened areas under her sphere of influence to reckless plundering by slave raiders and made participation in other economic activities extremely hazardous." It was from the declining years of the Oyo Empire and principally during the successive civil wars of the nineteenth century that the slave trade became an extremely important and decisive activity in Yorubaland. Though the motives for these wars have been the subject of controversy and debate among historians, it is undeniable that they converted the vast Yoruba hinterland into a major supplier of trade slaves which made the ports of Lagos, Badagri, Porto Novo and Whydah notorious for slave exports. The wars between Ibadan and the other Yoruba states, especially the Kurunmi war of 1862, produced a great number of Yoruba slaves that would find their way especially to Cuba and Brazil where the slavery system reached maturity in the second half of the nineteenth century. Indeed, Lagos had replaced the ports of the Bight of Biafra as the greatest exporter of slaves from the Nigerian region.

The Niger Delta Region and its Hinterlands

Slavery and slave trade were important institutions in the areas of present day Rivers, Bayelsa, Delta, Edo, Ebonyi and Enugu States especially between the 17th and 19th centuries when the Bight of Biafra gradually replaced the Bight of Benin as the major areas for trade slave exports into the oversees trade. As Abi Derefaka has shown, both institutions enjoyed considerable antiquity, probably as early as the period of settlement and development of social, cultural and political institutions. However, as elsewhere in our study area, persons of subordinate status were not too differentiated from other members of the society as they were often integrated. Derafaka observes that domestic slavery was an important institution in the socio-economic structure where emphasis was placed on increasing the population of the compound and later trade *houses*. However, the so-called slaves were regarded as members of the extended family as their owners usually assigned them to one or the other of his wives who were expected to treat them as their own children, especially after they might have undergone some rituals of enculturation and been integrated into the kinship of their owners. Demonstrated competence on tasks assigned them ensured rapid ascendancy up the slippery political and economic ladders of the society. They were allowed to own their properties and could even inherit the properties of their owners as any of the biological children. However, newly arrived slaves were subjected to greater indignities such as sale and use for human sacrifice. With the emergence of the coastal trading *houses* in the Niger Delta city states, people of subordinate status were offered greater opportunities and successful traders could marry slave women and their offspring. Indeed, as Derefake has stressed, a well-behaved and hard working slave who was successfully acculturated and socialised could be fully integrated into the family, *houses* and community. This was the kind of slavery that Olaudah Equiano described in his autobiography which is often quoted as the prototype of slavery in Africa.

The Niger Delta area was to play an important role in the Atlantic slave trade as her principal ports of Elem Kalabari (New Calabar), Bonny and Opobo would compete and eventually overtake Old Calabar as the major ports of embarkation from the late 18th century, Derefaka explains. The Niger Delta city states of Kalabari, Bonny, Okrika, Nembe, Andoni, Ogoni, Ikwerre, Ndoki and Opobo as well as the Itsekiri, Urhobo, Edo and Ika Igbo were deeply involved in the trade which substantially shaped relations between them as well as those between them and the Europeans. A substantial number of merchants and merchant families emerged and benefited from the slave trade.

However, the coming of the slave trade and even its abolition did not represent any major departures from the patterns established in the early periods because trade and commerce remained the major activities. Slaves were used in the trade in a variety of ways which allowed the enslaved great latitude to excel depending on their abilities and competences. Enterprising slaves like Jaja of Opobo could aspire to and indeed attain positions of eminence.

Most of the slaves sold through the Niger Delta ports were recruited from the Igbo and Ibibio hinterlands by the Aro. They were either captives during inter-communal wars and conflicts, pawns-turned slaves, social miscreants and criminals, "troublesome" children or weaker members of society looking for protection and sustenance. The coastal areas became frontiers of opportunity, attracting populations from the hinterland towards the coast. The growth in power, prestige as well as wealth of the slave traders, principally Ijo-speaking, "led to re-orientation of power away from traditional political and religious authorities in favour of new forms of social organisation centered on protecting the commercial interests of the slave trade", the Canoe House system. The *house* served to advertise the *house* as an important actor in local affairs and the procurement of new slaves. Essentially, then, slavery and slave trading remained integrative and absorptionist, confirming, once more, the absorptienist theory. As Falola and Heaton have concluded for the Niger Delta region:

> Overtime slaves became assimilated into their new houses, and through marriage, or bravery in battle or slave raiding, could become fully integrated into the house, even to the point of becoming the house head[7].

This substantially meant increase in the number of lineages or kingdoms in the era of the slave trade whose impact on the political landscape especially in Rivers and Bayelsa states have remained to this day.

The Cross River Region

As in the case of the Niger Delta city states, slavery and slave trade were dominant institutions in the Cross River region of Akwa Ibom, Cross River, lower Benue, parts of Ebonyi and Abia states and the Southern Cameroons, areas which historically made up the Cross River region. Okon Uya's analysis confirms that although there were varying forms of use of unfree or subordinated labour in the small-scale trade, artisinal and farming activities in the area, the coming of the slave trade was to transform relations between the Efik City States of Old Calabar and the Ibibio, Annang, Ogoja, Ekoi and Igbo hinterland communities from whence the slaves were extracted.

The analysis shows clearly that the Cross River region communities involved in the slave trade can substantially be classified into three, namely, the slave trading communities which principally were the Efik city states; the slave raiding communities, principally the Aro and their Abam collaborators; and the slave raided communities of present day Akwa Ibom, the Ogoja communities of the Cross River and the Igbo hinterland far and near. The impact of the trade differed substantially in the three groups, with the first two qualifying to be regarded as gainers while those in the third group were losers in the trade.

It is within this context that Uya has located the rise of Calabar to fame and prosperity which enabled her to exert considerable influence and authority over the hinterland. Indeed, it was the slave trade that integrated the hinterland communities into the Efik economic and cultural orbit which has substantially compounded the problem of boundary demarcation between Cross River and other states in the region.

The analysis also shows how the patterns established by the slave trade were responsible for the expanding European, mainly British, influences in the region even before the establishment of formal colonisation. The Efik were the principal beneficiaries of the British presence especially as they were able to resist European penetration into the interior thus denying the hinterland communities direct access to the Europeans until well into the first decade of the twentieth century. The slave trade and slavery thus left lasting imprints on the social, political and economic life of the region.

Uya also highlights the dominant role of the Aro as slave recruiters for the Bight of Biafra from the 17th to 19th centuries which can be attributed mainly to the effective manner the Aro manipulated their oracle for commercial and slave raiding purposes. Falola and Heaton have similarly concluded that:

The Aro applied the religious authority of the oracle to maintain a stranglehold on the slave markets in the interior of the Bight of Biafra throughout the eighteenth and nineteenth centuries[8].

Indigenous Slavery and Slave Trade in the Nigerian Region: General Comments

The analysis in this book has brought out some of the peculiarities and variations in indigenous use of slave labour and practices as well as highlighted the impact of the external slave trade, both trans-Sahara and trans-Atlantic, on the Nigerian region especially between the fifteenth and nineteenth centuries. From the sub regional analyses, we are in a position to make some assertions about the changing nature of those largely pernicious institutions on the society, politics, economy and cultures of the region.

Firstly, it is clear that both slavery and slave trade as institutions pre-dated the Arab and European trading activities in our region. The use of unfree labour or people in subordinated status, although on a small scale, was widespread among the indigenous peoples of the region. However, it is clear that those people of inferior status enjoyed a large measure of freedom approximate and sometimes superior to other people in the society. The critical asset they lacked was kinship and this is what set them apart, especially as kinship was the prevailing idiom of association and access to the socio-political and economic goods in those societies. Thus, although somehow stretched, Susan Meiers, Kopytoff and Paul Lovejoy are right to insist that lineage kinship was the ideology of slavery and alienation in the Nigerian region. Indeed, as shown in the various chapters, because new kinship ties could be acquired or forged, slavery based on its rather flexible, elastic and fluid statues, by and large, never constituted a distinct class in their societies. In fact, there were several avenues through which people of subordinate status could ascend the social, political and economic ladders, some even climbing to the top. It is thus clear that the use of the words *slaves* and *slavery* in their Western context especially in the Americas and the Caribbean, substantially distorts the meaning of indigenous slavery as it does not adequately translate the variety of forms captured by the many

Nigeria words that were used to designate unfree labour. It is also clear that though indigenous slavery was essentially absorptionist and integrative, these were not automatic but dependent on the prevailing social, political, and economic challenges confronting the societies. Indeed though people of subordinate status enjoyed a large measure of peculiums in all societies, being regarded as members of the extended families of their patrons, they were also denied psychological benefits, especially identities, in these societies. Their pompous traditional titles in Yourba land, Hausa land, Borno and in the Niger Delta region could not blot out the stigma of inferiority.

Secondly, contrary to the widespread notion that slavery was endemic in Africa, our studies show clearly that slavery was a historic institution and subject to changes, depending on the challenges facing the societies. Social differentiation and stratification resulting in denial of certain rights to some in the population were brought about by such factors as disparate migrations, population concentrations following sedentary living, economic specialisation brought about by extensive farm cultivation, and above all, short and long distance trade especially in the early stages of state formation. It is not surprising therefore that slavery and slave trading expanded in the Hausa states, Kanem Bornu, and the Middle Belt areas under the impact of the trans-Saharan trade just as those in the Niger Delta, Yoruba and Old Calabar regions did under the impact of the trans-Atlantic trade. It is also clear that although some persons of subordinate and unfree status were the early victims of the external demands, most slaves that entered the trans-Sahara and trans-Atlantic trades were created through factors induced by these trades. Kidnapping, raiding, inter-communal wars, prostitution of the existing judicial processes and oracles, *panyarring* and pawnship, were brought about or expanded by the demand for trade slaves. In other words, the direct linkage between domestic slavery and slave trading and the development of the Atlantic slave trade is rather stretched.

Thirdly, as we have seen, the slaves that entered both the trans-Saharan and the Atlantic trades were recruited largely by African middlemen, especially the noblemen and royalties, in the African states. Indeed, it is correct to argue that mutually beneficial partnership between the Nigerian middlemen and the European traders was essential for the success of the trade in slaves. Similarly, it was mostly the African agents like the Aro that recruited slaves from the hinterland for the coastal sellers. We cannot, therefore, blame the atrocities that accompanied this pernicious trade on the Europeans alone, even where we are able to show that the partnership was unequal.

Fourthly, we have shown that the transition from the slave trade to the so-called legitimate trade, or more correctly trade in commodities, did not represent any major break in the patterns established in the slave trade period. Indeed, the production and processing of the commodities such as palm oil and kernel in the coastal areas led to expansion in the use of slaves in the coastal plantations. As aptly stated by Adiele Afigbo, the result was that "legitimate trade emerged in the interior as a twin brother of the illegitimate trade; indeed the two developed as a sort of Siamese twins"[9].

Fifthly, we have stressed the role of slavery and slave trade in state formation in the Nigerian region. Our analyses confirm that slavery and trading in slaves were important activities in the Sudanic, Savannah and Coastal city states of Nigeria. We have highlighted the roles played by slaves in commerce, food production and general agriculture, the military, and administration of these states. Indeed, it is difficult to refute the conclusion that, "by the turn of the nineteenth century, slavery and the slave trade had become integral aspects of the economies and societies throughout the greater Nigeria area" [10].

Sixthly, we have shown that the Atlantic slave trade was a major factor in shaping and determining the relationships between the southern coastal city states of Nigeria and their hinterlands. It was the trade that bound the majority hinterland communities into the commercial, political and cultural orbits of their minority coastal neighbours thus elevating the Efik and Ijaw, for example, into prominence and reputation far beyond their numbers. The attempt to re-order this pattern in the colonial and immediate post-colonial periods accounts for much of the inter-ethnic rancour even to the present day[11]. We have similarly shown how the trade in slaves shaped the relationship of the Europeans, mainly British, and the coastal middlemen, and how these enabled the coastal dwellers to become the agents for mediating European influences such as Christianity and western education throughout the Nigerian region.

Seventhly, on the impact of the trade, we have shown that, on balance, the Nigerian region lost while the Europeans gained from the trade. Though the economic balance sheet is difficult to draw with accuracy given the paucity of the extant records, there is no question that the slave trade transferred to the West, "part of Africa's relative advantage in production of commodities for the evolving world market, retarded the growth and development of commodity production which in turn delayed and frustrated general commercialisation of economic activities" in our region. Joseph Inikori had further asserted that the social costs to Africa involved in the enslavement processes completely *dwarfed* whatever private gains a few members of the African elite would have made from their slaving activities[12].

Eighthly, the diaspora dimension of the slave trade and slavery for Nigeria has been stressed in our analysis. As shown in the different chapters of the book, the Nigerian Region was the largest contributor of slaves for the Atlantic trade and a major one for the trans-Saharan slave trade. The demographic implication is that the export slave trade was an important, indeed the most important factor, for the Nigerian diasporas to North Africa, the Middle East, Europe and most importantly, the Americas and the Caribbean Islands before the twentieth century. The existence of vibrant Nigerian derived cultures, religion and languages, such as those of the Yoruba in Brazil, Cuba and Southern United States; "the Calabar", Moko or Agbisherea in Cuba, Jamaica and Virginia; and Igbo in South Carolina, Virginia, and some of the Caribbean islands testify to this. These, in turn, are important cultural enclaves and extensions which can be exploited for foreign exchange in this era of globalisation and cultural tourism. As we have explained elsewhere:

> The Atlantic slave trade was most significant in that it represented the forced migration of millions of African peoples especially to Europe, the Americas and the Caribbean in significant numbers to enable them create vibrant living communities whose culture and

social institutions were discernibly African, varying in scale and intensity depending on such factors as geography, demography, the nature of the economic enterprise in which the slaves were involved, the ideological disposition and commitments of the enslaving white society, and the nature of their contacts with Africa[13].

Slave Trade Routes, Relics and Cultural Tourism

The Slave Trade Routes Project, to which the Nigeria government has subscribed and is fully committed, was conceived initially by African diaspora scholars in the Americas and the Caribbean to retrace the trans-Atlantic routes through which Africans in the West came into their host societies. It was to examine the importance of African cultures to a proper understanding of the cultures of blacks in the West, especially given the then prevalent thesis that most of what was African was lost in the trans-Atlantic crossing or the Middle passage. The debate sought to resolve the controversy generated by the disagreement between E. Franklin Frazier, black sociologist, who in his many works on black American institutions had concluded that the African American experience during slavery had generally disconnected him from Africa, and the white social anthropologist, Melville Herskovits who postulated that the African heritage and traditional organisations of the blacks had not been destroyed by enslavement of the African American. It was indeed the effort to resolve this 1930s Herskovits-Frasier debate that led to a revival of interest in the African roots of the African American experience and its proper conceptualisation as African Diaspora studies in late 1970's and 80's[14]. The effort was initially directed towards the building of a prototype of a slave ship which would carry students and professors from the embarkation ports of West Africa through the Atlantic to their landing in the Americas and the Caribbean. That way, they would be better able to appreciate the impact of the journey on the slave inmates of the ships.

It was this essentially academic interest that was redefined and appropriated by the United Nations Educational, Scientific and Cultural Organisation (UNESCO) and designated the Slave Trade Route Project, modeled after her Silk Routes Project in Asia in 1993. Expectedly, Nigeria, a major contributor of slaves to the Americas,

Caribbean and Europe and the Moslem world has embraced the project and the publication of this book in collaboration with UNESCO represents the first concrete effort to document slave routes in the Nigerian region in book form.

As detailed in this publication, most slaves that entered the slave trade were recruited in various ways from areas distant from their home territories or ethnic groups. These hinterland communities were the raiding and war devastated lands from which slaves were extracted. In the circumstance, the enslaves had to be transported through initially imprecise routes, sometimes by a combination of land and water, to their points of embarkation. Over time and through regularity of use, these became established as slave trade routes, linking villages, collection centres and traders in a relay fashion to the coastal ports of embarkation such as Old Calabar, Bonny, Elem Kalabari, Ikot Abasi, Brass, Benin, Badagri, Lagos, Whydah, Abomey and Port Novo.

Slaves exported to North Africa, the Middle East and Europe were transported overland to the major trading centres of trade like Kano, from where they were "moved across the Sahara Desert to North Africa and the Middle East." Given the nature of the desert, it is rather difficult to trace the routes and we are reduced to just mentioning the major trading centres through which they passed. As Mahdi-Adamu has correctly concluded "there were no routes set aside for importing or exporting slaves".

From the careful examination of the sub-regions in this book, we are able to identify the following regularly used routes in the Nigerian region for the Atlantic trade.

1. Katsina or Kano-Zaria- Nupe-Ilorin - Ijebu-Lagos (Eko) Route.
2. Sokoto-Birnin Kebbi-Kotongora-Mokwa-Jebba-Old Oyo Route.
3. Mokwa-Labzhi-Sakpe-Gbara-Muregi-Kabba, Ikare-Benin Route.
4. Kotongora-Dabban-Kutigi-Mokwa-Old Oyo-Gwanja Route.
5. Niger River-Eggan-North East Yoruba-Lokoja-Idah-Onitsha Route.
6. Old Oyo-Ekun Osi-Borgu-Whydah-Allada-Abomey-Porto Novo Route.
7. Oyo-Yewa-Badagry Route.
8. Ibolo-Ede-Apomu Ijebu-Epe-Lagos Route.

9. Yagba-Ijumu Owe-Ekiti-Akoko-Akure-Ode Ondo-Ikale-Ilaje-Mahin Route.
10. Awa River-Ibeno-Effiat-Ikot Ebong Beach Route.
11. Arochukwu-Enyong Creek or Umon Island-Calabar Route.
12. Odot Ikpe-Ikot Nkon-Ibakesi-Ndinya Mfia-Nung Ukim- Edene-Itak-Ifayong Uruan- Calabar Route.
13. Middle Benue-Boki-Calabar Route.
14. Cameroon grasslands-Mamfe-Ododop-Anyang-Calabar Route.
15. Uzuakoli-Ena-Edda-Biakpan-Cross River-Calabar Route.

For the trans-Saharan trade, the following routes may be identified:
1. Ngazargamo-Kawar-Fezzan-Tripoli Route.
2. Ngazargamo-Nguru-Hadeji-Kano Route.
3. Kano-Iferuan-Ghat-Ghadamer-Tunis Route.
4. Darazo-Gwaram-Birnin Kudu-Kano Route.
5. Bauchi-Ningi-Zaria-Kano Route.

It must be stressed that the routes described above were not as precise as could be inferred. Many routes criss-crossed each other and were supplemented by irregular and meandering foot paths as well as streams and rivers.

Relics

The slave trade relics in the Nigerian region varied from tangible material remains to intangible impact on the people and cultures of the region. Among the relics are: trade currencies; forts and baracoons especially in Old Calabar and Badagri, imported pre-fabricated buildings especially in Old Calabar, Badagri, Lagos, Bonny, Opobo, Ikot Abasi; important beaches which served as custody areas for slaves awaiting embarkation; abandoned market sites; squares and compounds used to custody slaves at the coast; clocks, paintings, Bibles, lanterns, alcohol bottles, other items for which slaves were exchanged and important chieftaincy titles. Among the intangible relics are the not-so-cordial relationships between the coastal dwellers, the principal traders with the Europeans, and the hinterland peoples who suffered most from the trade; boundary demarcation problems between the states in the slave trade corridor; and certain sense of "inferiority" arising from the popular view that to be a slave was to be inferior; and continuing sense of being the "exploited" among some communities. There are also memories from slavery and slave trade which are being converted into popular culture entertainments like music, poetry and other literary expressions and television drama.

Slavery, Slave Trade and Cultural Tourism

A major concern of UNESCO as well as the nations affected by the slave trade has been how to convert the tragedy that this most inhuman episode in world history represented into something positive and beneficial. It is in this context that the slave trade routes and relics become important, especially in the context of cultural tourism and globalisation. It is for this purpose that all the states in the slave trade corridor, especially Cross River, Akwa Ibom, Rivers, Bayelsa, Lagos and Abia have invested in establishing Museums where the slave trade relics can be properly custodied and put on display. The Cross River State government, for example, has established the Slave Trade History Museum in Calabar, just as the Lagos State government has done in Badagri. These "museums of conscience", apart from being foreign currency earners, are serving to attract African diaspora populations in Europe, the Americas and the Caribbean interested in the "roots phenomenon" to reconnect with their historical roots in this age of globalisation and cultural interconnectivity. They thus serve to promote better understanding of the issues involved in the relations between Africans at home and those in the diaspora. They also advertise in concrete forms how the adversities and tragedies of the slave trade era can be converted into significant props for positive development of Africa and the diaspora.

Conclusion

This volume was structured to examine critically the variety of forms of slavery in the indigenous communities of the Nigerian region, the impact of both the trans-Saharan and trans-Atlantic slave trade, as well as the enduring legacies of both institutions for Nigeria. The careful analysis of the sub-regions should serve to warn against the tendency to generalise about the nature, role, status and ideology of indigenous slaving and slave trade in Africa. In all cases, we have shown that the two institutions are better appreciated when located within the social, cultural and political challenges these communities faced, especially those associated with state formation, long distance trade and food production. Our studies have shown that the trade in slaves across both the Sahara desert and the Atlantic ocean had the effect of expanding the scale of slavery and slave trading in the Nigerian region and converting them into very major economic and political activities especially between the seventeenth and nineteenth centuries. We have shown that, contrary to the prevalent view, the abolition of the slave trade and slavery through Acts of the British Parliament in 1807 and 1833 respectively did not substantially affect the two institutions. Indeed, the production of "legitimate goods" had the opposite effect of expanding slave use especially in the plantations set up to produce the new articles of trade. We have also shown that slavery and exploitation of Africa seems to be continuing in new forms such as children and women trafficking, brain drain and illegal immigration. The picture that emerges from our studies of the different sub-regions is that slavery and slave trade were in fact extremely important institutions in the history of the Nigerian region between the tenth and early decades of the twentieth centuries.

Notes and References

[1] For details, see Okon E. Uya, *Contemporary Issues on Slavery and the Black World* (Calabar: Cats Publishers, 2003).
[2] *History of Nigeria* (Cambridge: Cambridge University Press 2008), p.44.
[3] *Ibid*, p. 48.
[4] *Slavery in Africa.*
[5] Folola and Heaton, *A History of Nigeria*, 47. See also Rachel Ama-Asaa Engmann, *African Muslims in the Atlantic World*, Conference Paper, Accra Ghana, 2009.
[6] Falola and Heaton, p. 50.
[7] *Ibid*, p. 57.
[8] *Ibid*, p. 59.
[9] See Adiele Afigbo, "Africa and the Abolition of the Slave Trade" cited in Uya, *Slave Trade and Slavery Abolition*, p9.

10 Falola and Heaton, *History of Nigeria*, p59.
11 For details, see for example, Uya *et al*, *The Efik and their Neighbours* (Cats Publishers, 2006).
12 See, Inikori, *Forced Migration: The Impact of the Export Slave Trade on African Societies* (Hutchinson University Library, 1982); and with Stanly Engerman, *The Atlantic Slave Trade: Effects on Economies, Societies and Peoples in Africa, The Americas and Europe* (Durham: Duke University Press, 1992)
13 Okon Uya "African Diaspora and Human Capital Abroad" in *Foreign Policy in Nigeria's Democratic Transition* (Abuja: Presidential Advisory Council on International Relations, 2006), pp. 157-185.
14 For details of the debate see Okon E. Uya, *African Diaspora*, chapter 1.

BIBLIOGRAPHY

Abubakar, S. *Lamibe Fombina* (Ibadan, 2008).
Alkasum, Abba. *History of Yola* (Zaria, 2003).
Bala Usman Y. and M. N. Alkali. *Studies in the History of Pre-colonial Borno* (Zaria, 1983).
Barbour, K. M. *Northeastern Nigeria: A Case Study of State Formation*, The Journal of Modern African Studies, 9, 1 (1971).
Boahen, A. A. *Britain, the Sahara and the Western Sudan*, 1964, p.128
Bovill, E. W. *The Golden Trade of the Moors* (London, 1968).
Brenner, L. *The Shehus of Kukawa* (London, 1973).
Denham, D., Clapperton H. and Oudney. *Narrative of Travels and Discoveries in Northern and Central Africa in the years 1822, 1823 and 1824* (London, 1826).
El-Masri, F. H. (trans/ed). *Bayan Wujub al-hijra [Uthman ibn Fudi]* (Khartoum, 1977).
Fremantle, J. M. *Gazetteer of Muri Province* (London, 1922).
Gwani, U. S. *Administrative Systems in Tangale Kingdom before and since Colonial Rule in Nigeria*. Vol.1 I, (Maiduguri, 1999).
Henry Barth. *Travels and Discoveries in North and Central Africa*, 5 vols
Hodgkin, T. *Nigerian Perspectives* (London, 1960).
Hogben, S. J. and A. H. M. Kirk-Greene. *The Emirates of Northern Nigeria* (Oxford, 1966).
Hogben, S. J. *The Muhammadan Emirates of Nigeria* (London, 1930).
Ikime, O., *Groundwork of Nigerian History* (Ibadan, 1980).
Kirk-Greene, A. H. M. *Adamawa Past and Present* (London, 1958).
Low, V. N. *Three Nigerian Emirates: A Study in Oral History* (Evanston: North-eastern University Press, 1973).
Lugard, F. D. *The Dual Mandate in British Tropical Africa* (London, 1923), p. 465.
Mahmud Hamman, *The Middle Benue Region and the Sokoto Jihad, 1812-1903* (ABU Zaria, 2007).
Migeod, C. O. *Gazetteer of Yola Province* (Lagos, 1927).
Mijah, S. E. *The Mbula of North-eastern Nigeria* (Jos, 2008).

Monteil, P. L. *De Saint-Louis a Tripoli par le Lac Tchad* (Paris, 1895), p.248-55.
Njeuma, M. Z. *Fulani hegemony in Yola* (Yaounde, 1978).
Palmer, H. R. *Gazetteer of Borno Province* (London, 1929).
Palmer, H. R. *History of the First Twelve years of the reign of Mai Idris Alooma of Bornu.*
Palmer, H. R. *Sudanese Memoirs*, vol. 1 and 2, (Lagos, 1928).
Palmer, H. R. *The Bornu, Sahara and Sudan* (London, 1936).
Usman, Y. B. *The transformation of Katsina* (Zaria).
Whittaker, C. S. Jnr. *The Politics of Tradition, Continuity and Change in Northern Nigeria, 1946-66.*
Passarge, *The German Expedition to Adamawa.* Geographical Journal, vol. 5, January 1894

Archival Materials
Rosedale, W. O. P. 'History of Balala' NAK, Acc. 77.
Ryan, H. B. 'Report on Yola Province, 1911' NAK, J.2.
Namtari District Note Book, (DNB) Local Authority Yola.

Theses
Ahmed, M. B. PhD (1989) 'The Refugee Emirate: Misau's Bornoan Origins and Relationship with its neighbours', University of Birmingham.
Aliyu Yahya Abubakar, (PhD) 'The Establishment and Development of Emirate Government in Bauchi, 1805-1903', Ahmadu Bello University, Zaria.
Pongri, J. (PhD) 1986, 'Political development in northern Adamawa, 1809-1960, A Study in the Development of Inter-Group Relations' Ahmadu Bello University, Zaria.

INDEX

Abolitionist movement, 123
Absorptionist theory, 186
Adim, (slave category) 67
Administration of Emirates
 – role of slaves, 61-63
Administrative title, 62
African
- Association, 110
- diaspora studies, 1, 198
- oral literature, 180
- roots of the African American experience, 198
- slave traders, 174
- Trade Act, 109
Agrarian slave settlers, 35
Ahmed el-Baghdadi, 40
Ajia title for slaves, 62
Akesan market, 167
Ango, Muhammadu Sani, 10
Anikwe, Ferdinand, 146-147
Aniwura, Efunsetan, 176
Antiquity of Slave Trade and Slavery, 29-32
Arjunoma Zanna (titled slave),. 56
Aro Long Juju of European records, 115
Arojubobaku, 167
Atlantic Slave Trade, 4, 103-105, 107-108, 110, 123, 127, 191, 196

Atlantic trade, 137
 - regularly used routes in Nigeria, 199-200
Awlad Sulaiman (an Arab Group), 38

Back-to-roots cultural tourism, 123
Bara System, 22
Bashai, Haruna Jada, 10
Bawa system, 22
Biological reproduction by slaves, 31-32
Birth through slave parents, 12
Black slavery, 184
Borno '
- military expeditions, 186
- slave titles, 66
- Mandara joint attack, 55
- North African Trade in Slaves
  – decline in, 58-60
Brain drain, 202
British colonial
- rule, 9, 21, 29
- government, 8
Buduma pirates, 55
Bungudu, Usman Dangwaggo, 10

Calabar Museum Society, 131
Caliph Abdurrahman, 41
Captives, 144, 192
Capture in Wars and Raids, 9-11
Categories of slaves, 67-68
Child
- abandonment and sale, 115
- abuse, 96
- labour, 153
Children and women trafficking, 202
Classical slavery, 107
Communal
- achieves, 147
- slave achieves, 150
- work, 146
Community relations, 44
Conquests of non-Islamic communities, 34
Conscription of labour, 45
Contemporary Slavery, 96
Crowther, Samuel Ajayi, 81, 92, 96, 179
Cultural tourism, 151
Cuncunawa (children of male slave), 12

Debt pawnship, 106
Deconstructing Slave Trade Literature in Yorubaland, 177-178
Dependency theory, 88
Diplomatic correspondences, 53
Domestic
- duties, 187
- service, 185
- slaves, 30, 43, 52, 84, 136, 144,154,188
  – duties of, 150
- slavery, 13-14, 51, 67, 81-82, 101, 187- 188, 191, 195
    - in Akwa Gross Region, 103-108
- social miscreants, 145

Dumde
- *(agricultural settlements)*, 63-64
- or Slave Settlements, 63-64
- type of slavery, 43

Dynastic instability, 28

Eastern route, 75
Efik
- cultural Zone, 102
- politics, 112
- trading agents, 113

Ekpe imperium, 113
El-Karemi, 11
Emirate administration, 45
Enslavement of war captives, 9
Euro-American racism, 184
European
- commercial capitalism, 81, 85

- imperial powers, 60
- imperialism, 184
- imperialists, 54
- powers, 49
- trade, 108

Export slave trade, 101-102, 187
External slave trade, 1, 194

Fansa
- arrangements, 21-22
- (self –redemption), 13

Farm hands, 146
Foreign trade, 56
Free people becoming slaves
 – how, 8-12
Freeborn
 – descendants of, 148
Fulani Jihadists, 163, 171
Fulata invasions, 44

Garkuwa, 71
Gifts
 – as a means of acquiring slaves, 55
Globalisation and
- cultural tourism, 197
- inter-cultural connectivity, 127

Gobir kingdome, 6
Gold trade, 19

Hausa kingdoms, 6- 7, 9
Hereditary monarchy, 163
Historical imagination, 1
Historiography, 1
Household
- servants, 68
- slaves of King, 68

Human
- pawnship, 106, 112
- sacrifice, 105
- subordination, 1054-106
- trafficking, 180
- tragedy, 1

Ibadan Wars, 164
 - and the trans Atlantic Slave Trade in Yorubaland, 171-172
Idillalan (slave brokers), 20
Illegal immigration, 202
Impact of slave Trade, 175-176
Indigenous
- communities, 201
- internal slave trade, 1
- slave trade, 2
- slavery 82, 84-90, 95, 101-132, 146, 187- 188, 194-195
 - and slave Trade, 194-198
 - ideological foundation of, 85-89
 - in Ghana, 2

Industrial revolution, 46

208

Inheritance, 49
Institution of slavery, 164
- nature of, 135-136
Inter
- class conflict, 170
- communal conflicts and raids, 116
- communal wars, 144, 146, 195
- and conflicts, 192
- community
- conflicts, 154
- relations, 151
- ethnic rancour, 196
- group warfare, 162
- state wars, 171, 185
Intra-community relations, 151
Internal slavery, 29
Isakole, 165, 167
Islamic
- principles, 52
- scholars, 9
- state, 7
Iwofa system, 177-178

Jihad
- campaigns, 74
- captives, 33
- conflicts, 33
- wars, 15
Judicial sentences, 12
Jukun Kingdom of Kwararafa, 28

Kalia, 67
Kidnapping, 11, 31, 49, 115, 119, 173, 185, 195
Kinship linage, 106
Kofar Bayi, 72
Kofar Fada, 72
Kurunmi war, 171, 190

Land routes, 137
Legal sentencing, 31
Legitimate
- commerce, 123
- trade, 54, 142, 196
Lineage kinship, 194
Local expeditions, 34

Madam Tinubu, 91-92, 176
Majidadi, 71-72
Makama, 71
Manifesto of the Jihad, 60
Mega Political system, 51
Middle Passage or Atlantic crossing, 126
Military
- campaigns, 10, 15
- of Sokoto Caliphate, 17
- engagements, 9-10, 185
- field, 35
- intelligence, 12

- invasion of Sokoto Caliphate, 11
- republicanism, 171
- services, 15
- strategies in battles and raids, 9

Modern day slavery, 49, 153
Mohammed el-Bashir b. ahmed tirab (Wazir of Borno), 54
Monarchical system, 163
Muhammed al amin el kanemi, 54
Murgu arrangement, 13,. 21-22
Museums of conscience, 123, 201
Muslim emirates, 30

19th Century Civil Wars and Slave Trade, 170-171
National Museum,
- Old Residency, Calabar, 123, 131
- Uyo, 123

Nike slave market, 146
Normadic and sedentary population, 52
Northern route, 75

Ogar, Ukonghmer, 105
Ohu system, 134
Old Calabar
— rise of, 110-114
Olokun Esin, 166-167

Olori Eru, Kudefu, 166, 188
Oral
- data, 75
- evidences, 104, 121, 114-115, 183
- history, 1-2
- informants, 9-10, 20-21
- traditions, 1-2, 105, 141, 143-144, 149, 162

Organization of Trade in Slaves
  – in Borno in 19th Century, 56-57

Ownership of slaves, 34
Owu kingdom, 163
Oyo
- elite, 190
- royal slaves, 167

Palace
- administration, 167
- courtiers (dogarai and Fadawa), 14
- slaves, 187

Pawnship (poverty), 105-106, 144, 195
Pawns-turned slaves, 192
Political
- achievement, 136
- agents, 123
- centralization, 112
- disputes, 10
- economy, 186
- Environment, 163

- geography of Yorubaland, 171
- history of Hausaland, 9
- history, 28
- landscape, 192
- power, 56, 84, 162, 164, 170
- relationships, 8
- system, 135, 169

Population
- movements, 124
- transfers, 93

Prisoners of war, 33, 154
Property value, 85

Quartering Slaves at the Coast, 122

Raiding, 87, 195
Rasheed, Muhammadu Haruna, 10
Recruiting Slaves for the Market, 114
Relics, 200-201
- and Monuments
  - in Ebonyi State, 150
  - of Slavery and Slave Trade, 43-46
- and Social Scars
  – connected with slavery and slave trade, 20-21
- of Slave Trade, 178-179
- of Slavery, 66-72
- Sites and Monuments, 95-96

Religious belief system, 160
Religious wars, 33

Repatriation records, 17
Reservoir theory, 103
Restitution, 145
Role Slaves in the Economy, 63-66
Royal
- African company, 109
- Domestic Slavery - physical reminders of, 72
- pilgrimages, 53

Ruling classes, 34-36 43-44, 91, 93,170,175,190

Rumdes
- system, 63-64
- or slave settlements, 74

Runji
- settlement, 15
- system, 20

Salt trade, 20
Self enslavement, 115
Shehu Usman dan fodio
– Jihad of, 54
Shrine keepers, 146
Silk Routes Project, 198
Slave
- acquisition, 30
- agents, 115
- ancestry, 93, 151
- based caste system, 148, 151
- business, 119
- captives, 51

211

- Capture and Exploitation, 32-34
- cargoes, 109
- catching, 44
    - expeditions, 115
- class, 66
- control, 95
- dance and narratives, 179
- definition of, 8 ,29, 82-84
- descendants, 67
- elite, 86
- exports, 38, 109
- farm settlements or hamlets, 96
- generals or Kachellas, 68
- History Museum, Calabar, 123
- holdings, 122, 165
- hunters, 11
- importation, 92
- labour, 36, 84 146, 152, 187
- marketing, 32
- markets, 20, 39, 42, 88, 91, 95, 117, 119,74
- merchants, 115
- military titles, 62
- owing communities, 147
- Ports and Exit Points, 173-175
- raided communities, 193
- raids, 49, 124, 173
- rebellion, 93
- recruiters, 193
- recruitment, 116, 122
- reservoir for raiding, 990
- revolts, 186
- rock shelter (imolegboja), 95
- routes
    - project, 1-2, 37-42, 94, 133, 144, 152
    - long-distance in South Eastern emirate, 74-77
- settlements, 33, 63, 74, 89
- titles, 61- 62, 66-67, 78
    - in Borno, 67-72
- Trade
    - corridor, 201
    - Currencies, 121
    - impact of, 175-176
    - in Cross River Region –
    organization of, 110-114
    – impact of, 123-127
    - period, 196
    - Relics, Artifacts, Routes and cultural Tourism, 122-123
    - route, 37
    - Routes, 94, 149
    - and Hinterland markets, 118-121

- and Markets, 172-173
- into and in the Niger Delta, 137-141
- project, 198
- Relics and Cultural Tourism, 198-201
- trading, 101, 120
- communities, 151, 193
- network, 138

Slavery, 134-135
- and Colonial Rule, 42-43
- and Slave Trade
  – external dimensions of, 90-94
  – in Sokoto and Kebbi, 8-18
- as historic institutions, 195
- as Social Institution
  – status, rights and privileges of slaves, 164-165
- definition of, 29, 49
- in Kanem and Borno, 52-63
- in South-Eastern of Sokoto Caliphate, 60-61
- Slave Trade and Cultural Tourism, 201
- system, 190
- under

- Kanemis and Rabih in borno, 54-56
- Saifawa in Kanem and Borno, 52-54

Slaves
- and Executioner or *Abenilori*, 169-170
- as private property, 101
- as Tribute, 63
- categories of, 67-68
- deployment in the economic sector, 16
- how they were utilized, 13-16
- import and export of, 16-18
- in Administrative and Religious Duties, 165-169
- in Enugu State Communities
  – nature and role of, 146-149
- sources of 61
- turned-chiefs, 188
- use on farms, 15-16
- used as Public officers, 14

Slaving voyages, 102

Social
- differentiation, 134, 138
- and stratification, 195
- group in the society, 30
- institution in Yorubaland, 164

- Isolation of Ex-slaves, 149
- miscreants, 192
- misfits, 105
- prestige, 105
- security institution, 177
- stratification, 49-50, 85-86, 97
- structure, 187-188
- subordination, 183

Socio
- cultural institutions, 135
- economic consequence of slavery, 151

Sokoto
- Caliphate 7-8, 10-11, 16, 18-20, 29, 31,33,36-37,41-42,51,74,90-91,185, 187
- jihad, 6-7, 10, 17, 22
- Province, 8

Songhai Empire, 19
Sources of slaves, 61
South-Eastern route, 76
Southern route, 76
Standard of exchange, 56
State security, 12
Stubborn and Unruly children, 145

Themes in slavery and slave trade studies, 2-3
Titled slaves, 166
Trade

- currencies, 122, 200
- fairs, 117
- routes, 17, 31, 37, 39-42, 65-66, 74
  - in Yorubaland, 172
- settlements, 125
- slave, 18
  - exports, 190
  - marketing, 90

Trading expeditions, 136

Trans
- Atlantic
  - routes, 198
  - trade, 152-154, 171-173, 177-180, 183-186, 188
  - Experience and Global Yoruba Cultural Influence, 178-179
  - slave activities, 47
  - Slave Trade, 1, 4, 17, 46, 81-82, 84-85, 90, 92, 95, 97, 134, 195, 140, 144, 148
  - and Human Sacrifice, 176-177
  - Indian Ocean trade, 1
- Saharan
  - routes, 177
  - salve trade, 197
  - trade, 4, 7, 18-20, 53,89, 177, 195
  - route, 6, 39

Tribute and gifts (Shahu), 34

Tribute slaves, 18
Umar el-Kanemi, 55-56
United Nations Education Scientific and Cultural Organisation (UNESCO), 1

Virginia Slave communities, 126
Voyages Database, 102

War captives, 18, 184, 187
Warrior slaves, 15
Water routes, 137

Waterways, 118-119
Ways of acquiring slaves, 34
Western route, 76-77

Yoruba
- civilization, 160-161
- Homeland, 160-164
- inter state wars, 175
- Political system, 164
- settlement, 162

Zamfara Kingdom, 7
Zusanna, 67

www.ingramcontent.com/pod-product-compliance
Lightning Source LLC
Chambersburg PA
CBHW021944290426
44108CB00012B/961